MAKING A DIFFERENCE

MAKING A DIFFERENCE

Leadership and Academic Libraries

EDITED BY PETER HERNON
AND
NANCY ROSSITER

LIBRARIES
UNLIMITED
A Member of the Greenwood Publishing Group
WESTPORT, CONNECTICUT • LONDON

Library of Congress Cataloging-in-Publication Data

Making a difference : leadership and academic libraries / edited by Peter Hernon and Nancy Rossiter.
     p. cm.
  Includes bibliographical references and index.
  ISBN 1–59158–291–1 (alk. paper)
  1. Academic libraries—Administration. 2. Leadership. I. Hernon,
Peter. II. Rossiter, Nancy.
  Z675.U5M325 2007
  025.1'977—dc22   2006031713

British Library Cataloguing in Publication Data is available.

Library of Congress Catalog Card Number: 2006031713
ISBN: 1–59158–291–1

First published in 2007

Libraries Unlimited, 88 Post Road West, Westport, CT 06881
A Member of the Greenwood Publishing Group, Inc.
www.lu.com

Printed in the United States of America

The paper used in this book complies with the
Permanent Paper Standard issued by the National
Information Standards Organization (Z39.48–1984).

10 9 8 7 6 5 4 3 2 1

CONTENTS

ILLUSTRATIONS

Figures

Tables

PREFACE

"There are a multitude of ways to finish the sentence 'Leadership is . . .'."[1]

The popularity of articles, books, and Web sites devoted to leadership indicates that "people are captivated" with the topic[2]—whether the focus is on an individual and that person's behavior, the process by which leaders influence others to achieve a common vision or goal, leadership theories and styles, motivational strategies, or even words of wisdom from successful leaders about what makes them effective. Commenting on the research literature, Peter G. Northouse points out that collectively the findings paint "a picture of a process that is far more sophisticated and complex than the often simplistic view presented in some of the popular books on leadership."[3] Despite the many writings—both popular and scholarly—new insights continue to emerge and support Northouse's conclusion: leadership is indeed a sophisticated and complex process.

The study of leadership might focus exclusively on leaders, either those in formal leadership positions or those lacking such positions but for whom people respond (*emergent leadership*). Such study might examine the interaction between leaders and followers, perhaps in particular situations. Making the picture more complex, leadership might be viewed from the interaction of different approaches, dimensions, or theories; this book addresses a number of them. Furthermore, at the institutional level, library directors interact with college and university deans, provosts, chancellors, and presidents. In some instances, the director becomes a leader, and it is doubtful that the others could be simplistically labeled as followers. Colleagues or partners therefore might be a better word than "followers."

At this point in time, no single work or body of research in library and information studies (LIS) can address all aspects of leadership and produce a cohesive whole that would gain universal acceptance. There is a need to examine leaders themselves, their effectiveness, nurturing, and renewal, and their interaction with followers and other leaders. *Making a Difference: Leadership and Academic Libraries,* which addresses different aspects of leadership, includes the perspective of different academic library directors and recognized leaders. Of particular note is Chapter 8, which offers the perspectives of eight directors to a set of questions related to leadership. Chapters 17 and 18 introduce and define managerial leadership, which modifies the previously mentioned depicted of leaders and followers/colleagues/partners by substituting "leaders in managerial positions" for "leaders." The doctoral program discussed in Chapter 17 is built around a leadership model, which originated in health care, that has great potential for recasting the discussion of critical leadership traits that can be learned and developed.

The topics covered in this book should be of interest to LIS students, participants in and instructors of leadership institutes, library managers, and, for that matter, any one interested in advancing the quality of leadership within LIS and in the term *managerial leadership*. Still, there is a need for more case studies and scenario plans that cover different topics from the perspective of academic librarianship and that reinforce the themes highlighted in *Making a Difference*. Clearly, this book does not (and cannot) represent the final word on leadership; however, it provides a foundation from which others can build, and it offer insights into the present state of leadership in academic librarianship.

Peter Hernon

NOTES

1. Peter G. Northouse, *Leadership: Theory and Practice* (Thousand Oaks, CA: SAGE, 2004), 2.
2. Ibid., 1.
3. Ibid.

ACKNOWLEDGMENTS

The editors and publisher gratefully acknowledge permission for use of the following material:

Excerpts from Bennis, Warren, *On Becoming a Leader*. Reading, MA: Addison-Wesley, 1989.

Excerpts from *When Generations Collide*, Lynne C. Lancaster and David Stillman, HarperCollins Publishers, 2002.

Excerpts from *Cross-Cultural Approaches to Leadership Development* by C. Brooklyn Derr, Sylvia Roussillon, and Frank Bournois. Copyright © 2002. Reproduced with permission of Greenwood Publishing Group, Inc., Westport, CT.

Figure 4.1, Model of Cross-Cultural Leadership Effectiveness, Reprinted from *Business Horizons*, Vol. 48, Illan Alon and James Higgins, "Global Leadership Success through Emotional and Cultural Intelligences," 501-512, Copyright (2005), with permission from Elsevier.

Table 9.1, reprinted from *Leadership Quarterly*, Vol. 11, Michael D Mumford, Michelle A. Marks, Mary Shane Connelly, Stephen J Zaccaro, Roni Reiter-Palmon, "Development of leadership skills: Experience and timing," Pages 87-114, Copyright (2000), with permission from Elsevier.

Tables 11.3, 11.4, and 11.5 reprinted from *The Journal of Academic Librarianship*, 32, no. 5, Arthur P. Young, Peter Hernon, and Ronald R. Powell, "Attributes of Academic Library Leadership: An Exploratory Study of Some Gen-Xers," pages 492-499, © 2006, with permission from Elsevier.

1

ACADEMIC LIBRARIANS TODAY

Peter Hernon

"Leadership and accountability go hand in hand."[1]

Discussions in the literatures of education, management and business, and the social sciences frequently address the changing nature of work, collaboration, entrepreneurship, innovation, and managing both change and a diverse workforce. To some extent, the literature of library and information science (LIS) covers these topics. It also discusses related subjects, such as recruitment to the profession, change management (e.g., the development of the hybrid library [a ubiquitous digital library provided by the commercial sector]) and new information services, blurring the distinction between information services and the creation of information products (often resulting from digital repositories), and strategies for helping an organization better meet its mission and that of its parent institution. The vision statements of academic institutions are challenging the institutions and everyone associated with them to excel. Clemson University, for instance, envisions itself as becoming "one of the nation's top-20 public universities."[2] To help achieve this aspiration, the university will need to develop its strategic direction, library collections, services, and staff.

Typically, libraries at research institutions develop mission statements that focus on leadership in a global setting (serving, for instance, as one of the world's leading research libraries), as well as on collecting, organizing, providing, and preserving access to (and services for) "a rich and unique record of human thought and creativity." Such libraries foster "intellectual growth and . . . [support] the teaching and research missions of . . . [the] University and scholarly communities worldwide."[3] Other academic institutions—focused less on research and graduate education—place greater emphasis on teaching and student learning. For example, the University of Nebraska at Kearney sees itself as "the state's premier institution for undergraduate education. It aims to graduate persons who know the accomplishments of civilizations and [are] disciplined [in] thought and are prepared for productive careers, further education, and responsible citizenship."[4]

As institutional accrediting organizations emphasize, academic institutions should not develop mission and vision statements and then ignore them. These critical components of strategic planning create the institution's identity, and the accreditation process holds the institution accountable for that identity. These accreditation organizations might demand a partnership between the teaching faculty and librarians regarding information literacy. As this chapter discusses, with library services and roles within the institution changing, there is increased need for librarians to become leaders at all levels of the organization. Clearly, leaders will emerge among those with line authority—middle to senior managers. Leadership, however, is not confined to those in formal managerial positions; it also appears among others—ones whom the staff respect but who are not managers.

WORKFORCE

According to Peter Hernon, Ronald R. Powell, and Arthur P. Young, various commentators have identified a national shortage of librarians in the workforce and, despite recruiting efforts, an inability of accredited LIS master's programs to graduate a sufficient pool to keep up with the number of retirements and individuals leaving the workforce.[5] Various writers have documented that "librarians are, as a group, substantially older than those in comparable professions, and they are aging at a much faster rate." Moreover, "as a group, ARL [Association of Research Libraries] university librarians are older than comparable professionals and even older than U.S. librarians in general, and they are aging quickly."[6] Commenting on these findings, Stanley Wilder, Associate Dean at the University of Rochester Libraries, writes:

retirement levels are already high, and will grow much higher in the near future, especially for catalogers, directors, Asian librarians, and Canadian librarians. At the same time, ARL libraries are shifting their hiring priorities to accommodate their need for new kinds of expertise. This shift is significant to the degree that it represents a movement away from traditional library skills and library education generally.[7]

Complicating matters, a number of academic and other institutions are not replacing all retiring or departing librarians, at least with staff who have a master's degree from a program accredited by the American Library Association. They might rely more on paraprofessional staff or seek individuals with other expertise and educational backgrounds. As a consequence, academic libraries manage a diverse workforce and senior managers serve as leaders—developing and focusing on a shared mission and vision statement, and goals.

SUCCCESSION MANAGEMENT

Although not widely discussed in the LIS literature, a number of libraries engage in succession planning, which is more than replacement planning. It involves the adaptation of specific procedures to ensure the identification, development, and long-term retention of talented individuals at the upper-level of management in libraries.[8] It "seeks to anticipate the future job requirements of . . . [an organization] in light of strategic or environmental changes."[9] Those engaged in such planning analyze the job market and their competitors, possible retirements within the library for the next five years, long-term organizational needs, and budget priorities. Succession management is not synonymous with replacing those same traits and skills held by retiring personnel. Positions vacated by retirement might be restructured to reflect better the current and future needs of the library. The analysis includes a review of job descriptions and how positions might be merged or moved into new directions. Furthermore, succession planning should determine if the possible retirements include significant leaders and, if so, the planning should address leadership development. Succession planning should also seek to ensure that library managers and leaders racially reflect the broader institution and society. As one unnamed library director interviewed for background information relevant to this chapter explained, "the number of people of color in top professional positions is improving but not at the rate it should." This aspect of succession planning goes beyond immediate organizational needs and confronts the profession as it seeks to provide a workforce that reflects a society that is diverse in many different ways. (Chapter 18 offers additional discussion of succession management.)

LEADERSHIP DEFINED

Management and leadership are not synonymous terms. Abraham Zaleznik believes that managers "seek order and control and are almost compulsively addicted to disposing of problems before they understand their potential significance."[10] They use "well-established techniques to accomplish predetermined ends."[11] Leaders, on the other hand, "tolerate chaos and lack of structure and are thus prepared to keep answers in suspense, avoiding premature closure on important issues."[12]

Leadership, which has more than 100 definitions,[13] focuses on social influence—influencing others to attain group, organizational, and societal goals. The purpose is to motivate people to develop, accept, and carry out a shared vision. It is not, however, a function confined solely to library directors and their senior management team; leadership should be evident at all levels of the organization, including teams and groups. In the case of teams, leadership should not be confined solely to the team leader. Anyone on the team should demonstrate leadership at one time or another. Leadership involves attributes such as trust, creativity, adaptability, innovation, and imagination, whereas management, perhaps as an oversimplification, focuses on problem solving, effectiveness, efficiency, and continuous quality improvement in the services offered.

For the purposes of this book, leadership is defined as "a function of knowing yourself, having a vision that is well communicated, building trust among colleagues, and taking effective action to realize your own leadership potential."[14] This definition takes into account the previous description of leadership and sets up the discussion of emotional intelligence, which is "the ability to manage ourselves and our relationships effectively,"[15] in subsequent chapters.

In today's environment, library directors should lead the organization in meeting its mission and vision. They should influence organizational climate through their leadership style or the way that they motivate others, gather and use information, make decisions, manage change, and handle crises. There are different leadership styles, and leaders need to master as many of them as possible, switching among different ones as conditions warrant. Daniel Goleman identifies leadership styles that are appropriate to emotional intelligence. For example, he notes that at times managers who are leaders might be *coercive* (expect staff to do as they instruct) and at other times *authoritative* (state a goal but be flexible in how the staff meet it) or *democratic* (give staff a voice in shaping a decision).[16]

ACADEMIC LIBRARY LEADERS

During the winter and spring 2005, the two editors of this book studied library directors whose institutions are ARL members.[17] Those participating in the interviews did not see a shortage of individuals qualified to lead university research libraries through the position of library director. They tended not to see any difference in the traits that these individuals will need to possess in the near future—the next five or so years. They also thought the talent pool among those serving immediately below them (assistant/associate/deputy directors) was strong. They recognized, however, that all senior managers could improve their leadership skills and abilities. Of greater concern to them was the long term, as many librarians do not want to become middle managers; they prefer to be project managers. After all, projects are short term and have clearly defined completion dates. These librarians have no long-term interest in management because they do not want work to consume their daily lives, and they do not want to assume responsibility (e.g., in making personnel decisions).

What leadership skills and abilities will middle managers need to possess? How will they build on their present skills and abilities? More fundamentally, how can the most talented librarians (better managers and leaders) be persuaded to become middle managers? Once they do, will they enjoy the experience and be willing to mature as managers and leaders?

Challenges

Not every librarian or library school student wants to be a leader or is capable of effective leadership. The challenge for those with potential is to realize that they can participate on teams as both leaders and followers. J. Richard Hackman, the Cahners-Rabb Professor of Social and Organizational Psychology at Harvard University, adds a further challenge: more important than leadership style in determining how well a team performs is to design and support a team so that its members can manage themselves. He identifies five conditions that set the stage for exemplary performance of teams: actual use of teams, a compelling direction, an enabling team structure, a supportive organizational context, and the availability of competent coaching (see Chapter 10).[18]

Some of the directors participating in the aforementioned published interviews commented that, if the most talented staff (ones who contribute to the team success and who seek advancement) are to advance in the library or other libraries, they need to gain line authority, benefit from nurturing, gain personal maturity, and develop an appropriate skill set. Another challenge, the directors noted, is to minimize the likelihood that team members will suffer from stress and burnout. Interviewees suggested that librarians look for partnership opportunities and take initiative to remind upper administration to include the library in formulating campus-wide policy. They also asked whether those in upper administration differ from library directors in the set of traits they consider most essential for effective leadership.

Generational differences, which have not yet been widely investigated, surely have an impact on the library workforce and workers' expectations. For example, library staffs include baby boomers (born between 1946 and 1964), a group likely to retire within the next two decades; generation X (gen-Xers, born between 1965 and 1979); and the millennial generation (also known as Generation Y, Nexters, or entitlement generation, born in the years after 1980), a group currently joining the workforce as student assistants and paraprofessionals. They expect to receive such benefits as travel allowances and compensation for attending conferences, and generally are more demanding, but this should not be viewed negatively.

According to writer Brien Smith, "the success of socializing new generation X workers is dependent on an organizational commitment to doing so. As such, . . . [any] organization needs to assure accurate expectations, a job-relevant knowledge base, and other insiders to ease the transition."[19] Managers need to understand and value generational differences and to recognize that managing a workforce containing all of three generations "will be a challenge."[20] It is therefore necessary that leaders from each generation emerge and interact, and that organizations nurture leaders from each generation, especially gen-Xers and millennials.

Once millennials replace the other groups at the professional level in an organization, there will likely be a subset of them interested in becoming senior managers. Some critics maintain that generation X professionals lack a commitment to their work.[21] A more realistic assessment is that this generation is one of latch-key individuals, who are independent, seek original solutions to problems, and do not engage in long-range planning; gen-Xers tend to be self-oriented and focused on the short term. "Managers should give Xers opportunities for 100 percent responsibility for specific goals and greater creative freedom to achieve those goals."[22] This implies that there are those in this generation who will assume leadership positions and will be effective in those positions.

Both generations, especially the millennials, do not read extensively. There is some evidence that many Xers working in libraries share a different value system from that of some library directors, believe that their role and opinions in the library have been undervalued, and have a misunderstanding about the research process. They also want their opinions to be sought, heard, and valued, and they want to gain the necessary experience as well as opportunities to build on their strengths.[23] Any widespread dissatisfaction has implications for staff retention, professional development, and the type of work performed, especially at institutions where the librarians hold faculty status, or an equivalent, and are expected to pursue scholarly publication.

Despite the previous comments, it is important to avoid stereotyping a generation,[24] to become acquainted with younger librarians as individuals, and to produce research based on facts. After all, gen-X is service-oriented and wants to help library users fulfill their information needs and expectations. As Rachel Singer Gordon notes, "if we truly want to bring our NextGen enthusiasm, outlook, and skills to bear on our institutions and professions, then we must be able to inspire our colleagues. We need to be able to show when and why change is necessary and to build excitement about where we and our organizations are headed."[25] She continues, "leadership depends less on a person's place on an organizational chart than on the personal qualities and actions of a given individual."[26] Leadership does not occur in a vacuum; it enables the organization to achieve its potential (mission and vision), as well as bridge communication gaps within and across generations.

Perhaps an excellent starting point in the education of future LIS professionals is to implement program outcomes—expectations that program graduates will have mastered as a result of their program—that focus on the set of competencies that the Association of Southeastern Research Libraries (ASERL) developed. Noting dissatisfaction with the pool of graduates of LIS programs to help research libraries become "key partners in higher education," ASERL identified the "attributes of the successful research librarian" as "intellectual curiosity, flexibility, adaptability, persistence, . . . the ability to be enterprising, excellent communication skills, [and a commitment] to life-long learning and personnel career development." Additional attributes are grouped under the following headings. The research librarian:

- Develops and manages effective services that meet user needs and support the research library's mission;
- Supports cooperation and collaboration to enhance service;
- Understands the library within the context of higher education (its purpose and goals) and the needs of students, faculty, and researchers;
- Knows the structure, organization, creation, management, dissemination, use, and preservation of information resources, new and exiting, in all formats; and
- Demonstrates commitment to the *values and principles of librarianship*.[27]

Additional attributes might be an ability to engage in critical thinking and problem solving. Exposure to research as a process of inquiry develops a person's problem-solving ability. As well, we would add self-motivation, self-awareness, the ability to listen, intelligence, values and a strong commitment to professional and personal ethics, inquisitiveness, and an interest in learning and helping the organization improve its services. A key question is, "Might one's leadership potential comprise a factor in the hiring decision?"

Those graduates of LIS programs who possess the previously mentioned attributes will have a good foundation on which to build. They will, however, need opportunities to develop and fine-tune their leadership potential. A critical role for senior management will be to provide leadership opportunities, observe people, and nurture those with potential. This question, however, has not been researched: "Is it harder to foster leadership at institutions where library staff are unionized or librarians have tenure?" Neither unionization nor tenure should become an excuse to maintain the status quo and fail to meet the shared vision and service potential of the organization.

Nurturing others is a responsibility of both directors and all senior managers. Some staff members may be more comfortable working with those immediately below the rank of director (assistant/associate/deputy directors), as these managers deal with them on a regular basis and do not make final decisions about promotions and salaries. Regardless, nurturing must come from somewhere; it might not emerge from inside the organization.

CONCLUSION

As Donald E. Riggs, Vice President for Information Services and University Librarian at Nova Southeastern University, explained, the profession does not face an immediate leadership crisis. Rather, he sees "the wake-up call" as being received: "now is the time to better understand leadership, take it seriously as part of our daily working lives, and become more conscious of the potential for a leadership crisis."[28] Thus it is essential to focus attention on how to screen or train people to acquire essential leadership traits and to ensure that the senior management team collectively possesses those qualities deemed most valuable in a particular work setting. Managing and leading libraries further involve dealing with people outside the immediate organization. Daniel Yankelovich and Isabella Furth of Viewpoint Learning, a company that specializes in linking business and public policy, note that the climate of opinion in society has changed: leaders "can no longer assume that their words or actions will be given the benefit of the doubt."[29] They identify the ability to communicate as "a make-or-break skill" for leaders to succeed.[30] Among the principles for communicating under conditions of mistrust, they list "make a conscious effort to move toward a 'stewardship' ethic:"

Stewardship involves making a commitment to leaving the institution better off than you found it. It also extends the perimeter of whom the institution cares for, and how it cares for them, to include a much wider community.[31]

Any discussion of leadership should not omit such tenets, and the reason that a number of library directors have told us they became organizational leaders was to help develop a shared vision that would guide the library in the near future. Besides, good communication—combined with being a good role model—is an essential ability for leaders to practice as they help manage organizational change. We should not forget that others watch leaders and learn from them.

Changing organizational culture involves building trust. Leaders and managers must earn respect throughout the organization and be accountable for maintaining a bond of trust. Thus leadership involves doing things that accomplish the shared vision and being accountable for the results. In such an environment, some of the most essential leadership abilities become patient persistence in instituting organizational change, creativity, integrity, honesty, credibility, and innovation. Still, no single leadership style can be applied to all libraries and situations, and leaders apply different styles at different times. As this book stresses, everyone interested in the future of libraries and their place in society needs to care about leadership, which is concerned with how leaders affect or influence groups to achieve goals and an institution's mission. There is a positive relationship therefore between leaders and followers.

Finally, other abilities relate to directing an organization. Examples include the ability to think on one's feet, to listen, and to synthesize. Because managerial leadership combines both management and leadership, it expands the number of relevant abilities that a senior management team needs to possess collectively to function effectively in a complex, stressful, and political environment. Ultimately, the question becomes, "How well do the different traits and abilities come together to shape individuals?"

"Leadership complements management; it doesn't replace it."[32]

NOTES

1. Quote from an anonymous university library director.

2. "Clemson University's Mission Statement" (Clemson, SC: Clemson University, 2001). Available at http://www.clemson.edu/welcome/quickly/mission/index.htm (accessed September 7, 2005).

3. "Library Strategic Planning: Yale University Library Mission-Vision-Values" (New Haven, CT: Yale University Libraries, 2003). Available at http://www.library.yale.edu/strategicplanning/mission.html (accessed September 7, 2005).

4. "Role and Mission of UNK: Mission Statement" (Kearney, NE: University of Nebraska at Kearney, 2005). Available at http://www.unk.edu/about/index.php?id = 124 (accessed September 7, 2005).

5. Peter Hernon, Ronald R. Powell, and Arthur P. Young, *The Next Library Leadership: Attributes of Academic and Public Library Directors* (Westport, CT: Libraries Unlimited, 2003), 1–11.

6. Stanley Wilder, "The Changing Profile of Research Library Professional Staff," *ARL Bimonthly Report* 208/209. Available at http://www.arl.org/newsltr/208_209/chgprofile/html (accessed September 8, 2005).

7. Ibid.

8. Angela Bridgland, "To Fill, or How to Fill—That Is the Question. Succession Planning and Leadership Development in Academic Libraries," *Australian Academic Research Libraries* 30 (March1999). Available through Expanded Academic ASAP (accessed September 8, 2005).

9. Ibid.

10. Abraham Zaleznik, "Managers and Leaders: Are They Different?" in *Harvard Business Review on Leadership* (Boston: Harvard Business School Publishing, 1998), 87.

11. Donald E. Riggs, "The Crisis and Opportunities in Library Leadership," *Journal of Library Administration*™ 32, nos. 3/4 (2001), 6. He offers examples that clearly distinguish between management and leadership (p. 6).

12. Zaleznik, "Managers and Leaders," 86. See also Peter G. Northouse, *Leadership: Theory and Practice* (Thousand Oaks, CA: Sage, 2004), 8–10.

13. Riggs, "The Crisis and Opportunities in Library Leadership," 5.

14. Warren G. Bennis and Burt Nanus, *Leaders: The Strategies for Taking Charge* (New York: Harper & Row, 1985), 18.

15. Daniel Goleman, "Leadership That Gets Results," *Harvard Business Review* 78 (March-April 2000), 78.

16. Ibid.

17. Peter Hernon and Nancy Rossiter, "Emotional Intelligence: Which Traits Are Most Prized?" *College & Research Libraries* 67 (May 2006): 260–275.

18. J. Richard Hackman, *Leading Teams: Setting the Stage for Great Performances* (Boston: Harvard Business School Press, 2002).

19. Brien Smith, "Managing Generation X," *USA Today (Magazine)* 129 (November 2000). Available through Expanded Academic ASAP (accessed July 28, 2004).

20. Raul O. Rodriguez, Mark T. Green, and Malcolm J. Ree, "Leading Generation X: Do the Old Rules Apply," *Journal of Leadership & Organizational Studies* 9 (Spring 2003). Available through Expanded Academic ASAP (accessed July 28, 2004).

21. "Generation X Professionals: Assumptions and Realities," *Worklife Report* 14 (Winter 2002): 10.

22. Gillian Flynn, "Xers vs. Boomers: Teamwork or Trouble," *Personnel Journal* 75 (November 1996): 90.

23. These comments are derived from "Where the Jobs Are," *Library Journal.* Available at http://www.libraryjournal.com/article/CA434433 (accessed July 29, 2004); "Gen X Bites Back," *American Libraries* 35 (September 2004): 43–45; "Reader Forum" in *American Libraries* following publication of Arthur P. Young, Ronald R. Powell, and Peter Hernon, "What Will Gen Next Need to Lead?," *American Libraries* 35 (May 2004): 31–35.

24. See Carolyn Wiethoff, "Management Basics: Managing Generation X," *Indiana Libraries* 23 (2004): 53–55; Rachel Singer Gordon, "NEXTGEN: What We Really Want," *Library Journal* 129 (October 15, 2004): 46.

25. Rachel Singer Gordon, "Time to Make Some Change," *Library Journal* 129 (August 2004): 51.

26. Ibid.

27. Association of Southeastern Research Libraries, "Shaping the Future: ASERL's Competencies for Research Libraries" (Atlanta, GA: Association of Southeastern Research Libraries, 2000). Available at http://www.aserl.org/statements/competencies/competencies.htm (accessed September 9, 2005). See also Association of Southeastern Research Libraries, "Survey Report: ASERL Competencies for Research Librarians: Usage at ASERL Member Libraries" (Atlanta, GA: Association of Southeastern Research Libraries, 2003). Available at http://www.aserl.org/aserlcompetencies.pdf (accessed September 9, 2005).

28. Riggs. "The Crisis and Opportunities in Library Leadership," 8.

29. Daniel Yankelovich and Isabella Furth, "The Role of Colleges in an Era of Mistrust," *The Chronicle of Higher Education* (September 16, 2005), B8.

30. Ibid.

31. Ibid., B11.

32. John P. Kotter, "What Leaders Really Do (Managers Promote Stability While Leaders Press for Change)," *Harvard Business Review* 79, no.11 (December 2001): 85.

2

——•••••——

THE NEED FOR EFFECTIVE LEADERSHIP IS NOT LESSENING

Peter Hernon

"Smart academic leaders want innovative and successful leaders for their libraries. Often they seek out individuals who can change the organization and lead it into the future. On the other hand, I know provosts who intentionally avoid such risk takers and want status quo."[1]

As the twenty-first century unfolds, it is evident that academic librarians do not (and cannot) accept the adage of business as usual given the ever-changing climate of scholarly communication. In a diffuse, digital environment, that communication continues to evolve and present new issues, challenges, and opportunities for colleges and universities, scholars, students, scholarly publishers, and policymakers. Simultaneously, libraries are developing new information resources, creating information products from their digital repositories, and forging new partnerships (e.g., through consortia). Nobody questions any longer that information and communications technologies change the services that libraries provide and the way staff members work.

As well, statements of the mission, vision, and values for academic institutions and their libraries receive increased scrutiny from different stakeholders (e.g., institutional and program accrediting organizations) because they indicate the direction in which the organization is going—what is the organization trying to accomplish. Regional and program accrediting organizations, among others, might frame accountability in terms of mission statements and move beyond the use of simple metrics cast as *inputs* (the distribution of the budget) and *outputs* (characterization of use and the amount of service provided). They might embrace *outcomes* that indicate the impact of the library and academic programs of study on student learning. In the emerging culture of assessment and with scholarly communication still changing, academic libraries must leverage scarce resources to maximize the value of their collections to the audiences they serve while continually trying to improve the services they deliver as well as the preservation of, and access to, diverse collections.[2] As this chapter highlights, these and related issues require sustained leadership.

Denise Troll, Assistant University Librarian, Library Information Technology, Carnegie Mellon University, highlights part of the changing environment when she writes:

Libraries become publishers when they digitize collections, host journals that are "born digital," or assemble student or faculty works online. Librarians become politicians when they lobby faculty members not to sign away copyright to a print publisher, because this means that the authors or the libraries will have to pay for use of these works. Traditional library measures cannot capture these changing reasons for the simple reason that they were not designed to do so.[3]

Issues such as these have an impact on library infrastructure—namely, staff, facilities, collections, and technologies—and the services provided to the parent institution. Clearly, there are shifting patterns in library operations, the nature of the work that staff perform, job descriptions and expectations, and library collections. The word *collection* does not refer only to those materials that libraries physically own.

SOME KEY CHALLENGES FACING HIGHER EDUCATION

At a seminar of the Triangle Research Libraries Network (TRLN) Doctoral Fellows in 2005, the provosts from Duke University, North Carolina Central University, North Carolina State University, and the University of North Carolina at Chapel Hill identified the following challenges in higher education for public institutions:

- The need for them "to embrace diversity and accommodate diverse cultural backgrounds, especially of traditionally underserved populations, in all aspects of operations";
- "The challenge of redistributing finite resources for new initiatives on campus, the reorganization of space for new programs and services, and the associated reorganization of expectations of students and faculty";
- "The need for public research universities to develop a new research model that handles the intermingling of public and private resources without creating conflicts of interest between the needs of students, faculty, corporations and the university's mission"; and
- "The need to articulate the importance of a strong bond between public universities and their communities . . . [T]he public research university is highly qualified

to help solve public problems, such as social justice, managing immigration, globalization in technology and commerce, fairness in government, medical break-throughs, and moral and ethical values in all professions."[4]

Articles appearing in *The Chronicle of Higher Education* have discussed issues such as these:

- The decline in financial support from government;
- Higher insurance rates, which are linked to rate increases resulting from natural disasters (e.g., hurricanes);
- Higher operating costs resulting from increased costs of health care for faculty and staff, and price increases for natural gas and electricity;
- Modest growth in endowments (private support depending on the field of study remains strong);
- More borrowing is expected to cover infrastructure (e.g., renovation and new building construction) because of stable credit ratings for institutions;
- Enrollments are increasing and so are tuitions in order to cover expenses;
- Increased competition from for-profit education, as government restrictions decrease; and
- Greater public scrutiny of tenure.

ACADEMIC LIBRARIES

Some of the challenges that the TRLN provosts identified for librarians address their role as liaisons to the faculty; the need to understand and, by implication, carry out their institution's mission; the role of the library in distance education (e.g., Web-based); a realization that the library is more than a repository—it "has become a gathering place for learning communities;" and "the need for librarians to be proactive information providers and change agents of collaboration for the benefit of their institution;" "the future of scholarly publishing and the role of the university press;" and "the importance of affirming integrity in academia."[5]

Joseph M. Brewer, Sheril J. Hook, Janice Simmons-Welburn, and Karen Williams of the University of Arizona Library set the stage for change management by stating:

While all campus units face reduced budgets, academic libraries suffer additional pressures due to a unique set of economic factors affecting our budgets. Libraries are experiencing record increases in the cost of scholarly information, with six to twelve percent annual inflation in the price of journals alone. Complex licensing agreements with publishers of online journals and indexes often force the purchase of expensive packages of titles, or of duplicate print versions. Academic libraries have an imperative to invest in a technology infrastructure that will support the delivery of digital content and create high-tech, student-friendly environments. Critical shortages in trained librarians drive up costs for recruiting and retaining professional staff.[6]

Quoting from Carla Stoffle, Barbara Allen, David Morden, and Krisellen Maloney, they note that "together these elements are 'adding, not reducing, personnel and operating costs'" and that academic library directors "are under considerable pressure from our institutions to reduce staff size while increasing services and access." Stoffle et al. then ask, "How will we address these changes?"[7]

Change management focuses on the infrastructure of libraries and the relationship between libraries and the broader environment in which they function. Most likely organizational change relates to more than one part of the infrastructure. For example, the provision of effective library services 24/7/365 might involve staff, facilities, collections, and technology. Does the library provide staff all of the time and at what level—professional or other? Which facilities are open and are they set up and operated as an information commons, with technology, reference staff, and physical collections readily available? What role are libraries playing as institutional repositories for faculty research and the records generated by different institutional bodies (e.g., the faculty senate)? Another example is that academic library staff might assist faculty in placing components of their courses in Web course management systems and digitally integrating different resources into class assignments and readings—text, primary documents, videos, and so forth.[8] It merits mention that, by creating Web portals that integrate end-user searching of various resources and that rely on software to provide an individually customized search interface and direct links to content, academic libraries, perhaps together with commercial vendors, are showing that online public access catalogs (OPACs) clearly do not provide a comprehensive record of library collections. At the same time, many undergraduate students depend solely or largely on the pull-down menu of selected databases available on a library's homepage and are less reliant on OPACs for information access.

Such examples illustrate that "the librarian's role in the future library will focus on deploying current technology that best meets student and faculty needs for locating pertinent resources and creating a relevant information environment to support student learning and faculty teaching and research."[9] Furthermore:

With the wide array of resources and the deluge of information, robotics or artificial intelligence aides will help organize material. Highly trained and competent librarians will provide for students, faculty and researchers more skilled and precise retrieval. They will do this by teaching techniques that focus on formulating a research topic or question, evaluating information sources, locating the best information resource, and understanding the ethics of information and intellectual property.[10]

To realize this instructional role, librarians will have to partner with more faculty across the institution and realize that they alone cannot teach all aspects of information literacy. Some aspects normally fall under the scope of the teaching faculty.

Libraries as a place will continue, but the arrangement of the physical library will change as learning behaviors and preferences shift from one generation to another. With increased remote access to library collections and as classroom teaching continues to change, in part as a result of student learning outcomes having to do with changes in student knowledge, abilities, and skills throughout a program of study, academic librarians will play more of a teaching role and focus more on students as learners.

In *Improving the Quality of Library Services for Students with Disabilities,* Peter Hernon and Philip Calvert show that academic librarians must also be more proactive in identifying and meeting the service expectations of special populations such as students with disabilities, whether those disabilities are physical or other.[11] Community colleges will continue to focus on different populations (e.g., those needing remedial education before they advance beyond two-year education and those for whom English is a second language) and ensure that they are ready to enter prestigious institutions with notable undergraduate and graduate programs.

Catherine T. Flaga of Michigan State University focuses on community colleges and indicates that "historically, the bulk of the transfer student literature has dealt with 'transfer shock' . . . which is defined as a drop in grade-point average at the new four-year institution." Her research indicates that a more meaningful measure is the extent of students' initiative in seeking out and utilizing "resources on their own." They are "committed students who took considerable responsibility for their education."[12] As a result they should be receptive to outreach that academic libraries initiate.

INFORMATION POLICY

Information policy, a field encompassing both public policy and information science, treats information as both a commodity—adheres to the economic theory of property rights—and a resource to be collected, protected, shared, manipulated, and managed. Instead of characterizing information policy in the singular, we should recognize that there is no single, all-encompassing policy. Information policies tend to address specific issues and, at times, to be fragmented, overlapping, and even contradictory.

Information policies comprise a set of interrelated principles, laws, guidelines, rules, regulations, and procedures that guide the oversight and management of the information life cycle: production, collection, distribution/dissemination, retrieval and use, and retirement or preservation. Information policy, which often centers on government, also embraces access to, and use of, information and records; the latter relates to the conduct of official business and provides an audit trail for holding government accountable.

Information policy involves interaction among different stakeholders and often compromise to gain sufficient consensus to enact a given law or other type of policy. As a result librarians must function in a political environment and work outside the profession and academic institution. Policymakers may know little about libraries and prefer to interact with knowledgeable individuals who influence larger blocks of people. Excellent examples of information policies important to academic librarianship include policies regarding intellectual property rights, privacy rights, and the "chaos in scholarly communication."[13]

NURTURING FUTURE LEADERS

Both the LIS literature and discussions with various academic library directors indicate that a fundamental challenge for the future will be to attract good people to positions of middle management. As Rachel Singer Gordon comments, "It becomes apparent that many younger librarians [Generation X] are both dissatisfied with their own managers and uninterested in becoming managers themselves"[14]; apparently they are satisfied with their present lifestyle and want to avoid stress. She issues an important reminder: "In addition to building on the leadership potential of current staff, succession planning should also be a factor in hiring decisions. Such planning or management should focus on "personal qualities such as energy, enthusiasm, and the ability to adapt to change and help propel organizations forward."[15] Stated succinctly, it is important to identify and nurture those willing to become middle managers who also have leadership potential.

Understanding leadership and developing one's potential can be gained, for instance, from discussions, presentation, reading relevant works, and critical self-reflection. This book highlights how to strive to reach one's potential. Its underlying assumption is that a person always seeks self-improvement. In a study of directors of libraries that are members of the Association of Research Libraries (ARL), Peter Hernon and Nancy Rossiter received some relevant comments that we omitted from the article.[16] These included:

- I am less a believer in mentorship than I am in observing other successful leaders and assessing which traits they possess that I might be able to adopt myself or at least work toward acquiring. I have read a few articles and books on leadership— a keen understanding of one's strengths is at least as important—there is no prescription for successful leadership and different organizations and situations call for different types of leaders.

- Lee G. Bolman and Terrence E. Deal's book, *Reframing Organizations: Artistry, Choice, and Leadership* (Jossey-Bass, 1997), was particularly useful in helping me identify areas where I need more work to be successful.

- There is no substitute for getting your fingers burned and your butt kicked or, conversely, seeing a project that you have pushed and sweated over actually succeed. The lessons learned from these experiences are what truly shape people. As Benjamin Franklin said, "Experience is a dear school, but a fool will learn it in no other way."

- The ability to lead effectively, to chart a vision for an organization, to support others who are carrying out that vision, all of these traits, while inherent in a good leader, can be honed through practice over time. Mentoring is important to this learning process in which one can learn from mistakes and obtain continuous guidance. Having a role model who exhibits desired traits of leadership is another way to learn.

A complementary perspective is that of library directors who reflected on the hiring process of fellow directors. Among other unpublished findings, Hernon and Rossiter found:

Most of those who make the final hiring decisions for deans/directors of ARL libraries are seeking people who are knowledgeable, articulate, cooperative, and sometimes even compliant. They want people who report to them to be effective, but not especially demanding of time, attention, and resources. They value good citizenship to the institution and discourage those who strongly advocate for their unit or are aggressively independent. Increasingly, they want deans/directors who are experienced fundraisers. Especially in the largest libraries, they rarely hire potential rather than experience.

One director emphasized that, "by the time a librarian becomes a director, he or she has had extensive experience in all areas of management. This is not true of deans and department heads in academic units. Librarians self-select and advance as leaders so that the pools for these positions are strong, not because the search process seeks leadership and risk taking." Other relevant quotations include:

- Most ARL library director search committees are dominated by faculty, either as chair or members. Because of their experience on search committees for tenured positions or department chairs, faculty tend to evaluate librarian candidates using the same or similar criteria used for hiring faculty. These criteria emphasize qualifications that have little or no relevance to qualities necessary to a successful administrator. They stress publishing, reputation of the candidate's home institution, opinions of faculty from the candidate's home institution, and presence of a doctoral degree. These criteria are significant, but they reveal nothing about a person's ability to lead and be successful as an administrator. Another factor is the tendency of nonadministrator faculty to assign little value to administrative skills. Faculty frequently adopt the attitude, subconsciously or consciously, that administration is pretty easy, something anyone can do. Fortunately, faculty who become administrators are quickly disavowed of this misconception.
- Today's directors are a very different breed than those in ARL positions when I began as a young librarian. The increase of women in directors' positions has greatly changed the traits held by directors. The male directors today have adopted many traits from women leaders.[17]

As a summary to this section, Clemson University represents a good illustration of the need to relate effective change management and good leadership. The university's vision statement calls for "Clemson . . . [to] be one of the nation's top-20 public universities."[18] Without any familiarity with the university and its library, one can still image that, if the intention is to realize this vision, there will be heightened pressure on the library to meet challenges and create new opportunities. Undoubtedly, increased attention focuses on the university's and library's strategic plans and how each addresses institutional and organizational culture, maximizes the cost/benefit of the services offered, and so on.

CONCLUSION

The achievement of change and coping with the types of issues highlighted in this chapter require leadership, not only within the library and the institution, but also across the profession, as the profession interacts with society at large and its various stakeholders. Change management also applies to organizational culture and acceptance of a shared vision, one likely to alter the status quo. As Pamela L. Eddy of Central Michigan University writes, "College [and university] leaders serve important roles as guides for campus understanding during times of change."[19] With institutions and campus systems, leadership must exist at all levels—from within departments to the system chancellor.

Leadership within libraries—at either the team or group level or among the managers (middle to senior levels)—must focus on recruiting, educating, and retaining librarians and on the ability of the graduates of schools of library and information studies to meet the types of competencies stressed by the Association of Southeastern Research Libraries (ASERL).[20] At the same time, with more libraries engaged in team or group activities, leadership must cope with the results that teams or groups produce as well as the professional development and socialization of team members (see Chapter 10).

"Good mentoring is essential, but the literature suggests that . . . [it] comes from many places and people."[21]

NOTES

1. Peter Hernon and Nancy Rossiter, "Emotional Intelligence: Which Traits Are Most Prized," *College & Research Libraries* 67 (May 2006): 260–75.

2. For an excellent discussion of the emerging role of academic libraries, see Jerry D. Campbell, "Changing a Cultural Icon: The Academic Library as a Virtual Destination," *Educause Review* 41 (January-February 2006): 16–31. Available at http://www.educause.edu/apps/er/erm06/erm0610.asp?bhcp=1 (accessed May 25, 2006).

3. Denise Troll, "How and Why Are Libraries Changing," CLIS [Council on Library and Information Resources] Issues, No. 21 (May/June 2001), 8 (of 11). Available at http://www.clir.org/pubs/issues/issues21.html (accessed February 13, 2006).

4. University of North Carolina, School of Information and Library Science, "News Release: Provosts from the Triangle Discuss Issues Confronting Higher Education" (Chapel Hill: University of North Carolina, 2005), 1–2 (of 6). Available at http://sils.unc.edu/news/releases/2005/09_trlnpprovosts.htm (accessed February 9, 2006).

5. Ibid., 2–3.

6. Joseph M. Brewer, Sheril J. Hook, Janice Simmons-Welburn, and Karen Williams. "Libraries Dealing with the Future Now," *ARL Bimonthly Report* 234 (Washington, D.C.: Association of Research Libraries, June 2004). 3 (of 16). Available at http://www.arl.org/newsltr/234/dealing.html (accessed February 9, 2006).

7. Ibid., 3–4. Carla Stoffle, Barbara Allen, David Morden, and Krisellen Maloney, "Continuing to Build the Future Academic Libraries and Their Challenges," *portal: Libraries and the Academy* 3, no. 3 (July 2003), 365. [363–380] Available at http://0-muse.jhu.edu.library.simmons.edu/journals/portal_libraries_and_the_academy/v003/3.3stoffle.html (accessed February 15, 2006).

8. See, for instance, Danuta A. Nitecki and William Rando, "Evolving an Assessment of the Impact on Pedagogy, Learning, and Library Support of Teaching with Digital Images," in *Outcomes Assessment in Higher Education,* ed. Peter Hernon and Robert E. Dugan (Westport, CT: Libraries Unlimited, 2004), 175–96.

9. Gloriana St. Clair and Erika Linke, "The Library of the Future," in *The Innovative University*, ed. Daniel P. Resnick and Dana S. Scott (Pittsburgh, PA: Carnegie Mellon University Press, 2004), 282.

10. Ibid.

11. Peter Hernon and Philip Calvert, *Improving the Quality of Library Services for Students with Disabilities* (Westport, CT: Libraries Unlimited, 2006).

12. Catherine T. Flaga, "The Process of Transition for Community College Transfer Students," *Community College Journal of Research and Practice* 30, no. 1 (January 2006): 3, 17.

13. W. Lee Hisle, "Top Issues Facing Academic Libraries: A Report on the Focus on the Future Task Force," *College & Research Libraries* 63, no. 10 (November 2002): 2 (of 2). Available at http://www.ala.org/ala/acrl/acrlpubs/crlnews/back issues2002/novmonth/topissuesfacing.htm (accessed February 15, 2006).

14. Rachel Singer Gordon, "Nurturing New Leaders by Demonstrating Quality Leadership," *JLAMS* [*Journal of the Library Administration and Management Section of the New York Library Association*] 1, no. 2 (2004–2005): 24.

15. Ibid., 26.

16. Hernon and Rossiter, "Emotional Intelligence."

17. It would be interesting to examine the traits depicted in the study cited in the previous reference and determine the extent to which the traits might reflect gender bias.

18. Clemson University, "Vision Statement" (Clemson, SC: Clemson University, 2006). Available at http://www.clemson.edu/welcome/quickly/mission/index.htm (accessed February 16, 2006). To gain a fuller sense of the goals behind the vision statement, see http://www.clemson.edu/welcome/quickly/mission/goals.htm (accessed February 16, 2006).

19. Pamela L. Eddy, "Nested Leadership: The Integration of Organizational Change in a Multicollege System," *Community College Journal of Research and Practice* 30, no. 1 (January 2006): 41.

20. See Peter Hernon, Ronald R. Powell, and Arthur P. Young, *The Next Library Leadership: Attributes of Academic and Public Library Directors* (Westport, CT: Libraries Unlimited, 2003), 43–44.

21. Comment supplied by an anonymous library director in the research resulting in Hernon and Rossiter, "Emotional Intelligence."

3

THE RESEARCH LITERATURE ON LEADERSHIP

Nancy Rossiter

"Leadership is the art of getting someone else to do something you want done because [*sic*] he wants to do it."[1]

A search for books on Amazon.com using the word *leadership* produced 175,081 results that included titles such as *Leadership Secrets of Attila the Hun, Leadership Secrets of Santa Claus,* and *Leadership Lessons from Jesus.* Correspondingly, numerous titles discuss the importance of leadership in businesses today. In many cases the leader is synonymous with the organization; that person's goals, objectives, drive, values, vision, and ethical standards guide the organization. This chapter characterizes the scholarly writings on leadership for the past 100 years. As it would be impossible to focus on all research streams on the topic of leadership, this chapter sets up the literature on emotional intelligence (EI), which focuses on the self-awareness, self-management, social awareness, and relationship management of leaders for subsequent chapters to address.

LEADERSHIP CHARACTERIZATIONS

Leadership theory has been characterized within a framework that classifies leadership as preclassical, classical, progressive, and postprogressive.[2] This framework places emerging leadership theories and perspectives into historical context.

Preclassical

The preclassical school of thought, which reflects on the "great man" or "heroic" leadership, maintains that leaders are born, not made, and that leadership is bestowed on a chosen few. People such as John F. Kennedy, Abraham Lincoln, and Martin Luther King inherit characteristics that make them predestined to become great leaders.[3] To explain leadership and why a few people are chosen to lead the populace, this school relies on stories about profits, chiefs, and kings who were great leaders.[4]

Classical Leadership

Organizational stability, hierarchy, and efficiency are fundamental features of classical leadership, which focuses on trait theory, behavioral theory, and situational theory. Researchers started studying leadership traits in the 1920s and have developed trait theories that identify key qualities and characteristics that differentiate leaders from other individuals. William V. Bingham, who adheres to these theories, defines a leader as someone who "possesses the greatest number of desirable traits of personality and character."[5] Ordway Tead views leadership as a combination of traits that enables an individual to inspire others to accomplish a given task.[6] Trait theory posits that these differences exist and contribute to leadership effectiveness. Examples of traits associated with leadership include masculinity and dominance,[7] intelligence, persistence, initiative, and sociability.[8]

Trait theories have seen resurgence in recent years. Charismatic leadership[9] and EI[10] continue this line of research and help to show the link between the personal qualities of the leader and their relationship to effectiveness of the leader. Another trait that has been researched in the popular press is physical fitness. In *Fit to Lead*, which was based on a quotation ("Physical fitness is the basis for all other forms of excellence") from President John F. Kennedy, Christopher Neck posits that if potential leaders get their bodies into shape, their minds will soon follow. When their minds are sharper, they become stronger leaders.[11]

Behavioral approaches fall into the classical leadership category. In the 1940s, attention began to focus on an examination of what leaders did instead of who they were. The shift resulted largely from the failure of trait theory to produce a consistent list of qualities that ensure a leader's success. Behavioral approaches considered the actions that leaders took regarding their followers. The major studies that that were published at this time were conducted at the University of Michigan and The Ohio State University. The Michigan studies identified two forms of leadership behavior: job-centered behavior and employee-centered behavior. Job-centered leaders examine subordinates' behavior and performance and work procedures. Employee-centered leaders focus on the development of cohesive work groups and employee satisfaction. In these studies, the two forms of leadership behavior were considered to be polar opposites. If leaders were more employee-centered, then they would be less job-centered.[12]

Other research that contributed to this characterization of leaders was the Ohio State studies. Like the Michigan studies, this line of research focused on two forms of leader behavior, but it indicated that different leadership styles could be exhibited simultaneously. The research also assessed the degree to which leaders were involved in tasks of creating structure and considering their subordinates. In initiating structure, the leader sets expectations for the leader-subordinate roles. The leader might show concern for subordinates and attempt to establish a friendly, supportive climate.[13] Other behavioral models that came about at this time were McGregor's Theory X and Theory Y and Blake and Mouton's managerial grid.

In *The Human Side of Enterprise,* Douglas McGregor described two ways, Theory X and Theory Y, that leaders use to view employees. Theory X leaders believe that employees are lazy, are only motivated by money, and try to avoid responsibility. Managers have to coerce, control, or threaten them to work. Theory Y leaders believe that followers work hard, are cooperative, and have positive attitudes. Followers view work as natural and on par with play or rest. Under proper conditions, they learn to not only take, but also seek, responsibility. Motivated employees work hard to achieve the goals of the organization without coercion and punishment. Employees are imaginative and creative, and their ingenuity can be used to solve problems at work.[14]

The model, which was developed at the University of Michigan, provided the framework for the Managerial Grid, created by Robert Blake and Jane Mouton.[15] It consists of five leadership styles that depend on the leaders' concerns for production and for people. The model is termed a *grid*, as the two theorists placed concern for production on one axis and for production on the other. Leaders who scored high on each axis were considered to be the best. The leadership style corresponded to a place on the grid. For example, the effective leader who scored high on both people and production was labeled "team management" and received a 9, 9 on the grid (in the upper right-hand corner). Conversely, a leader who had little concern for people or production would be a 1, 1 or an "impoverished" leader in the lower left-hand corner of the grid. The other styles identified were "Country Club" (1, 9) "Produce or Perish" (9, 1), and "Middle of the Road" (5, 5).

Because behavioral approaches are too simplistic to explain leadership in complex situations, these theories gave way to the situational approach that differs from previous characterizations as it includes the subordinate for the first time. Depending on the situation, effective leaders use different behaviors depending on the needs of the subordinates. Paul Hersey and Kenneth Blanchard created a model of situational leadership that suggests that using one of four leader styles (delegating, participating, selling, and telling) maximizes employee productivity. Followers also have four styles (motivated and able, unmotivated and able, motivated but unable, and unmotivated and unable). Productivity results when the leader applies the correct approach to the follower readiness level.[16] Other situational approaches include the least preferred co-worker theory and path-goal theory.

The Least Preferred Coworker (LPC) theory assumes that leaders should be more relationship than task motivated. Relationships, power, and task structure drive effective leadership styles. Fred Fiedler developed the least preferred co-worker scale by asking employees to identify a person with whom they would least like to work again. Employees then rated this person on several positive (e.g., friendly, helpful, and cheerful) and negative factors (e.g., unfriendly, unhelpful, and gloomy). It is important to remember that leaders will not be effective in all situations. When the leadership style matches the situation, effective leadership results; if there is no match, leaders fail.

The path-goal theory developed by Robert House, is an extension of the expectancy theory of motivation, which states that a person's motivation level is determined by whether or not he or she values a reward, and the likelihood that the person will achieve that goal. According to the model, the leader's job is to coach the subordinate on the best way to achieve the goal. The leader's job is to assist followers in attaining organizational goals and to provide direction and support so that the individual's goals are in concert with the organization's goals. Path-goal theory posits that, depending on the situation, leaders are flexible with their style. The theory includes two contingency variables that moderate the leader-subordinate relationship; these are the environment and follower characteristics. Environmental factors include task structure, authority system, and work group, whereas follower characteristics include locus of control, experience, and perceived ability.

Progressive Leadership

In the 1970s, the progressive leadership approach emerged. Stability and hierarchy were no longer enough to keep businesses competitive. Because this line of research views the leader as a change agent,[17] the focus centers on transformational leadership. Transactional leaders guide or motivate their followers in the direction of established goals by clarifying role and task requirements. James Burns contrasts a transforming leader with a transactional leader in that transactional leaders are more like power wielders, whereas transformational leaders have an interest in the personal development of the follower.[18] A transactional leader receives what he or she wants, and followers gets something they want—the typical "carrot and stick" approach. Another way to characterize the relationship is one of cost-benefit; in return for the contracted services provided, subordinates benefit from an economic exchange that meets their current material and psychic needs.[19] Also, transactional leaders do not sublimate their own needs to the organization.[20]

Transactional leadership works well when the focus is on maintaining day-to-day operations in stable environments.[21] The problem is that subordinates are not motivated to work toward accomplishing a group goal unless they receive a personal incentive. As a result, transactional leaders do not achieve the benefits of outstanding performance and subordinates do not reach their true potential.

Transformational leadership builds on transactional leadership. The transformational leader goes beyond recognizing existing needs of potential followers by seeking to satisfy broader needs and to engage the full person or follower.[22] Transformational leaders move followers to transcend their own self-interest for the good of the group, organization, or country and provides individualized consideration and intellectual stimulation. Such leaders possess charisma and special skills that allow them to provide a supportive environment while motivating followers to achieve higher levels of personal action. A transformational leader inspires the members of the organization to aspire to, and achieve, more than they ever thought possible.

A transforming leader acts to maximize the needs of the follower—to stimulate the needs of the entire organization of people, constantly moving them to higher-order needs. The term *transformational* stems from the ability to develop people as resources and move them to a more satisfactory state of existence.[23] By appealing to higher-order needs, the transformational leader generates a subordinate's commitment to achieving the organizational mission.

A review of the literature on transformational leadership identifies the most frequently mentioned qualities as acting creatively, interactively, with vision and being empowering, passionate, and ethical. Creativity is revealed through challenging the status quo and seeking out new ideas.[24] Creative leaders see problems from many different angles and solve them. Interactive leaders, it is said, provide better direction and are better communicators. Transformational leaders are concerned more with people than with processes.

Transformational leaders act as visionaries in that they communicate a vision to their followers.[25] Warren Bennis and Burt Nanus found that these leaders are better able to create a shared vision. They empower their followers thanks to their ability to translate intention into reality and sustain it for the followers. This empowerment puts duality into motion; empowerment creates more empowerment, which in turn creates more power and allows followers to achieve their potential. The strength and compelling nature of this vision empower the organization's members to excel.[26]

The most surprising element in the listing of characteristics is that the leader must be passionate.[27,28] Transformational leaders are passionate about the tasks they perform and about their people. They forget their personal problems, lose a sense of time, and feel competent and in control. Without passion there is no direction, and vision is short-lived.

Another important characteristic of transformational leaders is their ethical values. This type of leader does the right thing at the right time and possesses vision, self-confidence, and the inner strength to argue successfully about what he or she perceives as right or good.[29] Another defining characteristic that emerges repeatedly throughout the literature is that the transformational leader is, above all, an agent of change.[30] A change agent serves as a catalyst, not a controller, of change.[31]

Some critics argue that transformational leadership may be unethical, although it requires leaders to be morally mature and morally uplifting.[32] Contrary to what the critics say, the transactional leaders are more likely to engage in unethical practices. Transformational leaders, on the other hand, concentrate on terminal values such as integrity and fairness. According to Bernard Bass, leaders are truly transformational when they increase awareness of what is right, good, important, and beautiful; when they help elevate followers' needs for achievement and self-actualization; and when they move followers to go beyond their self-interests for the good of the group, organization, or society.[33]

By contrast, *pseudo-transformational* leaders may also motivate and transform their followers, but in doing so, they produce support for special interests; they do so at the expense of what is good for the group. They encourage "we-they" competitiveness and the pursuit of the leaders' own self-interests instead of the common good.[34]

Postprogressive Leadership

Postprogressive leadership research focuses on the organization and the impact that outside forces exact on the leader. Because the environment had become increasingly networked, global, and turbulent, a new type of leader was needed. This new organization demanded that organizations learn and change.[35] These capacities are achieved by fostering employees' potential to achieve a competitive advantage.

Postprogressive leadership focuses on social change, shared responsibility for leadership, and taking risks. Distributed leadership characterizes this stream of research. Broad and engaged participation in the leadership of the organization influences change. Further, organizational structures are viewed as flat or as part of a networked environment. Peter Senge and Margaret Wheatly belong to this research stream.

Senge draws on concepts from the physical and social sciences, as well as management and engineering.[36] He calls for changes in mental models; traditional approaches to leadership and management emphasize breaking down problems into small parts, which result in long-term dysfunction for the organization—seeing the parts often results in destroying the whole. Developing the habit of mind that looks for patterns and interrelationships, rather than chains of cause and effects, is essential for leadership in situations in which complexity and excessive amounts of information exist. Systems thinking requires the capacity to view organizations as systems and interconnected webs that are continually in flux. Changes to part of the web or system ripple throughout the entire organization. These interconnected webs are in marked contrast to the organizational structures that are consistent with classical paradigms of leadership, characterized as top-down pyramid of control and influence. These webs connect horizontally across the organization, whereas change originates at the top of traditional structures and is filtered down the chain of command.

Wheatly adopted ideas from the so-called new science of physics, biology, and chemistry.[37] Her work also reflects chaos and evolution theories. She embraces chaos and change. She writes that the organization as machine must be replaced by the organization as organic system. She views change as inevitable because all organizations change, adapt, and grow as they maintain their identity. Her vision of leadership requires that all members of an organization participate in the building the organization.

Post-Postprogressive Leadership

In recent years, many leadership books have focused on the importance of effective leaders focusing on the positive. Empathizing with one's followers, connecting with them through participation, individualized attention, and building their strengths are some of the methods that successful leaders use. Representative of this research are Daniel Goleman, Jim Collins, Stephen Covey, Robert Goffee, Gareth Jones, Donald Clifton, and Marcus Buckingham.

Much has been written on the subject of EI in the last decade. Goleman has found that emotionally intelligent leaders are much more effective at producing results than those who are not. He and his colleagues found that "high levels of emotional intelligence . . . create climates in which information-sharing, trust, healthy risk-taking and learning flourish. Low levels of emotional intelligence create climates rife with fear and anxiety."[38] They point out that, because a leader's moods and behavior drive organizational success, a leader's task is to achieve and maintain emotionally intelligent leadership.

Goleman and his colleagues' theories have emerged from the science of moods, in particular what has been called the open-loop nature of the brain's limbic system. Contrary to a self-regulating, closed-loop system, the open-loop nature of our brains depends on connections with other people to control our moods. This open-loop limbic system was "a winning design in evolution because it let people come to one another's emotional rescue."[39] Golman and his colleagues support this idea with research conducted in hospitals, which shows that the presence of another person in intensive care units not only lowers patients' blood pressure but also slows the secretion of fatty acids that block arteries.

Goleman and his colleagues further state that the most effective leaders display moods that match the situation at hand, but they also show optimism. They have a healthy respect for what others are feeling. Whether their followers are overwhelmed or pleased, effective leaders move forward with hope and humor. Goleman and his colleagues call this *resonance,* and effective leaders resonate with their followers through the five components of EI: self-awareness, self-management, social awareness, self-motivation, and relationship management.[40]

In addition to using traits to describe leaders, part of the research conducted by Goleman and his colleagues includes situational leadership. Leaders have a style toolbox and choose between visionary, coaching, pacesetting, democratic, and commanding styles. Visionary, coaching, and democratic styles benefit the organization; and leaders should be careful when using the pace-setting and commanding styles, as they have the potential to backfire and to be stressful for the followers.[41]

Collins, who revisits trait theory in his research on "Level 5 Leadership,"[42] continues the research stream on the power of being positive and its effect on leadership results. Level 5 leaders are characterized by humility, will, ferocious resolve, and the tendency to give credit to others while assigning blame to themselves. These leaders show humility by consistently giving credit to others or crediting luck for their success. When results are poor, however, they tend to blame themselves. They manifest their will in their determination to do whatever it takes to produce great results. They also have a knack for choosing great successors, ensuring the organization's success into the future.

Marcus Buckingham also focuses on the positive. With Donald Clifton he examined positive aspects in organizations and made a connection to leadership effectiveness.[43] Their research was based on a Gallup poll of more than 1.7 million employees from 101 companies in 63 countries. They found that only 20 percent of those polled used their strengths every day. In looking at related research, they found that millions of articles covered depression, but little research addressed joy. Society pays more attention to correcting peoples' weaknesses than developing their strengths.

Buckingham posits that great leaders focus on developing the strengths and talents of their employees.[44] He states that these leaders have three levers to lead people well: what their strengths are, what the triggers are that activate those strengths, and how the person learns.

Stephen Covey, who also focuses on effective leaders who accentuate the positive, sees leadership as a "choice to deal with people in a way that will communicate to them their worth and potential so clearly they will come to see it in themselves."[45] He suggests that leaders can make a difference by using their unique talents; this message is similar to what Buckingham advocates. Covey also believes that leaders should discover their own voice. To be a great leader, a person, he maintains, taps into people's full potential. He sees four roles for great leaders:

1. They are proactive, begin with the end in mind, put first things first, think win-win, seek first to understand, are understood, synergize, and renew the four dimensions of a person's nature (physical, spiritual, mental, and social/emotional).
2. They are involved in path finding.

3. They align subordinates with the goals of the organization.

4. They empower their subordinates.[46]

Great leaders accomplish these roles by being models to others, articulating a clear and meaningful organizational vision, creating systems and processes that are aligned with their organization's mission, and empowering subordinates to achieve that mission.

Rob Goffee and Gareth Jones believe effective leaders excel at capturing people's hearts, minds, and spirits.[47] Like Collins, they believe that being humble, through the selective revealing of weaknesses and practicing what they call "thought empathy" (balancing respect for the individual with the task at hand), makes for effective leaders. Being humble, empathetic, and listening to one's subordinates contributes greatly to a leader's success.

Richard Boyatzis and Annie McKee, colleagues of Daniel Goleman, linked EI with resonant leadership. Resonant leadership occurs when leaders have developed their EI and connect with others, inspiring teams to move together in a positive direction and to maintain a balance of optimism and realism. Resonant leadership identifies three traits necessary for renewal and keeping resonant leaders from falling into dissonance: mindfulness, hope, and compassion. Mindfulness includes leaders taking time to reflect on their own thoughts and feelings. This may include keeping a journal, meditation, or other ways to keep track of thoughts and feelings. It also includes being open to other's opinions, particularly in difficult times. Hope involves developing a vision and believing in one's ability to attain the dream. Compassion includes showing and receiving compassion. It also involves listening effectively to move toward mutual understanding.[48]

THE BODY OF RESEARCH

Recent writings reflect a return to focusing on the positive aspects of leader behavior and leadership styles by discussing authentic and full-range leadership and EI. In 1988, Martin Seligman, who was then the president of the American Psychological Association, launched the positive psychology movement. He felt that insufficient attention centered on the positive strengths of people.[49] He insisted on the scientific hallmarks of theory and research in contrast to what is in popular "feel good" or "self-help" books.

Fred Luthans, who applied positive psychology to the workplace, built on Seligman's foundation. He defined the term *positive organizational behavior* (POB) as "the study and application of positively oriented human resource strengths and psychological capacities that can be measured, developed, and effectively managed for performance in today's workplace."[50] POB, which is grounded in theoretical and empirical research, differentiates itself from the popular bestsellers that have a positive message but are not supported by research.[51]

Another leadership model that draws from POB and positive psychology is authentic leadership. Luthans and Bruce Avolio define this type of leadership as "a process that draws from both positive psychological capacities and a highly developed organizational context, which results in both greater awareness and self-regulated positive behaviors on the part of leaders and associates, fostering positive self-development."[52] Authentic leaders have POB strengths related to confidence, hope, optimism, and resiliency; their behavior is also consistent over time.

Part of the emphasis on the positive aspects of leadership may have to do with the adverse impact that an atmosphere of negativity has on business and the achievement of desired outcomes. A recent study that examined the communication patterns of management teams engaged in strategic planning showed that the most important factor in the profitability and customer satisfaction was the ratio of positive to negative comments among team members. This ratio, in fact, is four times more powerful than any other factor in explaining team success. Positive comments express support, helpfulness, or appreciation, whereas negative comments show disapproval, blame, or criticism. The researchers conclude that teams need to be able to draw on the liberating and creative power of positivism.[53]

Another well-researched area of leadership is that of full-range leadership, which Bass and Avolio popularized. The full-range leadership model has three dimensions: transformational leadership, transactional leadership, and laissez-faire leadership. Transformational leadership consists of four factors, the four Is: individual consideration, intellectual stimulation, idealized influence, and inspirational motivation. Transactional leadership comprises conditional reward and management-by-exception: passive and active. Most studies of full-range leadership use Bass's Multi-factor Leadership Questionnaire (MLQ). The MLQ measures six factors: charisma, intellectual stimulation, individualized consideration, contingent reward, management-by-exception, and laissez-faire leadership.[54]

EI is a predictor of the full-range leadership style. Recent research has built on the theory of EI by defining and investigating noncognitive intelligence. EI, which is a capability, suggests that individuals who have high levels of EI can perceive emotion, integrate it into thought, and understand and manage it. Links between EI and transformational leadership have been established. It is believed that EI may be the new "X" factor that advances and reinvigorates a more complete understanding of social influence and leadership.[55]

Recent research has attempted to find a better understanding of EI. Three distinct approaches to EI have evolved:

1. A trait, meaning that it is an innate personal quality that indicates emotional well-being;[56]

2. An acquired competence, meaning that it is the set of acquired sills and competencies that underlie effective leadership and performance[57]; and

3. An intellectual capability, meaning that it is the capacity to reason with emotion in four areas: to perceive emotion, to integrate it in thought, to understand it, and to manage it.[58]

A significant predictive relationship exists among EI, laissez-faire leadership, and leadership outcomes. The leader's internal self-concept moderates the relationship among EI, transformational leadership, contingent reward leadership, and the accomplishments that leadership produces.[59]

CONCLUSION

No "one size fits all" style of leadership exists. Instead, leaders develop a leadership style or styles that work best for them. Although this chapter discusses different leadership approaches, dimensions, and theories, new ones will emerge. Such a likelihood will inform the practice of leadership and reminds us that leadership is a complex progress with multiple dimensions. Over time, thinking about leadership has shifted from simplistic characterizations of personality traits to more complex frameworks for understanding what constitutes effective leadership. Effective leadership incorporates ethical considerations and builds a values-based organization in which principles and values guide day-to-day decision making, and both leaders and followers avoid wrong behaviors and take active steps to do what is right. As Peter G. Northouse writes, "Because leadership involves influence and leaders often have more power than followers, they have an enormous ethical responsibility for how they affect other people."[60] Leaders therefore should be caring people who are "particularly sensitive to the values and ideas they promote," and how their actions impact their organization.[61]

"The quality of leadership, more than any other single factor, determines the success or failure of an organization."[62]

NOTES

1. Dwight D. Eisenhower, "4th State of the Union Address" (1956). Available at http://www.theamericanpresidency.us/1956.htm (accessed March 1, 2006).

2. Chris B. Crawford, Curtis L. Brungardt, and Micol Maughan, *Understanding Leadership: Theories & Concepts,* 3d ed. (New York: Wiley, 2004).

3. Ralph M. Stogdill and Bernard M. Bass, *Handbook of Leadership: A Survey of Theory and Research* (New York: The Free Press, 1974).

4. Crawford, Brungardt, and Maughan, *Understanding Leadership.*

5. William V. Bingham, *Leadership: The Psychological Foundations of Management* (New York: Shaw, 1927), 5.

6. Ordway Tead, *The Art of Leadership* (New York: McGraw-Hill, 1935).

7. R. D. Mann, "A Review of the Relationship between Personality and Performance in Small Groups," *Psychological Bulletin* 56 (1959): 241–70.

8. Ralph M. Stodgill, "Personal Factors Associated with Leadership: A Survey of the Literature," *Journal of Psychology* 25 (1948): 35–71.

9. Robert House, "Theory of Charismatic Leadership," in *Leadership: The Cutting Edge,* A symposium held at Southern Illinois University, Carbondale, October 27–28, 1976, ed. James G. Hunt and Lars L. Larson (Carbondale: Southern Illinois University Press, 1977), 189–207.

10. Daniel Goleman, "What Makes a Leader?," *Harvard Business Review* 5 (1998): 93.

11. Christopher Neck, *Fit to Lead* (New York: St. Martin's Press, 2004).

12. See Ricky Griffin. *Fundamentals of Management, Core Concepts and Applications,* 4th ed. (Boston: Houghton Mifflin, 2004).

13. Ibid.

14. Douglas McGregor, *The Human Side of Enterprise* (New York: McGraw-Hill, 1960).

15. Robert Blake and Jane Mouton, "Management by Grid," *Group and Organization Studies* 6 (1981): 439–55.

16. Paul Hersey and Ken Blanchard, *Management of Organizational Behavior: Using Human Resources* (Englewood Cliffs, NJ: Prentice Hall, 1969).

17. Rosabeth Moss Kanter, *The Change Masters: Innovation and Entrepreneurship in the American Corporation* (New York: Touchstone/Simon and Schuster, 1983).

18. James M. Burns, *Leadership* (New York: Harper and Row, 1978).

19. Bernard M. Bass, *Leadership and Performance beyond Expectations* (New York: Free Press, 1985).

20. Karl W. Kuhnert and Phillip Lewis, "Transactional and Transformational Leadership: A Constructive/Developmental Analysis," *Academy of Management Review* 12 (1994): 648–57.

21. Bernard M. Bass, "Transformational Leadership: A Response to Critiques," in *Leadership Theory and Research: Perspectives and Directions,* ed. Martin M. Chemers and Roya Ayman (New York: Free Press, 1996), 49–80.

22. Burns, *Leadership.*

23. Kuhnert and Lewis, "Transactional and Transformational Leadership."

24. Burns, *Leadership.* See also Michael Z. Hackman and Craig E. Johnson, *Leadership: A Communication Perspective* (Prospect Heights, IL: Waveland Press, Inc., 1991).

25. Ibid.

26. Warren G. Bennis and Bert Naunus, *Leaders: The Strategies for Taking Charge* (New York: Harper & Row, 1985).

27. Stephen Covey, *The Seven Habits of Highly Effective People* (New York: Simon & Schuster, 1989).

28. Tom Peters, *Liberation Management* (New York: Knopf, 1992).

29. Norman Vincent Peale and Kenneth Blanchard, *Power of Ethical Management* (New York: Ballantine Books, 1989).

30. Bass, *Leadership and Performance beyond Expectations.*

31. Warren G. Bennis, *Why Leaders Can't Lead: The Unconscious Conspiracy Continues* (San Francisco: Jossey-Bass Publishers, 1989).

32. Bruce J. Avolio, "Leadership: Building Vital Forces into Highly Developed Teams," *Human Resource Management Journal* 11 (1995): 10–15.

33. Bass, "Transformational Leadership."

34. Ibid.

35. Kimberly B. Boal, "Strategic Leadership Research: Moving on," *Leadership Quarterly* 11 (2001): 515–50.

36. Peter Senge, *The Fifth Discipline: The Art and Practice of the Learning Organization* (New York: Doubleday, 1990).

37. Margaret Wheatly, *Leadership and the New Science* (San Francisco: Berrett-Koehler Publishers, 1994).

38. Daniel Goleman, Richard Boyatzis, and Annie McKee, "Primal Leadership: The Hidden Driver of Great Performance," *Harvard Business Review* 79 (2001): 44.

39. Ibid, 46.

40. Ibid, 49.

41. Daniel Goleman, Annie McKee, and Richard Boyatzis, *Primal Leadership* (Boston: Harvard Business School Press, 2002), 44–45.

42. Jim Collins, "Level 5 Leadership," *Harvard Business Review* 83 (2005): 136–46.

43. Marcus Buckingham and Donald O. Clifton, *Now, Discover Your Strengths* (New York: Free Press, 2001).

44. Marcus Buckingham, "What Great Managers Do," *Harvard Business Review* 20 (2005): 20–26.

45. Steven Covey, *The 8th Habit* (New York: Free Press, 2004), 1.

46. Ibid. Covey refers to renewal as sharpening a saw.

47. Robert Geoffee and Gareth Jones, "Why Should Anyone Be Led by You?," *Harvard Business Review* 78 (2000): 62–70.

48. Richard Boyatzis and Annie McKee, *Resonant Leadership* (Boston: Harvard Business School Press, 2005), 111–200.

49. See Martin E. Seligman and Michaly Csikszentmihalyi, "Positive Psychology: An Introduction," *American Psychologist* 55 (2000): 5–14.

50. See Fred Luthans and Bruce Avolio, "Authentic Leadership: A Positive Development Approach," in *Positive Organizational Scholarship: Foundations of a New Discipline*, ed. Kim S. Cameron, Jane E. Dutton, and Robert E. Quinn (San Francisco: Barrett-Koehler, 2003), 731–39.

51. See, for example, Spencer Johnson, *Who Moved My Cheese? Little Nibbles of Cheese* (Kansas City, MO: Stark Books, 2001); Spencer Johnson, *Who Moved My Cheese? An Amazing Way to Deal with Change in Your Work and in Your Life* (New York: Putnam, 1998).

52. Luthans and Avolio, "Authentic Leadership," 732.

53. Marcial Losada and Emily Heaphy, "The Role of Positivity and Connectivity in the Performance of Business Teams," *American Behavioral Scientist* 47 (2004): 740–65.

54. Bernard Bass and Bruce Avolio, *Transformational Leadership Development: Manual for the Multifactor Leadership Questionnaire* (Palo Alto, CA: Consulting Psychologists Press, 1990).

55. F. William Brown and Dan Moshavi, "Transformational Leadership and Emotional Intelligence: A Potential Pathway for an Increased Understanding of Interpersonal Influence," *Journal of Organizational Behavior* 26 (2005): 867–71.

56. Reuvin Bar-On, *The Emotional Quotient Inventory: A Measure of Emotional Intelligence* (Toronto, ON: Multi Health Systems, 1996).

57. Daniel Goleman, *Emotional Intelligence* (New York: Bantam Books, 1995).

58. John Mayer, Peter Salovey, David Caruso, and Gill Sitarenios, "Measuring and Modeling Emotional Intelligence with MSCEIT V 2.0," *Emotion* 3 (2003): 97–105.

59. See Mark Burbach, *Testing the Relationship between Emotional Intelligence and Full-Range Leadership as Moderated by Cognitive Style and Self-Concept.* (Doctoral Dissertation, University of Nebraska, Lincoln. 2004), 246.

60. Peter G. Northouse, *Leadership: Theory and Practice* (Thousand Oaks, CA: SAGE, 2004), 326.

61. Ibid.

62. Fred Fiedler and Martin Chemers, *Improving Leadership Effectiveness* (New York: John Wiley, 1984), 8.

4

GLOBAL LEADERSHIP

Nancy Rossiter

"Leadership is the capacity to translate vision into reality."[1]

As the American workforce becomes more culturally diverse and organizations function more in a global environment, there is a need to understand how leadership styles vary in their effectiveness. Although the majority of leadership research has been conducted in Western culture using leadership theories such as transformational leadership (a process that changes and transforms individuals), the application of what is learned should be sensitive to cultural values. For example, what if a potential Vietnamese or Japanese library director were educated in the United States about the benefits of transformational leadership and attempted to behave like a transformational leader when arriving back in his homeland? Will the person to whom he reports value the transformational behaviors, be threatened by them, or perceive them as ignoring tradition and organizational culture? In some non-Western cultures, the change orientation advocated by transformational leadership is viewed as a lack of respect for tradition.[2] This chapter, which explores universal and cultural specific models of leadership, examines three types of intelligence needed for effective global leadership:

1. The intelligence measured by standardized IQ (intelligent quotient) tests;
2. Emotional intelligence (EI); and
3. Cultural intelligence (CI).

SHORTAGE OF EFFECTIVE GLOBAL LEADERS

Many studies have examined the performance of global leaders; unfortunately, most of them point to the ineffectiveness of cross-cultural leadership. For example, in an analysis of global leadership literature, Vesa Suutari discovered that:

- Leaders need to develop global competencies;
- There is a shortage of global leaders in the corporate world;
- Many companies do not know what it means to develop corporate leaders;
- Only 8 percent of Fortune 500 companies have comprehensive global leadership training programs; and
- There is a need to better understand the link between managerial competencies and global leadership.[3]

In another review of the leadership literature, Tracy Manning found that the global leadership of multinational organizations fell far short of ideal; for example:

- 85 percent of Fortune 500 firms surveyed had an insufficient number of leaders.
- 65 percent felt that their leaders needed additional skills.
- One-third of international managers underperformed in their international assignments based on the supervisors' evaluations.
- Organizations have erroneously promoted leaders to international assignments based on technical and organizational skills.[4]

These findings point to challenges that managers face when they hire, develop, and train individuals to lead multinational organizations. It is important therefore for both managers and leaders to understand what makes global leaders effective. The next section reviews the main leadership styles applicable across cultural borders.

LEADERSHIP STYLES

Bernard Bass, whose research has been replicated consistently across cultures, analyzed three well-known types of leadership: *laissez-faire, transactional,* and *transformational.* Laissez-faire leaders abdicate their responsibility, avoid making decisions, and leave subordinates alone to perform their job responsibilities. This leadership style is not practiced widely in U.S. businesses, but elements of it appear, to various degrees, in managers. Carried to the extreme, this type of leader adopts a "sink or swim" strategy. Research has found that laissez-faire leadership has an adverse effect on the performance of employees, as it does not help subordinates or followers grow and satisfy their work-related needs.[5]

Transactional leaders identify and clarify job tasks for their subordinates and communicate how the successful execution of tasks leads to desirable job rewards. They try to obtain agreement from subordinates on what needs to be done and what the payoff will be for the people doing it. They determine and define goals, make suggestions about how to execute tasks, and provide feedback. Research on transactional leadership shows that this style of leadership has a positive influence on the attitudinal and behavioral responses of employees across countries.[6]

Transformational leaders take a long-term perspective by focusing on the future, not just on the current, needs of subordinates or themselves. They view short-term problems as opportunities for the organization and look at them from a holistic perspective. Transformational leadership complements transactional leadership. Transformational leaders raise subordinates' awareness of the importance and value of designated outcomes, and get employees to transcend self-interests for the sake of the organization. To accomplish this, transformational leaders possess and display the following characteristics: charismatic leadership, inspirational motivation, intellectual stimulation, and individualized consideration.[7]

Charismatic leaders exercise strong influence over workers, and they demonstrate vision and a sense of mission. They instill pride in their subordinates and gain their respect. Employees have a strong sense of trust and confidence in these leaders, tend to adopt their vision, and develop a strong sense of loyalty. Leaders who show inspirational motivation communicate high expectations and important purposes in simple ways. They demonstrate self-determination and commitment in attaining goals, and they present an optimistic view of the future. In this way, they can persuade workers to accomplish more than they initially felt possible. A leader who provides intellectual stimulation encourages workers to explore new ways of handling problems and to use their intuition. Subordinates eagerly offer their ideas, become problem solvers, and tend to have a more developed thought process. Leaders who provide individualized consideration are attentive to the unique concerns of their employees and use such means as mentoring, coaching, and counseling for employee development and growth. Cross-cultural research on transformational leaders has revealed that individualized consideration is effective and positively related to subordinate satisfaction, motivation, and performance.[8]

Studies of global leadership, particularly those conducted by Robert House and Bernard Bass, have found that elements of transformational leadership exist across cultures.[9] These elements include behaviors such as being "encouraging," "positive," "motivational," "confidence builder," "dynamic," and "excellence-oriented," as well as demonstrating "foresight." Two contrasting perspectives explain why some leader behaviors are successful in one's native culture but not in other cultures; these are the universal perspective and the culture-specific perspective.

THE UNIVERSAL PERSPECTIVE

Leadership is a universal phenomenon in that some form of it exists in every society and that some concepts apply across cultures. Bass suggested a universal position regarding the cross-culture transferability of transformational leadership. His model suggests that core constructs of transformational leadership should not vary across cultures.[10] These constructs (the four Is) include:

- Idealized influence (charisma). These leaders display trust, take a stand on difficult issues, and emphasize the importance of purpose, commitment, and ethical consequences of decisions.
- Inspirational motivation. These leaders communicate an appealing vision of the future and convey enthusiasm.
- Intellectual stimulation. These leaders question old assumptions and stimulate new ways of thinking in their followers.
- Individualized consideration. These leaders consider individual needs and abilities; they also coach and teach.

Peter Dorfman and Jon Howell tested specific hypotheses related to the generalizability of leadership behaviors and processes in the United States, Mexico, Japan, South Korea, and Taiwan.[11] Their research supports Bass's findings regarding the validity of both the universal and culture-specific views of leadership research across cultures.[12] Dorfman and Howell showed that cultural universality for three leader behaviors (supportive, contingent reward, and charismatic) is perceived as positive in the five nations. They also found cultural specificity, which necessitates distinct leadership approaches in different countries, for three other leader behaviors (directive, participative, and contingent punishment). These behaviors had a positive impact in only two nations. Of these behaviors, the impact of contingent punishment was the most distinctive in that it had a desirable effect only in the United States; there were undesirable or ambiguous effects in the other countries.[13] This finding may be due, in part, to management training in the United States, which emphasizes the importance of giving feedback, either positive or negative. In countries such as Japan, individualized negative feedback is usually withheld or done with a great deal of subtlety to maintain group harmony and save face.

Dorfman and Howell also found that charismatic leadership was universal. Such a leadership behavior, which is emotional in nature, has the most consistent effect on subordinate satisfaction across the countries. Charismatic leadership leads to a positive attitude toward work in the countries studied; however, worker performance was unaffected.

One of their most surprising findings is that, when comparing the impact of leadership behaviors in Asian and Western cultures, the United States is as different from Mexican culture, as it is from Asian cultures. Although Dorfman and

Howell discovered patterns in universal leadership behavior, they noted that the United States differs in two instances. It is the only nation in which participative leadership had a positive effect on subordinate performance and in which the contingent punishment behavior of leaders had a uniformly positive effect on subordinates. Dorfman and Howell suggested that certain factors contribute to culturally different results regarding leadership behaviors in the United States. These results include uniquely high individualism, egalitarian management climate, changing attitudes toward formal authority, movements toward increased professionalism, team processes, and employee empowerment.[14]

In ground-breaking research, which involved 170 social scientists in 62 countries, Robert House and his colleagues discovered support for the universal perspective related to the effectiveness of transformational leadership. Certain behaviors (being "encouraging," "positive," "motivational," "confidence builder," "dynamic," and "excellence oriented," as well as demonstrating "foresight") were universally endorsed across the countries. These seven behaviors are characteristic of transformational leadership.[15]

A more advanced form of the universal perspective is what Bass labeled "functional universal," which holds when the within-group relationship between variables is the same across nations. He suggested that developing a vision of the future and motivating followers to work hard and to achieve exceptional performance should lead to excellence in any country.[16]

Evidence supporting the universality of transactional and transformational leadership has been gathered worldwide. It shows leadership as either a matter of the contingent reinforcement of followers by a transactional leader or moving of followers beyond their self-interests for the good of the group, organization, or society by a transformational leader.[17]

Walter Lonner advanced four types of universals that transcend cultures: simple, variform, functional, and systemic. A simple universal is a phenomenon that is consistent throughout the world, whereas variform universal is a simple regularity influenced, to some extent, by cultures or organizations. A functional universal, as previously discussed, indicates a uniform relationship among variables. An example of this is the correlation between laissez-faire leadership and perceived ineffectiveness. Laissez-faire leaders are ineffective because they give workers total freedom to make their own decisions and decide on the methods to use to complete their work; such an approach is often perceived as an abdication of responsibility. A systematic behavioral universal explains if-then outcomes across cultures and organizations.[18] Still, it merits recognition that the culture-specific perspective specifies that different cultures require different leadership approaches.

THE CULTURE-SPECIFIC PERSPECTIVE

Unique cultural characteristics (e.g., language, beliefs, values, religion, and social orientation) generally require distinct leadership approaches in different nations. Researchers who adhere to the culture-specific position often mention the idiosyncratic nature of North America as support for the argument that leadership theories developed there have limited application elsewhere.[19]

Prevailing theories of leadership, according to House, are North American in character and are based on individualism as opposed to collectivism. They tend to be hedonistic rather than altruistic in motivation, to favor the centrality of work, and to be democratic in value orientation. Cross-cultural psychology and sociological research show that many cultures do not share these beliefs.[20] Table 4.1 summarizes some culturally specific differences in leadership models, including the cultural definition of the leader; the importance of an elite; and selection, advancement, and diversity differences. Leaders are perceived differently across cultures and their selection, advancement, and differences in cultural and other types of diversity vary widely.

Leadership Definition

The idea of a leader can be culturally imbedded. For instance, in the United States, the leader is seen as a person who acts much like a sports superstar. That person takes an organization to new levels of performance, achieving impressive short-term goals, and spinning the organization off to the highest bidder. In France, individual leaders are predestined to reach a leadership position owing to their national examination scores, the schools they attend, and their roles in national networks. Leaders in Germany must demonstrate high levels of skill and be experts in their chosen career field. In Japan, leaders are male, loyal, wise, and a product of a group.[21]

Importance of an Elite

Another key cultural difference in how leaders are viewed relates to whether they come from a carefully accepted elite group. Countries that adhere to this perspective include France, Japan, and China, as well as nations in Latin America. To be a leader in France, one has to be part of a national elite, a group that is the source of leadership potential. In other countries such as the United States, Canada, Scandinavia, Israel, the Netherlands, and Germany, a leader is a self-made person who outperforms others and rises to the top; as a result, being part of an elite class is not necessarily important.[22]

Selection Differences

In the United Kingdom and the United States, human resource professionals usually select professionals by means of a variety of selection tools, including psychological tests, a careful reading of resumes, and checking references. References from the leadership elite are not usually valued or sought out. In the United States, recruitment is ongoing and leadership mobility is prevalent. In countries such as France and Japan, the most important

Table 4.1
Cross-Cultural Leadership Differences

		U.S.	Latin America	France	U.K.	Germany	Italy	Holland	Poland	Japan	China	Vietnam	Israel	Africa
Leadership Definition	What is the cultural leadership prototype?	Free agent star	General	Genius	Diplomat	Master	Godfather	Marathon winner	Baron	Senior statesman	Warlord	Communist party boss	Field commander	Tribal chief
Importance of an Elite	Is the idea of an elite encouraged?	No	Yes	Yes	Yes	Yes	No	Yes	No	Yes	Yes	Yes	No	No
Selection Differences	Do social/political networks dominate?	Somewhat important	Key	Key	Important	Somewhat important	Key	Somewhat important	Important	Key	Key	Key	Important (army)	Key
	How important is a certain educational degree?	Key (MBA)	Important	Important	Important	Key	Important	Important	Somewhat important	Somewhat important	Important	Important	Important	Not Important
Advancement Differences	Age measured performance	No / Yes	No / Yes	No / Yes	Yes / Yes	No Key (diplomas and apprenticeship)	No / No	No / Yes	No / No	Yes / No	Yes / No	Yes / No	No / Yes	No / No
Diversity Differences	Present and role of professional women	Yes	No (except Argentina)	Yes (Magreb, Africa)	Yes	No	No	Yes	No	No	No	No	Yes	No

Adapted from C. Brooklyn Derr, Sylvie Roussillon, and Frank Bournois, *Cross-Cultural Approaches to Leadership Development* (Westport, CT: Quorum Books, 2002), 290–302.

selection criterion is the institution from which a person gets an education. In Germany, it is one's degree (e.g., a PhD in engineering). In China, Africa, and Italy, as well as Latin America, the most important factor is one's social contacts. Social networks and references from elite educational institutions are also essential in France and Japan.[23]

Advancement Differences

Countries such as the United Kingdom and the United States use a variety of approaches for advancement into leadership positions (including measured performance, interviews, and similar other tools). France, Israel, Italy, and Latin America select their leaders early on, mainly through informal recommendations and are unlikely to measure or assess senior candidates. In Japan, China, and Vietnam, the age of the candidate is also significant; older leaders are viewed as better leaders.[24]

Diversity

Diversity is also a factor by which leadership perceptions differ. Governmental policies and equal opportunity laws in some countries, including the United States, require the inclusion of more minorities and women in educational programs and leadership positions. The number of women and culturally diverse individuals is perceived as an indicator of diversity; this statistic might become an output metric for making comparisons across industries. An output metric for cross-cultural diversity is that 60 percent of women in the United States work outside the home as compared to 35 percent in Italy.[25] A United Nations survey of countries that practice gender equality at work revealed that Scandinavia was the top country; Canada ranked 4th and the United States was 19th.[26] Variables relating to both the universal and culture-specific models of global leadership can be found in the theory of emotional intelligence.

GLOBAL LEADERSHIP EFFECTIVENESS AND EMOTIONAL INTELLIGENCE

EI is broadly defined as "the ability to monitor one's own and other's feelings and emotions, to discriminate among them, and to use this information to guide one's thinking and action."[27] This means that EI can be conceptualized relative to an individual's awareness of his/her own values and ability to perceive and be aware of emotions expressed by others. The five components of EI are self-awareness, self-regulation, motivation, empathy, and social skill. The first three components relate to self-management, whereas the other two address "managing relationships with others."

Daniel Goleman, Richard Boyatzis, and Annie McKee found that the most critical leadership skills in the United States were linked to EI. As much as 79 percent of leadership success in the United States results from a high EI, and between 47 and 56 percent of work/life success is the result of EI.[28]

Research on the global applications of EI is limited. In a study that focused on the *empathy* aspect of emotional intelligence (recognizing emotion in others), Howard Weiss and Russell Cropanzano identified six basic universal emotions within the United States: happiness, surprise, fear, sadness, anger, and disgust. Although there is agreement among national cultures and subcultures about the meaning of commonly accepted emotions and their nonverbal and verbal cues, the meaning of some emotions does not translate easily across countries. This theory of emotional recognition was tested in a study conducted on U.S. and Japanese citizens. The U.S. group identified the six basic emotions correctly in 86 to 96 percent of the pictures. When the Japanese were asked to identify the same pictured emotions, however, they could only identify surprise with a high rate of certainty (97%). The other five emotions ranged from 27 to 70 percent.[29] This suggests that recognizing emotions may be difficult to generalize among different countries. Ilan Alon and James Higgins believe that the concept of CI bridges the emotional gap.[30]

CULTURAL INTELLIGENCE

Research indicates a growing recognition of the multiple intelligences required for global leadership. Illan Alon and James Higgins found the following three intelligences form the core of global leadership:

- Rational and logic based verbal and quantitative intelligence, which is measured by traditional IQ tests;
- EI, which has become prominent as a determinant of leadership success in the past decade and can be measured by EI tests; and
- CI, which can be measured by CI tests that are currently coming into existence.[31]

Two major types of CI exist; these are organizational CI and geographic/ ethnic CI. Organizational CI, which is the knowledge of an organization's corporate culture, is important when leaders move into or work for a new organization. A lack of organizational CI contributes to individual and corporate failures. Geographic/ethnic CI is the knowledge of the cultural or subcultural nuances in which an organization functions.[32] For example, in the United States, business is frequently conducted during dinner or while playing golf. In countries such as Japan, it is essential for business people to eat or play first, then negotiate the business deal. Leaders who are unaware of ethnic nuances will fail.

The term *cultural intelligence* has become used only recently, and there are few academic conceptualizations of it. P. Christopher Early and Soon Ang define the term as "a person's capability for successful adaptation to new cultural settings; that is for unfamiliar settings attributable to cultural context."[33] According to them, CI is distinct from social intelligence and EI in that people must learn new patterns of social interactions, rely on their own abilities, and provide the correct behavioral responses. For example, in a new cultural setting, familiar cues are largely or entirely absent (or are present but misguided); thus a common attributional and perceptual perspective cannot be trusted. In such an instance, a person must develop a common understanding from available information, event, or thought; however, that person may not have an adequate understanding of local practices and norms.[34]

Early and Ang offer many examples of individuals who have social, intellectual, and emotional intelligence, which made them successful in their own environment, but they could not transfer skills to a setting in a different country where they lacked CI. Tracey Manning suggested that the need for cross-cultural leadership is immediate and widespread, and the need for global cultural diversity is critical for achieving effective global leadership.[35] Robert Rosen, Patricia Digh, Marshall Singer, and Carl Phillips, in research involving 1,000 senior executives, found that global literacies are the cornerstone of leadership universals. Furthermore, as the world becomes more economically integrated, it is important to manage cultural differences.[36]

MODEL OF EFFECTIVE GLOBAL LEADERSHIP

Figure 4.1 explains how the three intelligences (IQ, EI, and CI) impact global leadership behaviors. When these intelligences are present, effective leadership behaviors result. To go beyond domestic leadership success, CI must be present. Although a lack of IQ, EI, and CI has an impact on

Figure 4.1
Model of Cross-Cultural Leadership Effectiveness

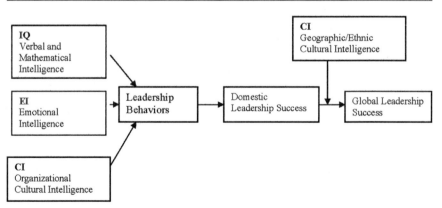

Adapted from Illan Alon and James Higgins, "Global Leadership Success through Emotional and Cultural Intelligences," *Business Horizons* 48 (2005): 501–512.

effectiveness for both work and leadership performance, those with low EI and CI are unlikely to realize the problem, thus failing in a different culture. Naturally, organizations must evaluate, reward, or correct those deficiencies.

CONCLUSION

There is a need for both managers and leaders to guide multinational organizations; managers should seek leadership behaviors and traits when they hire employees, especially those who assume managerial positions. They might even use intelligence, emotional intelligence, and cultural intelligence tests. Perhaps those making the hiring decision should seek out and probe examples of how the candidates displayed intelligences in their previous positions.

Also, although it may seem obvious to research the culture of the country with which one is doing business, leaders should be aware of differing perceptions of leadership (Table 4.1). Emotional intelligence tests provide a tool to assess the leaders in the organization. If a deficiency is discovered, the individual could receive training and education on the subject. Some organizations find it valuable to send leaders to a formal education program, such as those that result in a degree such as a master's degree in business administration or the doctoral program discussed in Chapter 17. In the short term, leaders could be given books, such as this one, language education, mentoring, and so on, to ensure they have the information needed to be effective globally. Other ideas include the use of case studies, role playing, scenario planning,[37] simulations, and other experiential learning tools to increase understanding of the country's cultures and subcultures. By providing the opportunity for global leaders to learn and develop their cultural awareness, organizations will be better able to thrive globally and to have productive global leaders.

"Leaders are those who consistently make effective contributions to social order, and who are expected and perceived to do so."[38]

NOTES

1. Warren Bennis and Burt Nanus, *Leaders: The Strategies for Taking Charge* (New York: Harper & Row, 1985).

2. Gretchen Spreitzer, Kimberly Hopkins Perttula, and Katherine Xin, "Traditionality Matters: An Examination of the Effectiveness of Transformational Leadership in the United States and Taiwan," *Journal of Organizational Behavior* 26 (2005): 205–27.

3. Vesa Suutari, "Global Leadership Development: An Emerging Research Agenda," *Career Development International* 7 (2002): 218–33.

4. Tracy Manning, "Leadership across Cultures: Attachment Style Influences," *Journal of Leadership and Organizational Studies* 9 (2003): 20–32.

5. Bernard M. Bass, *Bass and Stogdill's Handbook of Leadership* (New York: The Free Press, 1996).

6. Ibid.

7. Ibid.

8. Alexander Ardichvili, "Leadership Styles of Russian Entrepreneurs and Managers," *Journal of Developmental Entrepreneurship* 6 (2001): 169–88.

9. Spreitzer, Perttula, and Xin, "Traditionality Matters."

10. Bernard Bass, "Does the Transactional-Transformational Leadership Paradigm Transcend Organizational and National Boundaries?," *American Psychologist* 52 (1997): 130–39.

11. Peter Dorfman and Jon Howell, "Leadership in Western and Asian Countries: Commonalities and Differences in Effective Leadership Processes across Cultures," *Leadership Quarterly* 8 (1997): 234–64.

12. Bass, *Bass and Stogdill's Handbook of Leadership.*

13. Dorfman and Howell, "Leadership in Western and Asian Countries."

14. Ibid.

15. Robert House, Paul Hanges, Mansour Javidan, and Peter Dorfman, *Culture, Leadership and Organizations: The GLOBE Study of 62 Societies* (Thousand Oaks, CA: Sage, 2004).

16. Bass, "Does the Transactional-Transformational Leadership Paradigm Transcend Organizational and National Boundaries?"

17. Ibid.

18. Walter Lonner, "The Search for Psychological Universals," in *Handbook of Cross-cultural Psychology,* ed. Harry Triandis and W.W. Lambert (Boston: Allyn-Bacon, 1980), 143–204.

19. Gert Hofstede, *Culture's Consequences: International Differences in Work Related Values* (Beverly Hills, CA: Sage, 1980).

20. Ardichvili, "Leadership Styles of Russian Entrepreneurs and Managers."

21. C. Brooklyn Derr, Sylvie Roussillon, and Frank Bournois, *Cross-Cultural Approaches to Leadership Development* (Westport, CT: Quorum Books, 2002), 290–302.

22. Ibid.

23. Ibid.

24. Ibid.

25. Marc Boujnah, "L'inegalite des Femmes," *Air France Areo Magazine* 6 (2002): 43.

26. See "101 Facts on the Status of Working Women" (Washington, D.C.: Business and Professional Women/USA, 2005). Available at http://www.bpwusa.org/files/public/101FactsonWorkingwomen2005.pdf.pdf (accessed May 2, 2006).

27. Peter Salovey and John Mayer, "Emotional Intelligence," *Imagination, Cognition and Personality* 9 (1990): 185–211.

28. Daniel Goleman, Annie McKee, and Richard Boyatzis, *Primal Leadership* (Boston: Harvard Business School Press, 2002), 44–45.

29. Howard Weiss and Russell Cropanzano, "Affective Events Theory," in *Research in Organizational Behavior,* ed. Barry Staw and Larry Cummings (Greenwich, CT: JAI Press, 1996), 17–19.

30. Illan Alon and James Higgins, "Global Leadership Success through Emotional and Cultural Intelligences," *Business Horizons* 48 (2005): 501–12.

31. Ibid.

32. Ibid.

33. P. Christopher Early and Soon Ang, *Cultural Intelligence: Individual Interactions Across Cultures* (Stanford, CA: Stanford Business Books, 2003), 9.

34. Ibid.

35. Tracy Manning, "Leadership across Cultures."

36. Robert Rosen, Patricia Digh, Marshall Singer, and Carl Phillips, *Global Literacies: Lessons on Business Leadership and National Cultures* (New York: Simon and Schuster, 2000).

37. See Joan Giesecke (Ed.), *Scenario Planning for Libraries* (Chicago: American Library Association, 1998).

38. Dian Marie Hosking, "Organizing Leadership and Skillful Process," *Journal of Management Studies* 25 (1988): 153.

5

MODELING LEADERSHIP THEORIES

Joan R. Giesecke

"Leadership is one of the most observed and least understood phenomena on earth."[1]

Leadership theories abound in the literature and they range from very theoretical musings to very practical approaches to leadership development. Despite all of the work in the area of leadership, there is still no universally agreed on definition of leadership. Leadership definitions vary from field to field, often merging with management definitions. In his book, *Leadership for the 21st Century*, Joseph Rost identified more than 200 definitions of leadership from 587 books.[2] After reviewing numerous definitions, Rost defines leadership as "an influence relationship among leaders and followers who intend real changes that reflect their mutual purposes."[3] This definition helps identify some of the key characteristics of leadership that form the basis for many of the models and theories. The definition shows that leadership involves a relationship between leaders and followers, conscious desire to create change, and mutual understanding of goals. Followers in this definition are active participants in the relationship.

As Rost notes, "Passive people are not in a relationship. They have chosen to not be involved. They cannot have influence. Passive people are not followers."[4] Active people can be anything from very active and engaged in the leadership relationship to minimally involved with little influence on the relationship. Further, followers can change from very active to minimally active and back again based on circumstances and events. This change happens because the leader/follower relationship is a dynamic relationship where change is a part of the relationship. Rost also argues that followers are part of the leadership process. Followers practice leadership rather than followership. They are a dynamic part of the relationship and the relationship is a leadership relationship. Followers and leaders do different things in the relationship, but it is the relationship that sets the boundaries for leadership activities. Rost's definition and view of leadership provide an outline for analyzing the various theories of leadership. The various theories of leadership then describe how the relationship between leaders and followers can vary, how power is distributed within the relationship, how goals can vary, and how attention to people and tasks can vary.

Power is a key element in the leader/follower relationship and, like leadership, is a term with many meanings. Most definitions though include "an element indicating that power is the capability of one social actor to overcome resistance in achieving a desired objective or result."[5] Further, power "has been defined as the capacity to produce effects on others or the potential to influence."[6] Within these definitions, it is evident that power is tied to the relationship between actor A and actor B, whether the actor is an individual, a group, or an organization. John R. French and Bertram Raven identified five sources of power:

1. Expert power is based on distinctive knowledge, expertise, or skills.
2. Reference power is influence based on the strength of the relationship between the leader and the follower.
3. Legitimate power comes from one's role in a group or organization.
4. Reward power comes from one's perceived ability to give rewards to followers.
5. Coercive power, the opposite of reward power, comes from the perceived ability to give negative sanctions or remove positive events from the follower.[7]

Although research on these sources of power continues, Richard L. Hughes, Robert C. Ginnett, and Gordon J. Curphy note three generalizations that seem to hold. Effective leaders use various sources of power, leaders can be influenced by followers and power can move between the members of the relationship, and leaders vary in the extent to which they share power with others.[8]

This chapter reviews leadership theories, presents a model for understanding how the theories are related, examines the orientation of the leaders towards tasks and people, and explores the role of power in the relationship. These variables help to distinguish among the many theories of leadership that have been developed. Further, the chapter reviews the issue of gender and leadership, and considers the effect of social roles and perceived power in relation to gender.

TRADITIONAL VIEWS OF LEADERSHIP

One of the oldest and most well-known theories of leadership is that of the leader in control. The traditional leadership model sets the leader at the center of the organization or group. The leader sets the vision, enrolls others in the vision, and holds people accountable through measurement and rewards. In this model the leader acts as parent, setting the rules and monitoring performance. There is little input from followers and power is centered in the leader. There may be little concern for group members in this model. Rather, the leader focuses on goals and objectives to ensure that the group meets expectations. Two theorists who describe different ways of viewing the traditional model of leadership are Machiavelli and Max Weber.

Machiavelli

Perhaps one of the more interesting views of the traditional model of leadership was described by Machiavelli in *The Prince*.[9] He assumed that people are self-serving and self-interested. Without strong central government or organizations, the people will create chaos. Only by controlling the actions of others can the leader ensure order. For Machiavelli, power was used to manipulate and control people so that the leader could achieve his aims. He argued that a leader should be both a fox to recognize traps and a lion to defend himself against wolves. He said leaders need not keep faith with their followers when doing so would be against the leader's interest. He believed that rulers should inflict severe injuries quickly, murdering opponents if needed, to keep enemies from planning revenge. He wrote that leaders should keep their friends close and their enemies closer so that the leaders would have knowledge of any plots their enemies might be developing. His model is an amoral approach to leadership where he argued that the ends obtained justified the means used.

Max Weber

Max Weber, nineteenth-century German sociologist and the founder of modern public administration, described three models of leadership and authority: the traditional model, the charismatic/hero model, and the bureaucratic/rational model. He distinguished between the historical views of leaders as heroes or as those in control because of their position and his rational model where rules determine the scope of leadership.

In the traditional model, Weber argues that the leader's authority comes from the history and tradition of the society or organization.[10] Leadership is based on the person's place in the organization, institution, or government. Power and authority are centered with the leader. Power is handed down from leader to leader and may be exercised arbitrarily.

In the charismatic or hero model, the leader is followed or obeyed because of the hero's personal qualities rather than because of the leader's experience or skills. Followers trust the leader and have faith in the leader's ability to overcome crises. Power is centered in the hero rather than in institutions or organizations.

Weber is perhaps best known for developing the ideal model of the bureaucratic/rational organization. In the ideal bureaucracy, legal rules and regulations define leadership positions and outline the distribution of power and authority. There are clearly defined hierarchies in the organization and authority comes from the office rather than from the person. The ideal bureaucracies are formalistic, impersonal, yet highly efficient organizations. Authority and power are impersonal, bound by rules and regulations. As an ideal type, the bureaucratic leader follows the rules and maintains order.

TWENTIETH-CENTURY THEORISTS

Trait Models

By the twentieth century, leadership theories began to look at the personal traits or characteristics of leaders. Theorists argued that by identifying a core set of traits, one could develop programs to advance leadership skills. Numerous lists of traits were created, however, and researchers found it difficult to agree on one set of traits that seem to fit all leaders. Bernard Bass, in *Bass & Stogdill's Handbook of Leadership*, reviews many of the traits studies from 1904 through 1970 and notes the lack of consistency in the lists.[11] Traits work continues today as researchers investigate various types of leadership and seek to understand what traits are most helpful in today's leaders.

Behavioral Models

Kurt Lewin and his group were among the first researchers to conduct controlled experiments to examine what leaders do, what they emphasize, and how they relate to subordinates. They identified three major styles of leaders. Autocratic leaders centralize power and decision making. Democratic leaders encourage participation in decision making and distribute power. Laissez-faire leaders leave group members alone to make their own decisions. Similar studies conducted at the University of Michigan in the late 1940s also identified three types of leaders. These researchers found leaders who were predominately production centered, leaders who were predominately employee-centered, and those who were a mix of these two characteristics. The results of these studies, that showed that leaders who demonstrated concern for their followers were most successful, were contrary to the major belief of the time that people needed to be closely managed to be productive.[12]

Douglas McGregor

In his book *Human Side of Enterprise,* Douglas McGregor outlined his view of leadership. His work on motivation describes two theoretical views of leaders: Theory X and Theory Y. In Theory X, workers are assumed to be lazy and successful managers must closely supervise employees, establishing rules, directing production, and controlling their actions. Theory X leads to an autocratic leadership approach. In Theory Y employees are seen as self-directed and are motivated by an environment that promotes creativity, self-esteem, and self-actualization. Theory Y leaders are democratic and participatory, encouraging followers to succeed.[13]

Robert Blake and Jane Mouton

McGregor's theories can be seen in the work of Robert Blake and Jane Mouton who developed the "Managerial or Leadership Grid" to describe leadership in terms of the leaders' concern for people and the leaders' concern for production. They outline four types of leaders: impoverished, country club, authoritarian, and team leader. Impoverished leaders with low concern for people and production create impoverished organizations, with the leader having abdicated responsibility for the work. This is a lack of leadership model. A country club leader who shows a high concern for people with a low concern for production creates a friendly environment where goals may or may not be accomplished. An authoritarian leader who has great concern for production but little concern for people follows a Theory X approach to leadership. The operation may be efficient, but the results may still be limited. With leaders who have a medium concern for people and for production, adequate performance is likely to occur and a satisfactory environment will exist. Team leaders who show high concern for people and for production create a strong team environment where performance is high and an environment of respect exists. The descriptive work of Blake and Mouton helps leaders to understand the consequences of different behaviors and styles in accomplishing goals and objectives.[14]

James McGregor Burns

James McGregor Burns, who won a Pulitzer Prize for his book *Leadership,* reviewed the existing leadership theories and was the first to describe two general styles of leadership: transactional and transformational.[15] In transactional leadership, leaders see their role as a series of transactions with followers. In transformational leadership, leaders bring out the best in their followers and transform the organization by inspiring followers to achieve high goals. The work of James McGregor Burns has been expanded by researchers such as Bernard Bass and Bruce Avolio, resulting in a full range leadership model that includes four types of transactional leadership and four characteristics of transformational leadership.[16]

Transactional Leadership

In transactional leadership the leader motivates followers by appealing to the follower's self-interest and sets up a series of transactions or exchanges to accomplish goals. As Burns writes:

Leadership is the reciprocal process of mobilizing, by persons with certain motives and values, various economic, political, and other resources, in a context of competition and conflict, in order to realize goals independently or mutually held by both leaders and followers. The nature of these goals is crucial. . . . [T]wo persons may exchange goods or services or other things in order to realize independent objectives.[17]

Leaders and followers in a transactional relationship are not seeking joint efforts or collective interests, but rather bargain to advance individual interests. For example, a leader of a work unit defines tasks to meet unit goals, and in exchange for a salary, subordinates agree to perform those tasks. In a transactional relationship subordinates do not have to accept or support unit goals, but they do need to perform the assigned tasks to receive their salary.

In further work on the transactional model, researchers have identified four types of transactional leadership: laissez-faire, passive management-by-exception, active management-by-exception, and contingent reward. Laissez-faire leadership, as noted earlier, can be viewed as an absence of leadership. Leaders fail to take a stand on issues, do not follow employee performance, and do not appear to care if the unit or organization meets its goals. It is very much a hands-off approach to leadership. In passive management-by-exception, the leader uses corrective actions and punishment as a response to errors. The leader becomes involved in the organization or unit only when a mistake is noticed. In active management-by-exception, the leader actively monitors the subordinates, sets standards, and uses corrective action to address work concerns. This leader is more involved in the unit, but still emphasizes negative rather than positive behavior. In contingent reward, the leader sets clear expectations and uses rewards to recognize accomplishments. The leader actively monitors performance and looks for positive results to reward. This is a more positive approach to the organization than the other forms of transactional leadership.

Transformational Leadership

In contrast to transactional leadership, in transformational leadership, the leader and followers are united in pursuit of common goals. Burns writes that "leaders can also shape and alter and elevate the motives and values and goals of followers through the vital teaching role of leadership."[18] Whereas transactional leadership is concerned with individual goals, transformational leaders "raise their followers up through levels of morality, though insufficient attention to means can corrupt the ends."[19] Transformational leadership is an active leadership model, with both the followers and the leader engaged in the transformation process. Passive people are not likely to be transformed by the actions of the leader.[20]

Four key behaviors of transformational leadership are individualized consideration, intellectual stimulation, inspirational motivation, and idealized influence. Individualized consideration describes the compassionate leader who genuinely cares about followers, is encouraging, and makes personal contact with followers. Intellectual stimulation behavior leads to creative thinking, encouraging imagination by followers, challenging the status quo, and encouraging risk taking. Inspirational motivation behavior includes clarifying vision and mission, and inspiring others to achieve more than they thought they could do. Idealized influence behavior is seen in the cliché "walk the talk" where actions match the vision. Leaders develop trust among followers and exhibit great commitment. Using these four behaviors, leaders are able to motivate followers to transcend self-interest, promote higher achievement, higher morale, and greater change possibilities.

Robert Greenleaf

Transformational leadership has been extensively described and studied, but it is not the only accepted theory of positive leadership. In taking a different view of the relationship between leaders and followers, Robert Greenleaf coined the phrase *servant leader* to describe a new model of leadership that puts "the primary emphasis on the needs of the followers before the needs of the leader."[21] The leader is a servant first, willing to sacrifice self-interest for the good of the group. Leaders listen to the ideas of their followers and value the ideas of others. They stay aware of the needs of their followers and of the changing environment so that they can help followers respond positively to change. They help followers grow and develop. They do not try to convince others to do things through formal authority, but rather rely on persuasion. The desire to serve becomes the foundation for the desire to lead. The model focuses on altruism, simplicity, and self-awareness. This sets up a different set of interactions between leaders and followers.

Servant leadership has been criticized for being unrealistic, encouraging passivity, and sometimes serving the wrong cause. It is seen as a paradigm of weakness where followers can manipulate the leader.[22] Researchers also note, however, that servant leaders who "use proven transforming techniques such as developing a vision, enlisting others, fostering collaboration, strengthening others, linking rewards to performance, and celebrating accomplishments" can focus followers and leaders on a vision that avoids manipulation through mutual commitment to participation and community.[23]

Figure 5.1
Leadership Models

Leadership Model	Power Orientation	Task Orientation	Orientation toward People
Machaevelli	Centralized	Important	Obey leader out of fear
Max Weber-bureaucracy	Determined by rules	Important	Rules are more important
Charismatic leadership	Centralized in leader	May or may not be important	Willingly obey leader
Autocratic leadership	Centralized	Important	Not important
Democratic leadership	Shared power	May or may not be important	Important
Laissez-faire leadership	Dispersed	Not important	Not important
McGregor's Theory X	Centralized	Important	Not important
McGregor's Theory Y	Dispersed	May or may not be important	Important
Transactional passive	Centralized	Important	Not important
Transactional active	Centralized	Important	May or may not be important
Transactional contingent reward	Centralized	Important	Somewhat important
Transformational leadership	Shared	Important	Important
Servant leadership	Shared	May or may not be important	Important

BRINGING THE MODELS TOGETHER

One challenge in leadership theory is to find ways to bring the leadership theories together in models that can be used to describe a wide range of actions. Many models distinguish leadership theories by looking at leaders concern for performance or tasks versus the leaders concern for followers. These models are used to argue that leadership is most effective when leaders are concerned about both tasks and people.

Another way to look at leadership models is to look at how power is distributed. When power is viewed as the core of the relationship among leaders

Figure 5.2
Blake and Mouton's Leadership Grid

Leadership Theory	Power Orientation	Task Orientation	Orientation toward People
Impoverished	Dispersed	Not important	Not important
Authoritarian	Centralized	Important	Not important
Country club	Shared	Not important	Important
Team leader	Shared	Important	Important

and followers as the influencing factor in the theory, then power can be used to distinguish the different theories. Furthermore, adding in the level of concern by the leader for the followers and by the followers for the leader can further differentiate the leadership theories.

Figure 5.1 describes the various leadership models in terms of power orientation, task orientation, and orientation toward people. Figure 5.2 provides a description of Blake and Mouton's Leadership Grid using these same elements.

Centralized Power

In centralized power theories, power rests with the leader or leaders. Followers may be willing to participate with the leader to achieve goals, but the followers do not have the authority to make changes. Traditional leadership theories are based on a centralized power model, with power resting with the leader. Transactional models are also based on power resting with the leader. In the laissez-faire model, power rests with the followers, as leaders have abdicated their responsibilities and the group is left to set its own direction.

Shared Power Models

Transformational and servant leadership models are based on a shared power model, with followers and leaders having the ability to influence the relationship. These models emphasize shared visions, participatory processes, and mutual goals.

Concern for People

In the traditional leadership theories, leaders are more concerned with tasks than with the needs of the followers. This is also true in sectors of Blake and Mouton's Leadership Grid, and in transactional leadership behavior characterized by management-by-exception. Low concern for people can also be seen in laissez-faire leadership where leaders are not concerned with their followers and followers are unlikely to be concerned with the well-being of the leader.

Models that emphasize high concern for people include transformational leadership, servant leadership, sectors of the Leadership Grid, and transactional leadership that emphasize contingent rewards.

LEADERSHIP AND GENDER

Although many popular leadership and relationship books are based on the concept that women are naturally interested in relationships and that men are naturally hierarchical, research on leadership and gender is showing that there are more differences among men and among women than between men and women. Alice Eagly, a psychologist at Northwestern University, has done extensive work analyzing studies on leadership and gender. She and her colleagues find that social roles and stereotypes explain more about how women and men are perceived and how they act than do innate behaviors. Her extensive research shows that women are caught in a Catch-22 situation where they may find themselves being successful as leaders, but being criticized for not being feminine enough.[24]

Traditional arguments that have kept women from being seen as leaders include the hormone argument that women's lower levels of testosterone make them timid, the brain research argument that women's brains are not wired for leadership, the motivation argument that women are motivated to have children and raise a family rather than run a business, and finally the nature argument that women are violating their essential feminine natures when they try to lead.[25] Books, such as Carol Gilligan's *In a Different Voice,* Mary Field Belenky's *Women's Ways of Knowing,* or Deborah Tannen's *You Just Don't Understand,* all support the view that women are relational, spiritual, and inclusive, whereas men value excellence, mastery, and logic.[26] These arguments serve to limit options for both men and women and to perpetuate stereotypes that dominate society.

In their recent book *Same Difference: How Gender Myths Are Hurting Our Relationships, Our Children and Our Jobs,* Rosalind Barnett and Caryle Rivers describe the current research on gender and point out the problems that are created by the stereotypes that persist about women and men.[27] They note that many of the studies on women and men in the workplace compare women secretaries with male bosses and oddly enough conclude that women are less likely to wield power and influence in the organization and are more concerned about relationships. When researchers look at men in lower-level positions and women in upper-level positions, however, researchers find that the men are more concerned with relationships and women act more like their male counterparts. Barnett and Rivers conclude that the power differences among the levels of the organization are a better predictor of behavior than gender. Further, in reviewing leadership literature, they note that in hundreds of studies on "task oriented" versus "people oriented" leadership behavior, the research finds "no significant difference between men and women on these parameters."[28]

Women do benefit from the newer theories of leadership and leadership effectiveness that bring concern for relationships and people together with concern for tasks. Transformational leadership styles work well for women, as the style brings social role and work expectations together for women. Further, research by Eagly shows that women are slightly more likely to demonstrate transformational leadership behaviors than men.[29] Because research shows that both men and women can succeed as transformational leaders, the future for women as leaders may be brighter than the past has been.

CONCLUSION

Leadership is a well-studied concept that generates little agreement among theorists. Any number of leadership approaches can be effective. Today's research shows that leaders who have a more participatory style, share power, share decision making, and still keep goals and objectives in focus are likely to be successful. This is a style that works well for both men and women. Those who try to bully people, are dictatorial, and ignore the needs of followers may have limited success but will not achieve the great successes of those with a more participatory or transforming style. Good leaders create relationships with followers that lead to mutual acceptance of goals and mutual efforts to bring about change.

"It seems clear that organizations that maintain glass ceilings preventing the selection and promotion of women for positions of leadership may end up reducing the effective utilization of their personnel."[30]

NOTES

1. James MacGregor Burns, *Leadership* (New York: Harper & Row, 1978), 2.

2. Joseph Rost, *Leadership for the Twenty-first Century* (New York: Praeger, 1991), 44.

3. Ibid., 102.

4. Ibid., 108.

5. Jeffrey Pfeffer, *Power in Organizations* (Marshfield, MA: Pitman Publishing, 1981), 2.

6. Bernard Bass, *Bass & Stogdill's Handbook of Leadership,* 3d ed. (New York: Free Press, 1990), 226.

7. Ibid., 231–233.

8. J. Thomas Wren, *Leader's Companion: Insight in Leadership through the Ages* (New York: Free Press, 1995), 339–47.

9. Burns, *Leadership,* 444–45.

10. Harold Gortner, *Administration in the Public Sector,* 2d ed. (New York: Wiley & Sons, 1981), 167.

11. Bass, *Bass & Stogdill's Handbook of Leadership,* 59–88.

12. Barbara Moran and Robert Stuart, *Library and Information Center Management* (Englewood, CO: Libraries Unlimited, 2002), 353–54.

13. Douglas McGregor, "Human Side of Enterprise," *Management Review* 46, no. 11 (1957): 22–28.

14. Wren, *Leader's Companion,* 147.

15. Burns, *Leadership.*

16. Bernard Bass and Bruce Avolio, *Improvising Organizational Effectiveness through Transformational Leadership* (Thousand Oaks, CA: Sage, 1994).

17. Burns, *Leadership,* 425.

18. Ibid.

19. Ibid., 426.

20. Rost, *Leadership for the Twenty-first Century,* 123.

21. J. Thomas Whetstone, "Personalism and Moral Leadership: The Servant Leader with a Transforming Vision," *Business Ethics: A European Review* 11, no. 4 (October 2002): 389.

22. Ibid.

23. Ibid., 391.

24. Alice Eagly and Mary C. Johannnesen-Schmidt, "Leadership Styles of Women and Men," *Journal of Social Issues* 57, no, 4 (2001): 781–97.

25. Rosalind Barnett and Caryle Rivers, *Same Difference: How Gender Myths Are Hurting Our Relationships, Our Children, and Our Jobs* (New York: Basic Books, 2004), 174–76.

26. Ibid., 176. See Carol Gilligan, *In a Different Voice: Psychological Theory and Women's Development* (Cambridge, MA: Harvard University Press, 1993); Mary Field Belenky, *Women's Ways of Knowing: The Development of Self, Voice, and Mind* (New York: Basic Books, 1986); Deborah Tannen, *You Just Don't Understand: Women and Men in Conversation* (New York: Morrow, 1990).

27. Barnett and Rivers, *Same Difference.*

28. Ibid., 196.

29. Ibid., 197.

30. Bernard Bass and Bruce J Avolio, "The Transformational and Transectional Leadership of Men and Women," *Applied Psychology: An International Review* 45, no.1 (1996): 30.

6

THE LIS LEADERSHIP LITERATURE

Peter Hernon

"Throughout the world, leadership is generally perceived as something we need more of, while at the same time it is generally misunderstood."[1]

Anyone wanting to examine the recent leadership literature produced in library and information studies (LIS) might start with four excellent sources. First, a literature review of academic library leadership, which considered "published research studies, theories and models, literature reviews, books, and journal articles published between 1980 and 2003,"[2] "synthesize[d] what is now known about the characteristics and leadership style of university librarians and academic library directors."[3] The author, Sharon Gray Weiner, covered "recruitment, leadership potential, career development;" "roles and responsibilities;" and "characteristics and management style." Based on an examination of the research literature, she concluded, "many aspects [of leadership] have not been addressed and . . . a comprehensive body of cohesive, evidence-based research is needed. There is a dearth of published studies or dissertations that relate leadership to effectiveness of library directors, their organizations, or outcomes."[4] Of particular value in her article is the figure that identified study characteristics (e.g., method of data collection, number of respondents, and institution type studied) for a number of research studies. Although either a survey or interview was the most commonly used method of data collection, some researchers have used content analysis, the Delphi technique (a method of continual evolution to gather the opinions of experts on nonfactual issues), bibliometrics analysis (using quantitative analysis and statistics to describe patterns of publication within a given field or body of literature, for example, application of citation analysis), or modeling (statistical or conceptual).

Second, the 2001 volume of the *Journal of Library Administration*™ covered "Leadership in the Library and Information Science Professions: Theory and Practice." Ten articles discussed topics related to "the Crisis and Opportunities in Library Leadership," "Recruitment Theory," "Developing Library Leaders for the 21st Century," "Information Technology in the Virtual Library," "Financial Resources and What Leaders Should Know," "Diversity and Leadership," "Women and Leadership," "the Concept of Leadership in Technology-related Organizations," "Leadership Evaluation and Assessment," and "An International Perspective."[5]

Third, the spring 2002 issue of *Library Trends* covered topics such as leadership, renewal (or what is known as resonant leadership), career paths to advancement, mentoring, and job rotation.[6] For example, Catherine J. Matthews examined "midlife job change among librarians, particularly movement into senior academic library administration positions such as chief librarian." As she noted, "the new chief librarian, like others assuming new jobs, must 'build an image or role, build relationships, construct a frame of reference, map relevant players, locate themselves in communication networks, and learn the local language' among many other things."[7]

And, finally, the summer 2004 issue of *Library Trends* focused on organizational development, including organizational culture and change, as well as leadership.[8] Florence M. Mason and Louella V. Wetherbee provided one of the more relevant discussions for this book. They examined training programs for library leadership and note that these programs are "primarily multiday and residential in nature."[9] One of their conclusions was that "libraries will undoubtedly experience a loss of a large number of library leaders, and libraries and library organizations must continue to expand leadership training if there is to be a new cohort of leaders ready to take over."[10]

Given the scope and currency of these four sources, this chapter presents other writings that have appeared predominately from 2003 to the present (summer 2006), but gives particular attention to the research literature. Much of the nonresearch literature comprises press releases and highlights of conferences and seminars. Occasionally, there is mention of a leadership institute, graduate program, or for-credit course. Unfortunately, this chapter supports Weiner's thesis about a dearth of published studies on leadership effectiveness.

RESEARCH LITERATURE

Building on a body of research about leadership attributes, which they began in 2000, Peter Hernon, Ronald R. Powell, and Arthur P. Young used content analysis, the Delphi technique, and surveys to identify the leadership attributes that library directors considered most essential for academic and public library directors in the foreseeable future. These authors also identified leadership assessment tools, reflected on different ways to nurture the development of leadership qualities in senior library managers, and offered insights into the role of headhunters in helping institutions select the next generation of university library directors.[11]

A continuation of their research used the Delphi technique to explore the perceptions of gen-X librarians (born between 1965 and 1979) about which attributes are most essential for academic library leaders to possess and compared the perceptions of the 10 librarians to those of library directors. As Young, Hernon, and Powell cautioned, however, "Although the attributes that both groups value exhibit some noteworthy differences, any characterization of leadership attributes is multi-faceted and does not focus solely on generation."[12] In another extension of their research, Hernon and Nancy Rossiter used content analysis of job advertisements and a survey of directors whose library was a member of the Association of Research Libraries to examine emotional intelligence, which focuses on managing an organization's mood. Emotional intelligence encompasses self-awareness, self-regulation, motivation, empathy, and social skill. Among all of the attributes falling within these five categories, the researchers found the greatest consensus about two attributes: the importance of the director as a "visionary—able to build a shared vision and rally others around it" and "ability to function in a political environment."[13]

Although they do not specifically address leadership, Peter Hernon and Philip Calvert showed that some libraries were actively involved in ensuring that students with disabilities benefited from the receipt of high quality library services and, in other instances, some libraries were indifferent about meeting the information needs and expectations of this community of students. Librarians may not fully recognize the full range of disabilities and the fact that such conditions might also extend to the faculty. Furthermore, how aware are librarians engaged in information literacy instruction about different learning styles and need for accommodation that some students might require?[14] Clearly, there are opportunities for libraries to champion services for students with disabilities and other special populations.

Although the dissertation was completed before 2003, it is still worth noting that John W. Creswell gathered the perceptions of library faculty about the leadership practices and role of their department chair in faculty development. He found that library faculty members believed they have primary responsibility for their own professional growth and development.[15] Departmental chairs, the faculty thought, did not play active or nurturing roles in staff development.

James F. Williams II and Mark D. Winston, who examined publication patterns of academic librarians and administrators, considered one type of leadership—publication of research in leading LIS journals. Publication reflects analytical abilities and, in some instances, effective decision making.

Such attributes, they correctly noted, should not be forgotten in any investigation of leadership competencies.[16]

Finally, the work of Niels Ole Pors in Denmark merits mention even though he focuses on public libraries. He developed an instrument to examine and measure leadership. In a survey of academic and public library directors, he found that "openness and willingness to change" and "the ability to motivate and inspire" received the highest rating. The ranking of the other attributes varied between the two library types.[17] In another article, one co-authored with Carl Gustav Johannsen, Pors surveyed 562 library managers and reported that they "tend to perceive future roles as being greatly oriented towards people and towards values and see themselves as a kind of catalyst for change." Furthermore, they "are oriented toward values and value-based management."[18]

NONRESEARCH LITERATURE

There are numerous accounts in the literature about leadership development, leadership training programs, the need for nurturing leaders in the profession, and reflections of library leaders about challenges and opportunities.[19] Many of these descriptive works cover their topics in anywhere from a few paragraphs to a couple of pages and report on the effectiveness of various programs and institutes. As a result, this section selectively covers the nonresearch literature.

As more gen-Xers assume managerial roles, Pixey Anne Mosley believes that they will require cross-generational mentoring. She mentioned the body of research conducted by Hernon, Powell, and Young but concluded that the directors they surveyed misunderstand gen-Xers. That misunderstanding, she proposed, might result in miscommunication. The directors who were actually surveyed, however, identified attributes that they thought relevant for directors of the near future; they were not asked to factor in generation and did not do so.

Mosley concluded that "Generation Xers may be interested in taking on leadership roles, but they will do so on their own terms." She also characterized how gen-Xers would administer a library.[20] It seems that she fails to recognize that not all gen-Xers might function in the same way; there are different managerial and leadership styles. Furthermore, leadership, which she does not define, occurs more than at the director level. Libraries involved in team and group work benefit from staff who function as both leaders and followers.

Anne Page Mosby and Judith D. Brook explored different models for leadership development, team building, staff development, and success—making library services effective.[21] Esther S. Grassian and Joan R. Kaplowitz approached information literacy instruction from a managerial and leadership perspective. Their first chapter, "Developing the Leader within You," addressed "why leadership now?," "yes, you are a leader," some leadership qualities (vision, passion, courage, and integrity) and characteristics (persuasive communication skills, empowerment of others, encouraging diversity, risk taking, relationship buildings, and seeking learning opportunities), "leading within your organizational culture," and "leading change." The next chapter focused on management; Chapter 3 covered "cooperation and change," Chapter 4 dealt with "fostering growth in yourself and others."[22] Clearly, such a work suggests the need for more writings that connect different library activities and services to management and leadership or, as discussed in Chapters 17 and 18 of this book, managerial leadership.

Patricia Senn Breivik and E. Gordon Gee noted that the academic community has failed "to recognize or take advantage of the enormous potential of libraries."[23] Furthermore, "only vision and leadership on the part of presidents, academic vice presidents, and heads of libraries can create the necessary climate for academics to take a new look at their libraries and to integrate them into all aspects if campus life."[24] They envision leadership occurring through partnerships with faculty, campus administrators, and members of the broad community. Those partnerships should seek to enable libraries to take a new look at teaching/learning, research, and community service; to participate in campus initiatives; and to demonstrate their educational effectiveness—helping the institution to meet its mission and campus goals.[25]

"Because the library is a major information resource investment," Breivik and Gee maintained that it should become "a primary strategic tool in addressing campus priorities."[26] At a time of funding scarcity, it would be shortsighted not to examine that investment and how library resources and services contribute to meeting those priorities.

In *Leadership: Higher Education, and the Information Age,* Carrie E. Regenstein and Barbara I. Dewey offer a vision and a strategy for developing plans to improve the information technology (IT) infrastructure of higher education and the ability of academic librarians to achieve campus-wide IT leadership roles.[27] In a separate work, Dewey viewed the leadership of university library directors and staff from a cultural perspective and encouraged research libraries to "navigate at the interface of a hugely diverse set of campus and academic cultures. They approach learning and scholarship in very different ways. Librarians, themselves, need to work even more adeptly between the interface of scholarly, professional and management roles."[28] In fact, they need to "support the complete spectrum of academic cultures . . . emerging on our campuses."[29]

Glsela von Dran reviewed leadership styles, focusing on organizational change and transformation leaders. She identified and characterized a number of research studies that occurred outside LIS.[30] Mary Ann Mavrinac, who focused on transformational leadership, analyzed the changes that libraries must go through to become a learning culture. Her discussion centered on peer mentoring as a way to achieve such a culture.[31] She makes an important observation: "Organizations learn through individuals. Therefore, there is an inextricable link among leadership and change and individual wants and needs."[32]

Mary M. Somerville, Barbara Schader, and Malia E. Huston applied systems thinking as a strategy to prepare longtime employees to reconsider traditional roles. Their goal was to identify "improved ways of working, communicating, cooperating and interacting within the library organization and across the university community."[33]

CONCLUSION

The leadership literature, except within LIS, has grown at a phenomenal rate since 2002—the starting date for the writings highlighted in this chapter. From January 2003 to May 26, 2006, Amazon.com reported 16,865 books written on the topic in its database. For the same period, Elsevier's *Science-Direct* identified 791 articles on the topic, and *ProQuest Dissertations and Theses—Full Text* listed 4,393 works; however, the entire ProQuest database includes 30,163 relevant dissertations and theses. Furthermore, during the more than three-year period, there are more than 19,203 writings on the topic of leadership in *ABI/INFORM Global.* In comparison, the percentage of LIS literature produced in North America or elsewhere on the same subject is quite modest. The LIS literature draws heavily on the writings produced in management and other literatures, with infrequent reference to works produced in the LIS professional literature. This finding is not astounding; what is surprising, however, is that, with the focus on change management and becoming an institutional partner, there are so few substantial writings on leadership in LIS.

The LIS literature needs to examine the same types of issues pursued in other literatures. For example, how well do leadership theories apply to LIS? Conversely, how does LIS research inform or influence discussions of leadership in higher education and other nonprofit organizations? It might be beneficial for LIS researchers to place their research in *Academe, the Journal of Higher Education,* and other sources widely read by faculty and upper administrators, and to explore the research agenda identified in Chapter 18.

"Leadership is a relationship between leaders and followers, both individual and group, in mutual pursuit of organizational outcomes and in the fulfillment of individual wants and needs."[34]

NOTES

1. Donald E. Riggs, "The Crisis and Opportunities in Library Leadership," *Journal of Library Administration*™ 32, no. 3/4 (2001): 5.

2. Sharon Gray Weiner, "Leadership of Academic Libraries: A Literature Review," *Education Libraries* 26, no. 2 (Winter 2003): 6.

3. Ibid., 5.

4. Ibid., 14.

5. Mark D. Winston (Ed.), "Leadership in the Library and Information Science Professions: Theory and Practice," *Journal of Library Administration*™ 32, no. 3/4 (2001): 1–186.

6. Daniel F. Phelan and Richard M. Malinski (Ed.), "Midlife Career Decisions of Librarians," *Library Trends* 50, no. 4 (Spring 2002): 575–758.

7. Catherine J. Matthews, "Becoming a Chief Librarian: An Analysis of Transition Stages in Academic Library Leadership," *Library Trends* 50, no. 4 (Spring 2002): 578–602.

8. Keith Russell and Denise Stephens (Ed.), "Organizational Development and Leadership," *Library Trends* 53, no. 1 (Summer 2004): 1–264.

9. Florence M. Mason and Louella V. Wetherbee, "Learning to Lead: An Analysis of Current Training Programs for Library Leadership," *Library Trends* 53, No. 1 (Summer 2004), 187.

10. Ibid., 215.

11. Peter Hernon, Ronald R. Powell, and Arthur P. Young, *The Next Library Leadership: Attributes of Academic and Public Library Directors* (Westport, CT: Libraries Unlimited, 2003).

12. Arthur P. Young, Peter Hernon, and Ronald R. Powell, "Attributes of Academic Library Leadership: An Exploratory Study of Some Gen-Xers," *The Journal of Academic Librarianship* 32, no. 5 (September 2006): 482–502.

13. Peter Hernon and Nancy Rossiter, "Emotional Intelligence: Which Traits Are Most Prized?," *College & Research Libraries* 67, no. 3 (May 2006): 260–275.

14. Peter Hernon and Philip Calvert, *Improving the Quality of Library Services for Students with Disabilities* (Westport, CT: Libraries Unlimited, 2006).

15. John W. Creswell, *Department Chair Faculty Development Activities and Leadership Practices: University Libraries Faculty Perceptions* (diss., University of Nebraska-Lincoln, 2002).

16. James F. Williams II and Mark D. Winston, "Leadership Competencies and the Importance of Research Methods and Statistical Analysis in Decision Making and Research and Publication: A Study of Citation Patterns," *Library & Information Science Research* 25 (2003): 387–402.

17. Niels Ole Pors, "Dimensions of Leadership and Service Quality: The Human Aspect in Performance Measurement," *Proceedings of the 4th Northumbria International Conference on Performance Measurement in Libraries and Information Services, Meaningful Measures for Emerging Realities* (Pittsburgh, PA, 2001; distributed by the Association of Research Libraries, Washington, D.C.), 245–251. See http://www.arl.org/stats/north/index.html (accessed April 24, 2006).

18. Niels Ole Pors and Carl Gustav Johannsen, "Library Directors under Cross-pressure between New Public Management and Value-based Management," *Library Management* 24, nos. 1/2 (2003): 51, 58.

19. See, for instance, Carolyn A. Sheehy, "Synergy: The Illinois Library Leadership Initiative and the Development of Future Academic Library Leaders," *College & Undergraduate Libraries*™ 11, no. 1 (2004): 61–75; Amed Demirhan, "Developing Leadership through Mentoring," *Florida Libraries* 48, no. 2 (Fall 2005): 15–16; Janine Golden,

"Leadership Development and Staff Recruitment . . . Florida Style," *Florida Libraries* 48, no. 2 (Fall 2005): 17–20; Robin Kear, "Learning to Be a Library Leader: Leadership Development Opportunities in Florida and Beyond," *Florida Libraries* 48, no. 2 (Fall 2005): 22–23; Mary Spalding Edgerly, and D. Michele Beaulieu, "Bringing Effective Skills & Technology Together: Leadership Opportunities for Rural Librarians," *Rural Libraries* 23, no. 2 (2003): 7–19; Carole McConnell, "Staff and Leadership Shortages? Grow Your Own," *American Libraries* 35, no. 9 (October 2004): 34–36; Gregg Sapp, "James Neal on the Challenges of Leadership," *Library Administration and Management* 19, no. 2 (Spring 2005): 64–67; S. Cornell, "Growing Leaders," *Public Library Journal* 17, no. 4 (Winter 2002): 115–116, 118; "Leadership: What Makes Us Tick?," *Library Media Connection* 24, no. 6 (March 2006): 15–19; James Henri and Marlene Asselin, *Leadership Issues in the Information Literate School Community* (Westport, CT: Libraries Unlimited, 2005).

20. Pixey Anne Mosley, "Mentoring Gen X Managers: Tomorrow's Library Leadership Is Already Here," *Library Administration & Management* 19, no. 4 (Fall 2005): 185–90, 191–92.

21. Anne Page Mosby and Judith D. Brook, "Devils and Goddesses in the Library: Reflections on Leadership, Team Building, Staff Development, and Success," *Georgia Library Quarterly* 42, no. 4 (Winter 2006): 5–10.

22. Esther S. Grassian and Joan R. Kaplowitz, *Learning to Lead and Manage Information Literacy Instruction* (New York: Neal-Schuman, 2005).

23. Patricia Senn Breivik and E. Gordon Gee, *Higher Education in the Internet Age: Libraries Creating a Strategic Edge* (Westport, CT: Praeger, 2006), 1.

24. Ibid., 3.

25. Ibid., 4.

26. Ibid., xi.

27. Carrie E. Regenstein and Barbara I. Dewey, *Leadership: Higher Education, and the Information Age: A New Era for Information Technology and Libraries* (New York: Neal-Schuman, 2003).

28. Barbara I. Dewey, "Leadership and University Libraries: Building to Scale at the Interface of Cultures," *Journal of Library Administration* 42, no. 1 (2005): 42.

29. Ibid., 43.

30. Glsela von Dran, "Human Resources and Leadership Strategies for Libraries in Transition," *Library Administration & Management* 19, no. 4 (Fall 2005): 177–84.

31. Mary Ann Mavrinac, "Transformational Leadership: Peer Mentoring as a Values-based Learning Process," *portal: Libraries and the Academy* 5, no. 3 (2005): 391–404.

32. Ibid., 394.

33. Mary M. Somerville, Barbara Schader, and Malia E. Huston, "Rethinking What We Do and How We Do It: Systems Thinking Strategies for Library Leadership," *Australian Academic & Research Libraries* 36, no. 4 (December 2005): 225, 214.

34. Mavrinac, "Transformational Leadership," 394.

7

LEADERS IN INSTITUTIONS OF HIGHER EDUCATION: FROM DEANS TO PRESIDENTS

Peter Hernon

"Good leadership is necessary to ensure the strength of American higher education."[1]

Since the beginning of recorded time, there has been a fascination with leaders and leadership. That fascination, combined with recognition of the importance of leadership in improving organizational effectiveness (better meeting the organizational or institutional mission and vision), has resulted in scholarship examining leadership and the process of leading. Such treatises might focus on individual, interpersonal, or on institutional aspects of leadership. Examples of authors in different disciplines who have addressed leadership include James MacGregor Burns (political science), Michael D. Cohen and James G. March (higher education), Leila Gonzãlez Sullivan (higher education), Chester I. Barnard (business), Doris R. Fine (education in public schools), Philip Selznick (sociology), Fred E. Fielder (psychology), Janet L. Roseman (dance), and Doris Kearns Goodwin (history). John W. Gardner addresses political leadership in an interdisciplinary study that covers psychology, political science, and sociology.[2]

From such works, it is clear that some leaders are more effective than others, that charisma is not as important as other traits (e.g., self-awareness), and that trust is an integral part of successful leadership.[3] Furthermore, selecting and nurturing academic library leaders require identifying effective leadership characteristics and providing experiences for potential candidates who both test and challenge them. Clearly, scholarly interest in leadership is increasing and leadership remains a topic of substantial interdisciplinary interest. Leadership is not confined to a single person in an organization, and the person heading the organization might not be an effective leader or else might be one of several leaders. Or, the leadership might be "bad:" "ineffective" or "unethical."[4]

Leadership appears at all levels of an academic institution. Among the faculty and staff, there are recognized leaders. These leaders might be active on all issues that matter to their peers or just on selected issues. Members of upper administration, including the president, chancellor, provost, and/or deans, are often leaders. Holding a certain position, however, is no guarantee that a particular person is successful as a leader. For this reason, organizations have an interest in nurturing leadership so that highly qualified individuals become leaders at the highest levels, operating effectively within and outside the institution. To nurture leadership, there exist leadership institutes for college presidents, master's program in leadership, and so forth that focus on the development of selected traits. The institutes tend to be short term and to discuss leadership traits, challenges, and roles, as well as work on the development or refinement of key traits and an understanding of *strategic intent:* vision, mission, and strategic goals.

The purpose of this chapter is to set the stage for the next chapter, which provides commentary from some recognized library directors who are known for their leadership and, in some cases, their scholarly writings on the topic. This chapter highlights the importance of leadership to upper administration and shows that, when library directors become leaders, they function in an environment that nurtures leadership and expects those individuals to whom library directors report or who are of equivalent rank and authority to be leaders—helping the institution meets its mission (one stressing achievement and excellence) and to work toward accomplishing a shared vision. The higher education literature identifies key traits that reinforce the importance of trust but also highlights such others as being honest, innovative, a risk-taker, and a visionary, as well as meeting new challenges imaginatively. After all, higher education "requires leaders who are committed to quality, self-renewing change, and integrity in order to weather the current storms of uncertainty and forge a new model for higher academic achievement."[5]

COLLEGE AND UNIVERSITY PRESIDENTS

More than 750 college presidents and provosts at four-year institutions responded to a survey from *The Chronicle of Higher Education* that inquired about their positions, backgrounds, and views on issues confronting higher education. When asked to select two attributes they "consider most important to the success of their presidency," "strong leadership ability" was mentioned the most. Next in importance were "interpersonal skills" and "a strong vision of your institution's mission," both of which are actually components of leadership. Another question asked about how often they "attend to . . . various activities." "Fund-raising" was mentioned the most for a daily occurrence and "educational leadership" rated third—behind "budget/finance."[6]

Commenting on the survey results, Rita Bornstein, president emeritus at Rollins College (Winter Park, FL), surmised that "most presidents demonstrate an amazing capacity to push and pull their institutions toward evergreater levels of quality and financial stability. Their success is remarkable given the pressures, challenges, and vulnerabilities of the position."[7] She concludes, "Today's presidents can be counted successful if they are able to mobilize the human and financial resources necessary to strengthen the quality, reputation, and financial health of their institutions, and to collaborate in solving social problems."[8] She defines success in terms of the results emerging from leadership within the institution and from dealings with stakeholders.

This section notes some other examples of leadership traits. A task force of the American Association of Community Colleges, for instance, defined effective community college presidents as individuals who "thoroughly understand the community college mission. Armed with this understanding, he or she must be an effective advocate for the college's interests and must have skills in administration, community and economic development." The task force identified traits specifically related to "community and economic development" and "personal, interpersonal, and transformational skills." For example, "the personal skills needed for presidential leadership are extensive," but include "working with staff to promote the college's vision, values, and mission."[9]

At one college, some members of the governing board identified the traits that they thought the next president should have. They listed leadership and vision, combined with good people and communications skills to reach out broadly within the institution and to inspire everyone to improve educational quality and to work together as a team. For instance, the expectation is that "a good president would have vision and can articulate the vision and have others rally around the vision."[10]

The job advertisement for the next president of the University of Arizona captures essential traits: collegial leadership; involvement in shared governance; "a highly communicative relationship with faculty, staff, administrations, and students;" "highly-developed interpersonal relations and communication skills;" and "understand the importance of the . . . [university] to the state and the . . . [local] community and continue its leadership role in addressing community and statewide issues and advancing economic development through its research endeavors." Furthermore, the successful candidate should have "a proven record of leadership success," and be able to cultivate and strengthen effectively "relationships with alumni and the community and . . . [engage] them in the advancement of university goals."[11]

The literature links leadership with effectiveness, caring individuals, innovation, and the ability to influence planning and decision making within the institution and, more broadly, society as laid out in the mission statement.

The "charismatic" part of leadership is "ephemeral" or at least of lesser importance than the traits previously mentioned.[12]

CHANCELLORS

As the chief executive officer of a university system, the chancellor inspires internal and external constituency groups, represents the system to stakeholders, provides educational leadership, and, in conjunction with the board of trustees and in collaboration with the campuses in the system, develops policies, budgets, and plans. The leadership traits commonly identified in the literature include:

- Demonstrated ability to inspire and to lead the academic community;
- Demonstrated ability to link higher education with its constituencies and stakeholders;
- Strength of character, integrity, and high ethical standards;
- A record of successful implementation of strategic initiatives, with the determination to achieve objectives; and
- A demonstrated capacity for planning and the integration of planning and budgeting.

PROVOSTS

The literature portrays the provost as the academic leader of the university faculty and a member of the senior management team. As such, leadership responsibilities might involve:

developing and implementing an academic vision for the university; setting the university's academic priorities; working with the deans to develop the schools and colleges; identifying and cultivating interdisciplinary areas of excellence and collaboration within and between schools; . . . and ensuring the highest academic standards for our students and faculty throughout the University.[13]

Other roles of the provost include faculty recruitment, retention, professional development, promotion, and compensation, financial, and other.

DEANS

In many instances faculty members become deans but lack a background in management, and they might not be viewed as effective leaders. As Michael J. Johnson, Donald E. Hanna, and Don Okcott, Jr. point out, however, deans have both the responsibility and opportunity to lead dynamic organizations. These three educators view deans and chairpersons as "the heart and soul of the modern college and university."[14] The dean is an academic leader, who has excellent

Figure 7.1
Leadership Traits Appearing in Job Advertisements

Dean	Provost	Chancellor	President
Specified minimum number of years of leadership experience	Versatile communication skills and a strong background in mediation, coupled with a demonstrated ability to lead effectively in an institution with a tradition of substantive collective bargaining	Innovative	Ability to articulate the mission and goals of the university to both internal and external constituencies (visionary)—excellent communication skills
Demonstrated record of success in progressively responsible positions of leadership	Demonstrated success in valuing and enhancing diversity, also promoting global awareness	Energetic	A leadership style that emphasizes openness, collaboration, consensus-building, collegiality, and respect for shared governance
Strong communication skills	Skill as a successful team builder, fostering decisionmaking while rewarding innovation and productivity	Outstanding communications and interpersonal skills	Fundraising skills to build the university's resource base in support of its education, scholarship, and public service mission
Demonstrated ability to collaborate with, and relate effectively to, both internal and external constituents (build partnerships)—coalition builder	Ability to mentor emerging faculty leaders while affording new opportunities for senior faculty		An experienced, innovative and forward-thinking academic or business leader to build on the college's current and past successes and core competencies
Commitment to integrity	Strong leadership related to research activities (their promotion and accomplishment)		Support and nurture a climate that values diversity in students, staff, and community

Figure 7.1
Leadership Traits Appearing in Job Advertisements (continued)

Dean	Provost	Chancellor	President
Evidence of establishing a strategic vision and direction	A strong record of leadership and the proven ability to think strategically, prioritize effectively, and act decisively		
Inspiring and leading faculty and students	Broad, innovative, collegial, and visionary academic leader (articulate the university's vision)		
Innovative	Integrity		
An entrepreneurial leader (business school)	Able to achieve institutional goals		
Effective in collaboration	Effectively represent the university and its priorities with diverse internal and external audiences		
Create a climate, organizational structure, and managerial leadership team that encourage all members of the college community to contribute positively and productively to department, college, and university goals	Entrepreneurial leadership		
Record of garnering resources to support academic endeavors	Leadership in developing high quality academic programs		
Serve as a vital member of the university's overall leadership team			

Figure 7.1
Leadership Traits Appearing in Job Advertisements (continued)

Dean	Provost	Chancellor	President
Organizational structure, and managerial leadership team that encourage all members of the college community to contribute positively and productively to department, college, and university goals	Leadership		
Record of garnering resources to support academic endeavors	Leadership in developing high quality academic programs		
Serve as a vital member of the university's overall leadership team			

Source: Section C, *The Chronicle of Higher Education* (November 18, 2005; November 25, 2005; and December 2, 2005).

interpersonal skills and an eagerness to work interactively with others (president or chancellor, provost, other deans, faculty, and students), a fund raiser, a person able to motivate and inspire others, a visionary, and a team builder.

LEADERSHIP ATTRIBUTES APPEARING IN JOB ADVERTISEMENTS

As this chapter illustrates, leadership is important to the vitality of the college and universities. Figure 7.1 reinforces this point by taking job advertisements from three issues of *The Chronicle of Higher Education* and identifying the leadership component for college and university deans, provosts, chancellors, and presidents. There was no attempt to review advertisements for assistant deans, vice-provosts, vice-chancellors, and vice-presidents; to compare the qualities between those in the vice position and those to whom they report; or to relate the specific traits presented to the type of institution as characterized by *The Carnegie Classification of Institutions of Higher Education*.[15] In a number of instances, advertisements merely mentioned leadership without specifying particular qualities; for instance, the individual "possesses a demonstrated record of success in progressively responsible position of leadership." It is almost as if there is a common definition or view of the word "leadership," or the advertisement assumed that deans and others in high positions—especially those seeking the position of president or chancellor—are automatically leaders, or at least have a record of broad accomplishments that could be reviewed.

Reference to leadership is more common with the position of president, chancellor, and provost, than it is with a deanship. One university sought a provost who is a:

seasoned, courageous and dynamic leader with a strong entrepreneurial spirit who will set the standard of intellectual engagement and accomplishment, encourage a strong sense of collegiality, both internally and with external partners, and be a highly effective presence and voice of the institution, championing its work and its successes to extend their impact.

Some advertisements for a dean to lead a college of science or health care considered as desirable the "ability to advance the research agenda of the college and university," perhaps "with emphasis on interdisciplinary and cross-college initiatives."

CONCLUSION

The perception is that individuals in positions of upper administration in a college or university—from chairpersons and deans to the president—are (or must be) effective leaders and able to apply different leadership styles as the occasion demands. The literature of higher education identifies the leadership traits they should possess and offers strategies for obtaining them. In some instances, the leaders discussed in this chapter might have to "resolve problems with embedded moral issues."[16] When they do, they provide moral leadership. Various stories appearing in *The Chronicle of Higher Education* and other publications document moral and ethical lapses among academic leaders.

One important trait common to leadership from library director up to the college or university president or the university chancellor is *caring about people:*

Don't try to decide in advance which people will matter to your leadership development. Everybody matters. If you come to my university for a high level job interview, you'd better make a good impression on the support staff member who guides you from one important meeting to the next, because I'll ask that staff member for an evaluation. He or she will see you from a different perspective, and that perspective matters very much to me.[17]

"Leaders are the people who get things done."[18]

NOTES

1. Rita Bornstein, "The Nature and Nurture of Presidents," *The Chronicle of Higher Education* (November 4, 2005): B11.

2. James MacGregor Burns, *Leadership* (New York: Harper & Row, 1978); Michael D. Cohen and James G. March, *Leadership and Ambiguity: The American College President* (New York: McGraw-Hill, 1974); Leila Gonzālez Sullivan, "Four Generations of Community College Leadership," *Community College Journal of Research & Practice* 25 (September 2001): 559–71; Chester I. Barnard, *The Functions of the Executive* (Cambridge, MA: Harvard University Press, 1938); Doris R. Fine, *When Leadership Fails: Desegregation and Demoralization in the San Francisco Schools* (New Brunswick, NJ: Transaction Books, 1986); Philip Selznick, *Leadership in Administration: A Sociological Interpretation* (Evanston, IL: Row, Peterson, 1957); Fred E. Fielder, *A Theory of Leadership Effectiveness* (New York: McGraw-Hill, 1967); Janet L. Roseman, "On Leadership," *Dance/USA Journal* 14, no. 4 (Spring 1997): 15–19, 25; Doris Kearns Goodwin, *Team of Rivals: The Political Genius of Abraham Lincoln* (New York: Simon & Schuster, 2005). See also John W. Gardner, *On Leadership* (New York: The Free Press, 1990).

3. J. B. Rotter, "Interpersonal Trust: Trustworthiness and Gullibility," *American Psychologists* 35 (January 1980): 1–5.

4. Barbara Kellerman, "Howe Bad Leadership Happens," *Leader to Leader* 35 (Winter 2005): 41–46.

5. Charles J. McClain, "Leadership with Integrity: A Personal Perspective," *Innovative Higher Education (Historical Archive)* 17, no. 1 (September 1992): 9.

6. "The Chronicle Survey of Presidents of 4-Year Colleges," *The Chronicle of Higher Education* (November 4, 2005): A37.

7. Bornstein, "The Nature and Nurture of Presidents," B10.

8. Ibid., B11.

9. American Association of Community Colleges, "Community College Leaders; Today and Tomorrow" (Washington, D.C.: American Association of Community Colleges, n.d.). Available at http://www.ccleadership.org/leading_forward/characteristics.htm (accessed November 5, 2005).

10. Matthew Null, "Candidates List Desired Traits of College Presidents," *The Telescope* (October 31, 2005). Available at http://www.the-telescope.com/media/paper749/news/2004/10/11/News/Candidates.List.Desired.Traits.Of.College.President-746666.shtml (accessed November 7, 2005).

11. "Draft Leadership Characteristics: President, University of Arizona" (Tucson, AZ: University of Arizona, 2005). Available at http://www.abor.asu.edu/special_editions/UA%20Search/Leadership%20Characteristics.pdf (accessed November 7, 2005).

12. Stanford University, "The Cares of the University" (Palo Alto, CA: Stanford University, n.d.). Available at http://www.stanford.edu/home/stanford/cares/noframes/crystal.html (accessed November 7, 2005).

13. New York University, Office of the Provost, "About the Office" (New York: New York University, n.d.). Available at http://www.nyu.edu/provost/about-statement.html (accessed November 14, 2005).

14. Michael J. Johnson, Donald E. Hanna, and Don Okcott, Jr., *Bridging the Gap: Leadership, Technology, and Organizational Change for University Deans and Chairpersons* (Aldgate, South Australia: Webcite, n.d.). Available at http://www.webcite.com.au/prod14.htm (accessed November 14, 2005). See also Gary S. Krahenbuhl, *Building the Academic Deanship: Strategies for Success* (Westport, CT: Greenwood Press, 2004).

15. See *The Carnegie Classification of Institutions of Higher Education* (Menlo Park, CA: Carnegie Foundation for the Advancement of Teaching). For the last version and its predecessors, see http://www.carnegiefoundation.org/classifications (accessed February 8, 2006).

16. Shelley B. Wepner, Antonia D'Onofrio, Bernice Willis, and Stephen C. Wilhite, "Getting at the Moral Leadership of Education Deans," *The Qualitative Report,* 7, no. 2 (June 2002). Available at http://www.nova.edu/ssss/QR/QR7–2/wepner. html (accessed November 12, 2005). See also David G. Brown, *University Presidents as Moral Leaders* (Westport, CT: Greenwood Press, 2005).

17. University of Arizona, Office of the President, "Frey Leadership Institute Talk, Atlanta, Ga." (Tucson, AZ: University of Arizona, 2003): 3 (of 5). Available at http://president.arizona.edu/communications/public-addresses/public-address02/ (accessed November 14, 2005).

18. "The Neuropsychology of Leadership." Available at http://www.sybervision. com/Leaders/ (accessed November 7, 2005).

8

LIBRARY DIRECTORS' VIEWS
ON LEADERSHIP

"Those interested in leadership should think about the characteristics
critical to leadership success."[1]

Shirley K. Baker, Vice Chancellor for Information Technology and Dean of
Libraries, Washington University, considers "vision, courage [making difficult decisions], and the ability to make things happen through others" as
"key leadership characteristics."[2] She notes that:

Formal leadership opportunities, with title and authority, are often not as readily available as staff with desire and ability would like. Those interested in leadership should
look for informal opportunities which allow them to test their interests and ability,
without a formal appointment.[3]

She then identifies strategies for gaining experience in leading informally.

Viewing leadership from a different perspective, this chapter presents commentaries from eight nationally known directors of college and university
libraries who answered four questions that several library directors identified
as worthy of discussion and as complementary to the issues discussed elsewhere in this book. Those questions are:

- How do you stay attuned to the pulse of the institution?
- How do you keep the library aligned with that pulse?
- How do you keep the librarians focused on matters important to both the organi-
  zation and the institution?
- Is there a perception among library staff that the director is the sole leader of the
  library? Is such a perception correct or incorrect?

CAMILA A. ALIRE, DEAN EMERITUS OF UNIVERSITY LIBRARIES, UNIVERSITY OF NEW MEXICO

How Do You Stay Attuned to the Pulse of the Institution?

A university is a very complex organization and very multidimensional. Consequently, for me, the pulse of the institution comes from different "arteries." I think it is myopic for administrators to look to one source for the pulse or to assume that they themselves can determine/assess the pulse of the institution. Leaders must keep their eyes and ears open constantly.

When I first arrive as a new administrator at an institution, I immediately start to observe what is going on. It does not take to long to do what I call my "sphere-of- influence" campus assessment, where I try to determine who the power brokers and/or decision makers are. I do this assessment at all levels—board of regents, president, president's cabinet, president's office staff, provost, associate provost, provost staff, vice presidents and their staff, deans and associate deans, faculty, faculty governance, library administrators, library faculty, and library staff. (In the last four categories, I assess formal leaders and look for informal leaders.)

I make it a point to meet one-on-one and establish a first name relationship with the presidents of both the undergraduate student and the graduate student governments each year. This helps with knowing the pulse of the students. Additionally, I seek out well-established people in the community. They are identified from university formal functions, meetings, and community events.

My first "sphere-of-influence" list is not exclusive. As I work through the institutional culture, I will inevitably add and delete people. This can be due to new ones arriving on campus, internal people being promoted, and others leaving the institution.

Once I have identified the individuals for my mental sphere of influence list, I then work to establish solid relationships with them. And in many cases, they are business/social relationships. The relationships are developed for different reasons, but the ultimate goal is to maintain a pulse of the institution that could better position me and others to advocate for university libraries.

Specific Examples

First, the University of New Mexico (UNM) was searching for a new president when I arrived. All the noncabinet administrators were clamoring to get to know him the minute he arrived on campus. He was inundated and overwhelmed with the university, community, and legislature wanting his time.

In the first few months, he hired an executive vice president for administrative services and a chief of staff. I spent my time getting to know them; both came out of the governor's office. I knew I would have my time with the president at various functions and other gatherings. However, having a close tie to his two top associates has paid off unbelievably for university libraries. Those relationships have been predicated on mutual respect and confidence. Consequently, because I have a strong pulse on the university, I can put 2 + 2 together and be aware of forthcoming issues.

Second, everywhere I have been, I have established a "lady deans" luncheon group. Originally, it was because there were only two of us at most universities where I have worked; however, now with many more of us, we can develop a camaraderie that enables us to discuss anything and everything relative to the university. If I have otherwise missed something, I pick it up through this group.

And, third, for whatever reasons, I have always had a very strong relationship with my provosts and their entire staffs. (I would love to find out their perceptions of why that has been so.) I say this about the provosts I have worked with because they have shared much information in confidence not related to university libraries. Could it be that my perceived irreverence is refreshing?

How Do You Keep the Library Aligned with That Pulse?

In addition to my answer to the preceding question, I do this through:

- My visibility. I make sure that I am very visible throughout the university. I want to make sure that when anyone sees me, that person thinks libraries. This has worked extremely well with groups that I do not interact with on a daily basis such as the Board of Regents and other university officers above the dean and provost levels. It is absolutely amazing what one hears at a university social event or official dinner. Anyone in the "sphere of influence" can then corroborate this information.

- Visibility of key library personnel. I make sure that key individuals are visible at other levels of the university. We try to have library faculty and staff cover all functions, events, and so on. Again, I want the university to *think libraries* when administrators, faculty, and staff see any of us. Inevitably, information comes from those library faculty and staff who are visible representing university libraries. That information helps with monitoring the pulse of the university.

- Committee/task force appointments. I never shirked the responsibility of being involved in university committee and/or task forces. My involvement is usually at the provost's level or university level. I particularly like being involved in key university personnel searches. What I mean by *key* is a search to fill positions that support university units that cut across the university. This is a strategic activity. Most deans do not want to be bothered with direct involvement except for a provost or president. I suggest myself as the deans' representative on searches such as Vice President for Advancement or University Chief Counsel or any other search that will have the following representation: other university administrators, key faculty, and community representatives. This provides exposure to another level of individuals to develop a relationship that keeps me aligned with the pulse of the university.

- Communication with library faculty/staff. I do not want to be a leader on campus who continuously says "the dean is the last to know." Consequently, keeping the lines of communication open between library faculty and staff and me is critical. This does not mean that everyone is involved; it means that those people who are out and about in the university know that I have an open door for them to share any information they might have that would help me and others get a sense of the pulse on the university.

How Do You Keep the Librarians Focused on Matters Important to Both the Organization and the Institution?

The factors that help me keep librarians focused are:

- Engagement and communication. It is important to keep the library faculty engaged, that is, to let them know that you rely on them to help you with the pulse of the university. The majority of them like that role. Again, not everyone is involved, but the ones who have been instrumental in getting information back to me and my management team that helps us position the library better within the institution.

  With engagement comes communication. As a leader, I need to ensure that library faculty understand the issues/concerns/challenges du jour for the library (e.g., related to the strategic plan). They need to know what is important to us so that they can determine what information is helpful and should be brought back.
- Library strategic plan. It is critical that library faculty know our strategic goals because they are what keep the library management focused. We reiterate the goals and any new objectives to the faculty at the beginning of the academic year. Being reminded of those goals enables the faculty also to stay focused and be alert about what on campus might help us achieve those goals and related objectives.
- Active involvement on committees and task forces based on expertise. By encouraging library faculty to volunteer or be appointed to some university committee or task force as appropriate, I help them stay focused on what is important to the university. Ironically, sometimes a library faculty member does not see his/her role in a particular group until others or myself point out that their expertise is very appropriate for the situation. These also helps keep them (and the library) visible.

Is There a Perception among Library Staff That the Director Is the Sole Leader of the Library? Is Such a Perception Correct or Incorrect?

Yes, in every library where I have become the leader, the perception is that the director is the sole leader. For whatever reasons, previous administrators fueled that perception. I pride myself in changing that perception at each university library where I have worked. I do that through empowerment and communication. Empowering others to help "take the lead" has always been well received. Encouraging them to accept that delegation is part of the process. It only takes one good, successful example of empowerment that convinces others that I am serious about delegating to and empowering others. It has been my experience that library faculty and staff take the opportunity afforded to them to be leaders within the organization and outside the organization if allowed. However, a leader cannot empower others and then discourage risk-taking at the same time. Providing that opportunity for others in the organization to lead should be coupled with the strong support for risk-taking realizing that occasionally there will be setbacks. And they should not be punished for those setbacks.

There is enough room, enough work, and enough challenges to spread the leadership around! The dean does not have to be the only leader in the organization. As dean, I readily assume the role of facilitator when appropriate. By that I mean, making sure that the work and challenges are addressed by engaging others to take the lead to accomplish them.

I have to add that leading by example has helped every management team with which I have worked to become more empowering. It has also helped individual team members "to let go" and to delegate more. Everyone then becomes more engaged by knowing that he or she contributes to the library's efforts.

RUSH G. MILLER, DIRECTOR, UNIVERSITY LIBRARY SYSTEM, UNIVERSITY OF PITTSBURGH

How Do You Stay Attuned to the Pulse of the Institution?

I have employed different strategies for staying abreast of developments within the university over the years depending on the size and nature of the university with which I was associated. Because of the size and complexity of the University of Pittsburgh, I must rely on many individuals within the library system to assist me with this task.

The most important aspect of being "tuned in" is discerning which of the many voices on campus are most important. A director can be led astray very easily if he or she does not know who is credible and authoritative and who is attempting to manipulate. I make a point to verify information that comes to me. I also listen to every faculty member with whom I have contact. It is essential to keep in touch with various faculty perspectives (e.g., by discipline and rank). Active listening is a key to success for any director.

I serve on the Deans and Directors Council, which is the primary leadership body within the academic area. Important as a forum for information sharing, it is also essential for networking and being able to talk one-on-one over lunch or at breaks in meetings with deans and others. I also meet frequently with the Senate Library Committee, which is not always as representative body as I would prefer, but which does attempt to convey viewpoints of faculty and students through representatives to the libraries. I meet as often as practical with the provost and the vice provosts with whom I interact on a regular basis. I have developed professional relationships with a number of individual faculty members and often discuss issues of concern to them. I also attend meetings of the board of trustees and give reports to and interact with its Committee on Academic Affairs and Libraries.

I read the major campus publications such as the *University Times,* an independent newspaper published on campus; the *Pitt News,* the student newspaper; and the *Chronicle,* which is published by the Office of Public Affairs. I read a number of departmental and school newsletters as well.

Every single academic program at Pittsburgh is assigned a bibliographer and liaison responsible for not only collection development but also frequently communicating with faculty and students in each discipline. They often provide me with an advance warning of emerging issues needing our attention and faculty opinion of library services and policies.

But beyond all of this, we have been working toward a "culture of assessment" for a number of years. We have been an annual participant in the Association of Research Libraries' LibQual+™ because it was a pilot project and thus has longitudinal data on our users' perceptions of our services. We build assessment into every new program and service and monitor the utility of all of our services, including technology-based ones, on a continuous basis. We have a "feedback" mechanism on our Web pages and digital library projects, and receive very useful information from the responses to them. By keeping in touch with our users through our various assessment systems, and by keeping up with the issues that our faculty and administrators convey to us formally and informally, we have a good sense of the "pulse" of the institution.

How Do You Keep the Library Aligned with That Pulse?

Our strategic plan and the development of new services are aligned with the ambitions plans of the University. For the past 11 years here, I have worked hard to understand the aspirations of the university as a whole and individual divisions within it, and to align our goals so that we contribute directly to the attainment of those ambitions. For example, our aspirations to be globally focused led directly to the development several years ago of our major collaboration for electronic resource sharing with all of the major academic libraries in China, as well as others in Taiwan, Hong Kong, and Korea. The ambition to enhance the quality of the undergraduate experience at the University of Pittsburgh has led to a host of new projects and services designed to serve undergraduates better.

The need to align our library program to the aspirations of the university leads to conscious alignments of our services and resources to those areas of development that contribute most directly and concretely to the needs of the campus. For the most part, we reconcile them so that we focus on the libraries' long-term health. For example, we recently decided to consolidate two of our many departmental libraries to save cost and to utilize our recently added high density storage facility as a means of reducing collections in these librar-ies to allow consolidation. In years past, this might have resulted in major resistance from faculty in the disciplines affected. Now, however, these units needed space for newly endowed professorships and welcomed this change.

Our process of alignment is deliberate and so far very successful. In addi-tion, in some way, I try to meet every faculty or administrative request that I get. This is especially true for faculty who often have little access to depart-mental or university funding to meet their needs. Recently, for example, I found end-of-the-year funding with which to purchase expensive films/ DVDs. This assisted the film studies program in enhancing the media collec-tion. When the philosophy of science faculty expressed the need to build an online archive to support their discipline, we developed the PhilSci Archive, an open archives initiative, in partnership with the Department of History and Philosophy of Science, the Philosophy of Science Center, and the Phi-losophy of Science Association to meet this need. Since then, we have built and mounted five more discipline-based online archives for various disciplines on campus.

How Do You Keep the Librarians Focused on Matters Important to Both the Organization and the Institution?

Everyone in the library system must follow the goals and aspirations found in our strategic plan. Each year, departments write specific goals and plans for the unit, and librarians and staff develop individual professional goals for the year. Once approved, they are expected to achieve them and annual appraisals are tied to the attainment of these goals. In fact, upper management reviews these goals and appraisals for consistency before approval. Resources are allo-cated generally to highest priority activities, those that directly contribute to attaining institutional goals and objectives.

I find that, for the most part, staying focused is not a difficult task. We use highly trained and experienced librarians who are self-motivated to achieve positive and constructive results from their efforts.

Is There a Perception among Library Staff That the Director Is the Sole Leader of the Library? Is Such a Perception Correct or Incorrect?

I certainly hope not! It would be very incorrect in our case. I have worked very long and hard to develop leadership at all levels in the organization. As I look around the library system at the University of Pittsburgh, I see strong and able leadership being exerted at all levels. We are fortunate to have a strong senior staff team, and we act as a team in decision making and direction-setting. Supervisors are empowered to make most decisions in line with general policies and plans. We have a representative Council, with both elected and appointed members, that assists with decision making and policy formulation. We have working groups that manage programs and training. Librarians are organized for faculty governance as a faculty, and they elect officers to manage the Library Faculty Assembly and its various committees. All in all, many librarians are leaders in the organization and often take initiative in resolving or deciding issues well below the director level. I like to think I am considered to be the leader of the overall vision and sometimes have the authority to make decisions or set directions unilaterally where needed to ensure success, but that kind of action is and should be very rare.

That said, it is clear that every organization and leader on the Pittsburgh campus knows that I am the leader of the library system. I have been in my position for 11 years and am well known on campus. I have worked hard to establish credibility with all of them. Within the library system, the librarians and staff understand and in fact support the notion that the director is the final authority. My credibility on campus is the key to the respect for my authority within the library system. If a director is not respected by the university community, he or she will have little real authority within the system ultimately.

STEVEN BELL, DIRECTOR OF THE LIBRARY, PHILADELPHIA UNIVERSITY

How Do You Stay Attuned to the Pulse of the Institution?

It happens in formal and informal ways. At my institution the library director reports to the vice president for academic affairs (VPAA) and is a member of the Deans' Council. We meet every other week to exchange information, and this is where I generally hear about new and ongoing developments. For example, the VPAA is fairly new and we are setting course for some change. He has made it clear that we need to create change in the curricula. This enables me to anticipate and prepare for this change. I already know some of the new degree programs we are considering, and I can communicate concerns (mostly about resources) I might have about these new directions. My role as library director is not to impede progress but to support it and communicate to the VPAA and deans those ways in which they will need to support the library if we are to meet successfully accreditation standards or receive state approval. Finding out what is happening is critical for keeping librarians attuned to institutional change, and enabling them to participate in our decision-making process.

The governance structure provides additional opportunities for staying attuned to the pulse of the institution. At this institution librarians are not on the tenure track. Officially we are not committee members. Excepting an "advisory" role for the library director, we participate in several committees in nonofficial ways. For example, my information literacy coordinator is the co-chair of the Information Literacy Task Force, a committee made up mostly of faculty members. The core committees for me in terms of the "pulse" of the institution are the curriculum committees, both the undergraduate and graduate. Interaction with them provides access to information about curricular changes. I know when new courses in every school are proposed (I must sign off on all course proposals that go before the curriculum committee), and I have the opportunity to both work with faculty on determining the level of resources needed to support the course and have librarians work with faculty members to integrate information literacy skill building into any appropriate course.

The final formal channel comes by way of the Teaching, Learning, and Technology Roundtable. I have chaired the roundtable since its inception, and it provides a great opportunity to discover how faculty are using technology, what works and does not work for them, and what they want in the way of technology and support for integrating it into their courses. Access to this information allows the library to maintain a position as a technology leader on campus and to be more involved with the information technology department in meeting faculty and students needs.

Informal channels are also useful for finding out what is happening, as well as influencing what happens. Informal activities occur in a variety of ways. I have a librarian who eats lunch with faculty colleagues on a regular basis, and although some of what is heard is little more than institutional gossip, every now and then we hear of something important that may impact on the library. Other librarians are friendly with faculty, and friendship is a mechanism for learning what is happening within different colleges of the university. I share information with colleagues I work out with on a regular basis in our fitness center, and I also get work done during our weekly basketball game that involves faculty, administrators, student services employees, and others. We routinely exchange information, and I have used this time to sow the seeds of cultural events with faculty, as well as to have discussions about the library's technology infrastructure. It is not all that different from what we know about important decisions and deals being made on the golf course.

One challenge I have is to keep this information coming in on a regular basis, filtering and vetting it, finding out what is fact versus fiction (or what is likely to happen versus what may happen but not anytime soon), and then making it a part of the regular environmental scan I perform to help determine what direction the library needs to take in accomplishing stated strategic goals and fulfilling our vision.

How Do You Keep the Library Aligned with That Pulse?

Like a real pulse, the institutional pulse varies depending on internal and external pressures, influences, and shifting resource allocations. While we certainly want the library to adapt to and potentially anticipate those variations, it is important to be guided by essential values and a plan that keeps us focused on helping faculty in their effort to enable students to achieve institutional learning outcomes. We want to strike a balance between staying on course as a library organization and aligning ourselves to change within the organization. As the library director I also need to deviate from both when it may be beneficial to the institution, for example, taking advantage of an opportunity that may better position the library to serve future needs.

The process begins with a strategic plan. The entire academic affairs sector goes through a common process to achieve a united strategic plan. This is helpful in aligning the library with the pulse of the institution because we have access to the plans of the individual colleges, and we can have our plan reflect what the deans will seek to accomplish. This overarching strategic planning process occurs about every fifth year, but the library revisits its strategic plan at the beginning of each semester as it reviews accomplishments, confirms that our long-term goals are still appropriate to the needs of the institution, and determines which goals and objectives should be prioritized for the coming semester.

For example, my institution has been changing its curriculum and culture over the last decade. At one time it was primarily focused on the textiles industry, but that has since shifted to a variety of design fields. In recent years the shift became more prominent owing to the introduction of non-textiles engineering programs into the school of textiles. This presented some real challenges to the library. If we wanted to align with the pulse of the institution we needed to rethink our collection development and determine what and how much textiles resources to cut, but not so deeply as to drastically weaken a historical collection strength for the institution—and one that still resonated with many of the long time faculty. At the same time we needed to plan acquisitions for two new additions to the curriculum. Working with the dean and faculty, we identified a number of journal titles to cancel and determined what resources would help to meet new curricular subjects.

From my perspective the key to keeping the library aligned to the institutional pulse is to be vigilant by conducting ongoing internal and external environmental scans, using that information continually to review stated goals and objectives, and fostering collaborative relationships between librarians and academic colleagues that enable us to align with the pulse as needed.

How Do You Keep the Librarians Focused on Matters Important to Both the Organization and the Institution?

I use a combination of strategies to keep the librarians focused on our strategic goals and objectives, as well as those of the institution. Most important, as a library director I think the best thing I can do is have knowledgeable and competent librarians that I can trust to make good decisions and stay focused on their personal and organizational goals. I believe it is important to communicate with them regularly, but not micromanage their work. If we are communicating effectively, then I feel confident that the librarians and I will be in agreement about library and institutional priorities.

Not unlike the ways in which we align with the pulse of the institution, I can establish a working relationship with the librarians to have them align with strategic goals and objectives. This process is built into our annual evaluation process. I review the past year's goals set by each librarian, and we develop goals for the next academic year. Then we review the progress toward the current year's goals halfway through the academic year. In addition, I meet regularly with individual librarians to discuss ongoing projects and deal with any issues that may impact on their progress.

As much as regular staff meetings may be maligned, they are important for information sharing. This is when I can let the librarians know what is happening at the institution, particularly within the academic sphere. They also share with everyone the progress of projects on which they are working, information about current assignments, or a problem that requires staff discussion. We can, as a group, discuss the importance of these issues for the library and the organization, and we can determine how to respond to institutional challenges and change. Each librarian can also focus on the school to which he or she serves as liaison. I encourage the librarians to attend the school faculty meetings.

I would point to three final things that I think may help to keep the librarians focused on what is important to the institution and library. First, since I am sometimes too eager to try new things and incorporate new technologies, I need for the library staff to keep me focused and anchored on current challenges. They need to be able to let me know when adding a new program or service would be disruptive, and should be postponed or further questioned. Second, it is important to be as open as possible about the budgetary process and resources to let the staff know what we can and cannot do, and to allow them to have input into the allocation of resources. Third, it is crucial for me to listen to and focus on supporting their needs—giving them the resources they need to perform their jobs—as much as that can be done.

Is There a Perception among Library Staff That the Director Is the Sole Leader of the Library? Is Such a Perception Correct or Incorrect?

A few years back the "theme" of the Association of College and Research Libraries for the year was "every librarian a leader." I think that is true to an extent, but it depends on what we mean by leading. If we look at it from the more narrow perspective of decision making and having the final authority on resource allocations, the perception that the library director is the sole leader is largely a correct perception. As the director I must make the final decision on what initiatives we take and what resources we put into them. But that does not happen in a vacuum.

I do not know if my staff would think of themselves as leaders in their own right, but to the extent that I depend on their input in formulating the vision and in making resource allocation decisions, I think the perception that the library director is the sole leader in incorrect—and I think the library staff would agree. Yes, at times I have heard the statement, "You are the director and you will decide what you think is best," which suggests that I inadequately take the staff perspective into account. But if I feel strongly that something is the right thing for us to do, then I go ahead with that course of action. I would like to think that most of those decisions have worked out well for the library, institution, and library staff.

Where I do see that perception of library director as sole leader as incorrect is in our connection with the user community. The director alone cannot grasp all that is happening on campus, and how the user community feels about library services and resources. That is where I encourage each librarian to be a leader within the schools to which he or she serves as a liaison. These liaisons need to develop a vision for services and resources specific to that segment of our user population, and create the relationships with students and faculty that will allow them to be accepted as a colleague and educator. Although there is certainly an expectation that the library director will develop a vision and put in place those things needed to realize that vision, as a library director I depend on my library staff (professional and support) to serve as the antennae of the library in gathering information and data that shape the vision.

Another area in which every librarian can lead is in bringing innovation to the library. Developing good ideas for new services, discovering useful new technological utilities, recommending a better way to use space in the library building, performing research for publication and presentation, and other innovations are important forms of leadership, but they are not the sole domain of the library director. The challenge for the library director as leader is to create the right environment that is conducive to innovation. I certainly try to lead by example by maintaining a "keeping up" regimen that allows me to follow news and developments in librarianship, but more important in fields that are peripheral to this profession. Innovation often develops from activities that occur outside the profession. When I find things of interest I share them with the librarians to get them thinking about new possibilities, but I try to be careful not to overload them. I hope this will encourage them to also find and share information with colleagues that will inspire and motivate them to take more of a leadership role within our library and institution.

LARRY L. HARDESTY, INTERIM UNIVERSITY LIBRARIAN, WINONA STATE UNIVERSITY

How Do You Stay Attuned to the Pulse of the Institution?

As a dean, I am on the Deans' Council, which includes the deans of the various colleges; and the senior vice chancellor for academic affairs, to whom I report, leads it. I am also on the Administrative Council, which is led by the chancellor and consists of the senior administrators of the university. Both these groups are formal ways of keeping attune to the pulse of the institution. In addition, the deans have coffee each Wednesday morning in the library conference room where we have informal discussions of the events of the week and what may be coming up. I find this very helpful to find the meaning and reaction to what is going on in the formal meetings.

In the past at a smaller institution, I made sure I ate in the cafeteria with classroom faculty members, and I occasionally had lunch with the vice president of finance, although we tended not to talk shop. Also, at a small school I tended to socialize more with the classroom faculty. There is a Friday afternoon social hour here (University of Nebraska at Kearney), and I try to attend those just to meet and talk informally with people. I do have a regularly scheduled meeting with the person to whom I report. I also attend any lunches, dinners, athletic events, etc., to which the other deans, or the vice-chancellor or the chancellor invite me.

I also serve on several campus committees, some ex officio and some not, and I try to attend as much as I can. I watch for information coming out from any of the campus offices that might relate to the library, such as general education revisions. Because I am on a campus that is part of a state system, I pay attention to legislative news and also confer and meet with my counterparts at these other institutions.

In addition, I talk quite a bit (at least is seems to me) with the librarians, who, as faculty, serve on various campus committees. Oh yes, it pays to watch the local newspaper to see what is playing in the news.

How Do You Keep the Library Aligned with That Pulse?

I make sure the minutes of the dean's council are distributed. Also, I write up notes from the administrative council meetings and distribute them to the entire library staff via e-mail. The librarians have a weekly meeting where we discuss events going on campus. The associate dean of the library attends meetings I cannot attend and she writes up notes, which I often distribute further.

How Do You Keep the Librarians Focused on Matters Important to Both the Organization and the Institution?

This can be accomplished largely through informal discussions and the formal weekly meetings. The librarians are faculty here and they are involved in the faculty committee system. I do think there is a need here for some strategic planning and goal formation, and I am working on that.

Is There a Perception among Library Staff That the Director Is the Sole Leader of the Library? Is Such a Perception Correct or Incorrect?

This is not the situation here. The librarians are faculty and they are involved in the faculty senate committee system. They take this role pretty seriously. In a more hierarchical organization, such as the library, the more extreme elements of faculty governance do not work well. On the other hand, a dictatorial, or at least a nonconsultative style of management does not work well for the library, as it also does not work well with classroom faculty. Librarians are bright, articulate people who want a say in their day-to-day work lives and they should be involved.

TERRENCE MECH, DIRECTOR OF THE LIBRARY, KING'S COLLEGE, WILKES-BARRE, PA

How Do You Stay Attuned to the Pulse of the Institution?

Your position in an organization influences what you may see and hear, as well as your access to information. The library director's position, on most campuses, is an institutional middle manager's position—responsible for a significant organizational unit and reporting to a senior institutional level manager. From this vantage point, library directors must be able to peer into senior administration and to oversee their libraries to know what is going on. Being able to see and hear what is going on is relatively easy; rather it is the ability to recognize activity and decipher the implications that is the occasional difficulty. With obligations to both the institution and the library, a director's ability to environmentally scan the internal and external horizons and look side-to-side is a prerequisite for success. For other leaders within a library, their spot on the organization chart often determines the immediate nature and starting point of their leadership activities. At a college the size of King's College (2, 085 FTE [full-time equivalent] students and 140 FTE faculty) the institutional pulse is rather transparent.

Given the college's size and the library's function as a crossroads for many constituencies, the library is in an excellent position to observe student and faculty behavior and reactions unobtrusively. In the course of daily business, working relationships with student life, technology, and physical plant provide a network of sources and perspectives.

Academic institutions, even small tranquil-appearing colleges and universities, are complex multifaceted organizations teaming with life, stories, challenges, rumors, ideas, aspirations, agendas, trial balloons, and pronouncements. These daily messages to and among organizational members reinforce institutional cultures, reaffirm values, and signal directions. There are official channels that broadcast to the entire organization and the outside world, and then there are the smaller conduits closer to the organization's "shop floor," those parts of the institution where the organization's *real* work gets accomplished. Here new ideas form and float about, percolate and ferment change and on occasion trouble, as frustrations and unhappiness are vented. These conduits carry the observations, questions, suggestions, and calls for help or clarity that come from those doing the organization's work. A familiarity with academic and institutional culture reminds one that sometimes the process is as essential as the content.

A library leader needs to be attuned to the multiple signals that various academic constituencies generate. The ability to hear the different notes and sense the varied refrains, identify the important themes, and filter out the background noises is an acquired art that comes from listening and observing. With practice you are able to pick the potentially interesting exchanges, those with ramifications for the institution or the library. Library leaders must be careful to monitor several institutional frequencies. Monitoring only one channel limits your ability to recognize and understand the messages in the cacophony.

For library leaders, that means reading college publications, committee minutes, institutional research reports, knowing the organizational structures—administrative and governance—both the official and the unofficial, being aware of how things actually get accomplished both formally and informally. It means getting out of the building, being visible on campus, and establishing positive relationships with your boss, faculty, administrators, support staff, and colleagues. If you want to be "in the know," you have to be recognized and known by others, willing to serve the organization, and able to establish yourself as someone with a perspective that transcends the confines of your own organizational unit. A reputation for evenhanded, independent thought and action also builds trust and provides access to the thoughts of those shaping the institution. Knowing what issues are challenging the institution and how the organization might respond makes it possible to identify potential areas of common interest among or between the library, the institution, and different departments.

How Do You Keep the Library Aligned with That Pulse?

An awareness of what is important to the college is vital if the library is to support the college's work or even get ahead of it. At King's College, the emphasis on teaching and student learning makes it a natural fit for the library to emphasize the development and assessment of students' information skills. These efforts have resulted in a vibrant instructional program with a series of study guides and handouts for student and faculty use. The library's assessment of seniors' information skills provides department faculty with a comparison of students' information skills by major. With department identities masked, the general results are distributed college-wide, with the details going to the individual departments for use in their curricular discussions.

In this environment, knowledge of the curriculum and what faculty members are doing in the classroom and with assignments is helpful.

Given its location as an institutional crossroads and the director's role as an institutional middle manager with vertical access to senior administrators and horizontal access to other institutional middle managers, the library is in a position to not only align with an institution's pulse but also influence that pulse. The library encourages and supports curricular change through an assessment of students' information skills and publicly sharing the results for discussion.

A library mission statement that reflects the college's mission and the library's role in achieving that mission is a formal reminder of how the library is linked to the institution. Setting and measuring success toward annual or multiyear goals that are tied to the institution's strategic plan is a way to synchronize the library's pulse to that of the college. Collaborating on these areas of shared interest requires knowing the strengths, weaknesses, and potential of the library and the librarians. Being aware of how constituencies (students and faculty) view the library may mirror how well the library is attuned to various institutional pulses. Graduation or campus-wide satisfaction surveys, conducted by an institutional research office, provide libraries with an idea of how students view the library and its efforts. It also means using comparative data for benchmarking and monitoring trends. Knowledge of what an institution's peer-group libraries are doing or thinking may either confirm ideas or provide something to consider. A regular program review or internal self-study, formal or informal, helps to renew the shared understanding of the library's health and reassess the library's contributions to the institution's larger mission. Stepping back from the daily work, laying down the rose- or dark-colored lenses and looking objectively at the library provides an opportunity for librarians and staff to enumerate the challenges and the successes, as well as realign priorities. Any meaningful vision for the library must be illuminated with knowledge of the issues facing higher education-at-large, as well as the challenges of the particular institution the library serves.

How Do You Keep the Librarians Focused on Matters Important to Both the Organization and the Institution?

Keeping the library in sync with the institution means knowing where the library's and the institution's interests intersect with the personal interests, skills, and abilities of the librarians and support staff. Keeping the library aligned requires that individual librarians and support staff know where the library is going, how it is going to get there, and what their role is in that process. Change and realignment can be difficult even for those individuals who are thoughtful and aware of how their actions contribute to the library's collective success or failure. But to be successful, leaders at all levels within the library must be comfortable facilitating change in themselves and those around them. Libraries and colleges do not change; rather, it is the individuals who work within them that change or do not change. Individual employees provide the public with its perception of the institution. Even at small institutions, the positive adjustment to new organizational or environmental realities can be a slow and difficult process, as personnel individually recognize the need to adapt new ways or to abandon previous behaviors. The temptation to revert to old behaviors and attitudes can be a struggle until individuals understand and see the benefits of making the change. To keep everyone focused, it is important to continuously articulate the *big picture* and how the policy or their actions contribute. Harnessing the energy of others without wearing them down is an art form. At small colleges continued professional development is vital for keeping skills sharp and outlooks flexible and positive.

Is There a Perception among Library Staff That the Director Is the Sole Leader of the Library? Is Such a Perception Correct or Incorrect?

Frequently, at smaller institutions there is a perception among some librarians and support staff that library directors are the sole library leader. This perception is not confined to the library either. Being a library leader, whether or not a director, requires energy, courage, and being able to regularly step outside your comfort zone, take risks, and challenge assumptions or traditions. It means being able to set aside your bias and asking others to step out from behind theirs. There is a danger to having the director as the only library leader; there is no one to challenge the director's unconscious assumptions. All library leaders need a "reality check" on occasion that helps them stay in tune with themselves, the library, the institution, and various constituencies. Over time, perspectives need to be recalibrated because of fatigue, exuberance, or the blind pursuit of a vision. Sometimes a look in the "rear-view" mirror at past actions—yours, the library's, the institution's, or others'—provides an epiphany, or more likely a less pleasant revelation, that based on subsequent events and reflection, you or others are not as divine and all knowing as originally thought. The ability to learn from our mistakes and those of others adds further dimension and temperance to one's perspective.

For a library to be successful requires more than one leader. It means developing individuals who are comfortable with ambiguity and asking the big questions—like why, and how, or what if. Real team players must be confident enough to raise issues and directors must be able to listen when personnel tell you things you would rather not hear. To maintain momentum in a small academic library, it is vital that reluctant leaders-to-be are coaxed and stretched out of their introverted comfort zones. Everyone must understand that they do make a difference and be encouraged to contribute to the library's success and renewal.

THOMAS G. KIRK, JR., LIBRARY DIRECTOR AND COORDINATOR OF INFORMATION SERVICES, EARLHAM COLLEGE

How Do You Stay Attuned to the Pulse of the Institution?

This is in some sense an easy question to answer. In a small liberal arts college, especially Earlham, one is close to everyone. By virtue of my position, I sit in a variety of administrative-level formal meetings where other institutional leaders are present and discuss issues. This is my most formal mode of communication.

To be effective in this mode one has to ask lots of questions and be prepared to frame them in an appropriate context. What is important in these formal meetings is to be prepared. I need to know what the issues of the institution are, how they impact on the library, or how the library can meet the challenges faced. I need to think about those relationships ahead of time and develop a sense of what questions need to be asked. Attending these meetings is not a passive exercise; rather, it is an active engagement through which concerns of the library get expressed, not necessarily by making proposals, but by asking the important questions.

But the formal meetings are not the only means of staying attuned to the campus. In fact they are not necessarily the most important. Being in a small institution I can see the president, provost, other vice presidents, the officers of student government, among others, by sending an e-mail message asking for an appointment. Like the formal meetings it is important to go prepared. Because I have asked for the appointment I am able to some extent to "set the agenda." In such instances, I need to prepare and develop a sense of what questions I want to ask, and what kind of information I want to have.

I have not been part of a large academic institution, but I would imagine that getting appointments would require a longer lead time and time for preparation will be longer; however, I think the point I am making here applies in all situations. To be in touch with the pulse of the institution, it is essential that I be a proactive listener to the official channels of supervision and communication.

There also are a number of informal methods of staying attuned to the pulse of the campus. These are not particularly novel, but perhaps it is the degree of involvement that is important. I meet regularly with individual faculty. I also interview candidates for faculty teaching positions so I have reached out to them before they even get an appointment. I read the student newspaper. I interact with students at the reference desk. I talk to library staff about what they are hearing across the campus. I talk with hourly staff. I read reports from administrative offices. I attend workshops, faculty lectures, academic departments' programs, and campus-wide cultural and athletic events. As with the two more formal methods described previously, it is essential that

I consciously focus on learning from others. In response to what I hear, I ask more questions.

Finally, I need to have time to integrate the information I am hearing. As part of that process I like to be sure I am hearing multiple perspectives on the same issue. If I hear some information through an informal channel and I want to verify its accuracy, I make it a point to talk to those directly involved. I am not interested in spreading information further unless I know its veracity.

In summary, I use multiple channels, I engage people by asking questions, and I am constantly contextualizing the information I am hearing to form a multilayered sense of the institutions' pulse. On reflection, I realize I have placed a heavy emphasis on asking questions. This emphasis is probably a reflection of my personality as well as a reflection of my membership in the Society of Friends (Quakers) and my socialization to the ways of Earlham. The practice of asking questions is both a scholarly and religious activity that allows the questioner to understand the perspective of others. This questioning is important in the fact-finding stages of engaging any issue.

How Do You Keep the Library Aligned with That Pulse?

Conceptually, I maintain that alignment by constantly thinking about how the library's mission and goals fit with the institutional issues. When there is an issue that is relevant, it is important to put steps in motion to address the issue by developing plans. Let me illustrate this principle with an example, one that is still in process and for which the outcome is not clear.

For about three years there have been some concerns among students about library access. At one time it was a request to have additional 24/7 computer lab and associated study space available at the end of the semester. More recently the issue has become the lack of study space anywhere on campus throughout the semester between midnight and 2 AM.

I have been in regular contact with student government officers, the college Committee on Campus Life, and senior administrators. The issue of computer lab accessibility is clearly a library issue, but increasing study space is not only a library issue. However, the library does see itself as a place for study and so we have appropriated that issue rather than push it away to some other unit of the college.

I have therefore been developing multiple plans for addressing these issues, which, although linked conceptually, are separate projects with separate costs. There does not seem to be a single solution that addresses both student demands satisfactorily. Through the work of a number of people, two proposals are now on the *institutional table*. Which proposal will ultimately be chosen is unclear. But as one of the library staff put it in a recent staff meeting at which the proposals were being reviewed, "this is a win-win situation for the library." Addressing the issues demonstrates the library's engagement with larger campus issues. Whichever proposal is accepted, we will have extended the reach of the library in its efforts to support the college's academic program.

How Do You Keep the Librarians Focused on Matters Important to Both the Organization and the Institution?

I do not know that I do anything consciously except to be constantly engaged in asking the question "How do we better serve the academic needs of students and faculty?" This kind of question drives our regular planning processes. Certainly I keep library staff, not just librarians but the entire staff, informed about developments in the institution.

Structural circumstances also promote librarians' focus on matters important to both the organization and the institution. First, as members of the faculty, librarians serve in the many roles. (These activities are discussed in more detail in the next section.) Second, the criteria for assessment include both the quality of work within the specifics of a job description and the broader rubric of community and institutional service. (The next section provides more detail about these points.)

Is There a Perception among Library Staff That the Director Is the Sole Leader of the Library? Is Such a Perception Correct or Incorrect?

The perception certainly is *not* that I as director am the sole leader of the library. All of the librarians have liaison responsibilities, and, because of the small size of the institution and the development of close personal relationships, this liaison relationship goes way beyond the narrow questions of reference/instruction/collection development. These liaison relationships lead to the exchange of information about a broad range of institutional issues. For example, important staff and curricular changes are discovered through these channels faster than through the formal channels of college committees and governance structures. Library practice and policy can also be explained to our users through informal channels, and this dialogue often leads to questions about changes in policy and practice to meet changing user needs. Again, because of size we can make arrangements in response to the need for change, on a trial basis, before we implement an activity, program, or policy on a library-wide basis.

Equally important is the context in which librarians serve their professional responsibilities at the college. As librarians they serve as members of the faculty and, with privileges such as access to professional development grants and sabbaticals, they have responsibilities for student advising and service on all college committees. That includes such key committees as the curriculum, budget, faculty personnel, and nominating committees. With a presence on, even convenership of,[4] these committees, any librarian can be in dialogue with other faculty and administrators about college-wide as well as library issues.

Perhaps the most interesting example of this phenomenon is when a librarian serves on the budget committee, a faculty committee that advises the president on budget priorities. When the provost and I present the annual library budget to the committee, a librarian may be a member of that committee. Of course, that situation is of great benefit to the library. But it also means that the librarian must understand the budget more deeply than might typically be the case. Therefore it has also been my practice to keep the librarians and the rest of the library staff informed about many issues in which they might not normally be interested. Because they serve in many different roles within the institution, it is important to the library that they can represent the library effectively in the various venues in which they operate.

In addition to this institutional involvement beyond the library, librarians also work independently of the library. Examples of these activities outside the library include leading an off-campus study program to Africa or France, teaching a course, managing an extracurricular student development program, or convening an important institutional activity such as accreditation self-study. Whenever a librarian does such outside work, the library is reimbursed for the person's time. In this way the library can hire replacement staff. There is no doubt that this outside work periodically distracts librarians from focus on the library's program, but it also places librarians in a variety of other contexts within the institution. This type of activity extends the reach of the library and demonstrates librarians' integration across the institution. Finally, via these multiple roles, all librarians represent the library and connect with all parts of the institution. Their visibility and information gathering are important to their leadership roles.

In answering the question, I have focused on the leadership role that librarians play outside the library. There is also a strong tradition of shared leadership within the library. The organization is very flat and each staff member has a large amount of autonomy, but with the responsibility of consulting widely. Within the larger institution, our guiding principle is that "everyone affected by a decision should be consulted." Although designated people have administrative responsibility for decision making, they are expected to consult broadly. The consultation need not follow a precise organizational reporting structure in which all external decision-making communication is through the library director. Therefore librarians are seen taking leadership roles in the development of new programs and policies.

The responses to the questions I have given here are naturally shaped by both my personal philosophy of leadership and by the institution in which I practice that leadership. I suspect that the editors of this volume are interested in these individual stories to show both the diversity of forms that leadership takes and the common threads among the individual responses to the four questions. I see two threads that I believe the reader might see as important elements of leadership that I have tried to highlight in my individual response. They are (1) being engaged proactively in feeling the pulse of the institution, both through formal and informal channels of communication, and (2) the importance of broad and deep leadership from among the library staff both in operating the library and integrating the library into the work of the institution. Although these are not the only two important elements of leadership, they happen to be the two that I have highlighted in answering the questions.

MIGNON ADAMS, DIRECTOR OF LIBRARY AND INFORMATION SERVICES, UNIVERSITY OF THE SCIENCES IN PHILADELPHIA

As a library director, I am responsible not just for the running of the library, but also for making sure that I understand both its role as part of the larger institution and the institution's role in higher education and society. I cannot make reasonable budgetary requests or set appropriate goals if I do not understand the workings of my institution or the trends that are affecting higher education.

How Do You Stay Attuned to the Pulse of the Institution?

I do so by making and maintaining formal and informal contacts outside the library, by learning about the programs we offer, and by reading the same materials that the college's administrators read. Many years ago I started a custom that turned out to be even more useful than I had first imagined. Whenever new administrators (e.g., department chair, dean, vice-president, or controller) begin, I take them to lunch in the first month or so. Often I am the first person outside their immediate work unit they have met. I do not have any agenda, open or hidden, other than to get to know them in an informal way and understand the jobs they do. Almost always this has started a relationship that allows me to call the people I meet in order to ask a question, and always it has given me a perspective on how they contribute to the university. In return, it is my hope that I have given them a better idea of how the library helps to fulfill the goals of the institution.

Other kinds of social contacts are also important. In small-town colleges, the opportunities for social interaction are plentiful: in churches, school meetings, soccer games, or other community events. In an urban setting, where I am now, people disappear at 5 PM and we rarely see each other off campus. It is important therefore to attend retirement receptions, lectures, student activities, or other events where it is possible to speak to others and appreciate their viewpoints. Even discussions back and forth to the parking lot can be fruitful.

Of course, there are many opportunities for formal interaction. Serving on task forces and other committees that consider issues other than those of the library helps in seeing the institution as a whole. Library directors are asked to be on these groups when they have established a reputation for being a good committee member: showing up for meetings, doing the required home-work, participating in the discussion, and demonstrating that they are look-ing at the needs of the institution, not just their own parochial interests.

Working with the student government is an excellent way to understand the problems and wishes of the student body. I try to meet with the student government's executive committee once a year. Other directors I know take the newly elected president to lunch. Still others serve as advisors to student groups or visit residence halls regularly.

The largest program at my institution prepares students for a certain health profession, a profession I knew little about before accepting this position. Each profession has its own values and frames of reference, as well as its own literature. In addition, supply and demand go up and down in professions, affecting enrollment and the college's finances. Fortunately, the national orga-nization of the profession for which we prepare students welcomes librarians as members. For many years I attended its annual meetings, participating in sessions dealing with that profession, as well as those that focused on librar-ies. Another librarian now attends.

The most useful step I took was to interview both the faculty and others in the profession in preparation for writing an article on their information needs. Although I have not studied our other programs in such depth, I have sought to understand them by reading about them and asking faculty about them. They are very happy to tell me.

Finally, I make a point of reading what the top administrators read, both internal reports and published materials. After some discussion, I persuaded the director of admissions to send me, as well as program heads, the monthly admission reports. Since we are tuition-driven, as are most private institu-tions, the ups and downs of our enrollment translate directly into budgetary support. The university's annual report, its yearly compilation of statistics, and its budget give me an accurate picture of what is occurring. I peruse all of these and ask questions when I do not understand something.

The Chronicle of Higher Education is one publication that all administra-tors read. Its thick weekly issues detail the issues of concern to all of higher education—and its occasional library pieces can be influential, including the notorious article on "the deserted libraries."[5] The attendance at the library here, like most other college libraries, continues to rise each year. Knowing that my president was aware of that article was an impetus to make sure that he and others on campus were told about our wall-to-wall occupancy.

In addition to the *Chronicle*, there are other publications in higher edu-cation. On my campus, these tend to be *University Business* (sent free to administrators, including librarians), *Change*, and publications from the

Association for the Study of Higher Education. On other campuses it may be a different mix. My president reads popular business books so I keep up with those in the local bookstore to be ready for the next task we are asked to do.

How Do You Keep the Library Aligned with That Pulse?

By making sure that I understand my institution, the contributions that different units make toward its goals, its programs, the concerns of its administrators, faculty, and students, and its role in the context of higher education, I can keep the library aligned to the pulse of the institution. The goals of the library must follow the goals of the institution. We must make changes in the library when programs or students change; however, it is not enough that I work at understanding the larger picture. Librarians also need to do this. To ensure that they can, they should get out of the library, form relationships elsewhere on campus, and understand the issues that affect us all.

I have known of libraries where the expectation is that librarians work an eight-hour day inside the library. Going to a campus activity is to be done on one's own time. At those institutions the library staff probably know only other library staff and no one else on campus knows them.

Creating departmental liaisons for collection development meets other goals in addition to maintaining the library's collection. Individual librarians can get to know the members of the departments they serve and become more familiar with the problems faculty face. Going to a department meeting at least once a year lets the librarian become aware of the issues there. I give funding to liaison librarians to take a new faculty member in their departments to lunch—again a way to get to know others better.

Librarians have faculty status on slightly less than half of American colleges and universities. Faculty status can be a two-edged sword in its demands for research, but librarians who have it can participate fully on faculty committees. They are usually popular members, because they do indeed attend the meetings, do the homework, and complete the task. Popular members are asked to serve on other committees. Right now, library faculty here are involved in these ways: they serve as chair of the Arts and Sciences Curriculum Committee, a member of the search committee for a dean, a member of the faculty government's executive committee, and a member of one of the committees developing an institutional strategic plan.

Even without faculty status library staff can often participate meaningfully in other activities on campus. Our circulation supervisor is the cheerleading advisor, the night supervisor teaches Swahili, and the cataloging assistant lends her voice to concerts. Although they largely participate on their own time, these activities sometimes spill over into work time. Any loss in productivity, however, is more than offset by the visibility that the staff gains on campus and the relationships they form.

How Do You Keep the Librarians Focused on Matters Important to Both the Organization and the Institution?

Everyone in the library needs to be aware of the forces that affect the institution. I forward the enrollment reports to everyone, and comment on our progress. Those who understand the connection between enrollment and fiscal health will take time to help a visiting prospective student, greet the student's parents, or go an extra step to help a struggling enrolled student. Unfortunately, I have known a few teaching faculty who think that admissions is not part of their job and who can even be rude to parents and visitors.

Finally, librarians should know about higher education and its issues. In this library, I automatically forward the daily announcements from *The Chronicle of Higher Education;* the latest issue is kept at the reference desk.

Is There a Perception among Library Staff That the Director Is the Sole Leader of the Library? Is Such a Perception Correct or Incorrect?

The simple answer is certainly not. The staff expects me to be the official spokesperson, but they know that they speak for the library, too. Typically in half-day meetings during the summer, the entire staff engage in library planning. Groups composed of both librarians and staff select tasks, work on them, and report back to the entire group. Our strategic plan is not my product, but the result of the thinking and discussing of all of those who will be carrying it out.

Leadership skills need to be fostered and practiced. When I learned that some of the librarians had never chaired a committee, I suggested that responsibility for faculty meetings be shared. Rotating alphabetically, each librarian takes his or her turn as the facilitator, setting the agenda, conducting the meeting, and writing the minutes. This training has been helpful, I think, in giving them the confidence to take the leadership roles on campus committees that they do. And, I try to make sure that the rest of the library knows about their accomplishments.

At our summer meetings, I ask staff as the occasion arises to take responsibility for various activities. One staff person has extensive experience as a scout leader. She often does a "warm-up" exercise for the group. Another time, two staff members replicated a workshop that they had attended. Staff are often the ones to write up the group reports and schedule a meeting.

Academic libraries are not stand-alone institutions. If they are to survive, then the library director, the librarians, and the support staff need to understand their roles in the context of the entire university.

SARAH M. PRITCHARD, UNIVERSITY LIBRARIAN, NORTHWESTERN UNIVERSITY

The preceding essays by experienced leaders are excellent summaries of how directors work both within their libraries and across the institution. Using strategic planning and formal assessment as ongoing tools and frameworks, and developing leadership across all levels of the staff, is critical at almost all types of libraries (or organizations, for that matter). Each director reveals the need to use official and unofficial channels and structures concurrently to sustain communication and effectiveness. With the plethora of planning and assessment tools, the variety of higher education governance and political structures, and the diversity of staff styles and abilities at a large academic library, perhaps the challenge for a library director is to know when to use which tool, channel, style, or developmental approach. To do this year in and year out, it helps to view one's work as a series of shifting "cultural constructs" that shape the desirable or allowable choices.

How Do You Stay Attuned to the Pulse of the Institution?

Each library and institution has a different style, different traditions, and different resource trade-offs, and of course those change over time within a single institution as well. There is an old-fashioned anthropology of every organization; you do not have to agree with it, but you absolutely have to understand it in order to thrive. We need to be aware of power, ritual, kinship, and barter. The power structures can be formal or informal, as Steven Bell notes: the deans' council, the capital planning committee, or the faculty senate must be navigated, and the director must discover which deans are out of favor, which building deals are cut behind closed doors, or which senate committees have members to whom the president pays attention. This can take a new director, especially if not an internal promotion, a year to learn—then beware if all of a sudden a new provost or president is appointed, for much of it may change!

The usual "tribal rituals" include graduation, convocation, and family weekend, but I try to know which ones really require my presence as opposed to that of my key department heads. I focus my own efforts on any ceremony or event with implications for fundraising, institutional prestige, or external visibility at the board/trustee/community level, while making sure, for example, that public services librarians are at all student orientations, and that collection development and research liaisons cover events for new faculty. Again, it can take almost an entire academic cycle to discover whether the library's absence from a given event is noticed, or whether it is worth the effort to be included in an event from which the library previously was excluded.

The rituals and the power dynamics are built on "kinship," that is, not only which departments are connected to or recently divorced from the power dynamics, but who is friends with whom (or pretends to be), who has old bad blood with whom, who has family or college buddy connections to the trustees or the state legislature, and myriad other allegiances. Kinship and barter—"you scratch my back and I'll scratch yours," or "I'll trade you three goats for a cow and one of those really special baskets"—are the norm in any workplace, and the library director needs to excel at both to stay informed and to have the confidence of superiors and subordinates. One must take the long view of these dynamics; many people who work in universities, particularly the faculty, are there for decades and the relationships and enmities can build up and become more enmeshed over the years.

This may seem like a roundabout way to answer the question, "How do you keep attuned to the pulse of the institution," but it is by understanding these structures and relationships that I know where to focus my attentions and those of my key senior staff.

How Do You Keep the Library Aligned with That Pulse?

Liaisons, committees, and planning documents have all been described in this chapter and are all very effective processes for keeping the library externally aligned. Here, too, I like to conceptualize my role as one of meshing library processes with relevant external structures. There are so many possible committees and projects and issues, so choosing which ones to engage in is itself a matter of strategic positioning. I am always looking for a good, and easy, opportunity to keep the library visible and relevant to the campus, while at the same time helping the librarians and library staff see that they must take campus priorities into account. By "easy," I mean an opportunity that takes advantage of work we might already be doing or skills we have or want to develop. Perhaps the best such campus-wide processes are when an institution develops a formal academic plan, undergoes accreditation, adopts entirely new majors or programs, launches a major fundraising campaign, or lays out 5- and 10-year capital building proposals.

In each of these mechanisms, not only does the library need to be integrated programmatically, but there will be some sort of committee, task force, or leadership group that is coordinating the work. Needless to say, these processes are also very political and sensitive, even when seemingly routine. It is an important part of my work to try to track, ideally well in advance, when my campus will be doing one of these undertakings, and to lay the groundwork for ensuring library inclusion in the substance, as well as library representation on the group or at least on some subgroup. It is not at all to be taken for granted, and I have had both successes and failures in each of the processes I listed. Sometimes it is a matter of timing, over which one may have no control; you are too late to get into the act, it is happening so fast that consultation is circumvented, or you have not laid enough political groundwork to get general acceptance of your right to be there. It may make a big difference if it is the first time a campus has undergone a campaign, or if a new president decides to combine academic planning, accreditation, and campaign planning. In that last case (yes, it is true), the specific requirements of those three initiatives are just different enough to create the possibility of real traps and contradictions in how the director makes the library case.

The library may also be seen as an obstacle—too much expensive space, hard to get donors, blocking faculty from launching new majors (our simple wish to have adequate collections for a new program can often be seen as unnecessarily controlling), and dragging down the accreditation review with bad data. One needs some intuition about how senior administration views a given process. Are they extremely nervous and keeping it tightly held, or are they conversely demanding massive involvement even for a plan you consider tangential? It is my job to assess the costs and benefits each time I want to get us involved. It is often as much a matter of charm and personal persuasion as it is one of logic that helps ensure a good reception for library issues in these critical institutional processes. Then I have to get the library staff to see the relevance and to do a lot of background work in getting information, evaluating services and collections, and working up presentations. This is the most effective strategy for aligning the library with the institution, however, and, in fact, the best way to keep librarians focused on priorities that count.

How Do You Keep the Librarians Focused on Matters Important to Both the Organization and the Institution?

As outlined previously, explicitly engaging the librarians in work related to external institutional processes is key. As earlier essays have demonstrated, using these processes to define services and thus, ultimately, performance evaluation is important and pretty direct. But there is an equally effective indirect way to ensure focus, which is for the director to ignore behaviors or activities that do not contribute to the right goals. By choosing which internal meetings to attend, by deciding whether to give funding to a project, and by selecting particular librarians to represent us, I am sending signals all the time. I may sit in on a library meeting where I am not the chair, but may need to hear, for example, from collection development groups, instructional coordinators, or search committees; their suggestions may help me realign priorities or values. Usually alignment is a problem when the previous director was very inwardly focused or so heavily externally focused (i.e., not even on campus but always gone at national meetings) that the librarians were not routinely aware of student and faculty and institutional trends, or left to their own devices to set goals that only addressed staff's own workplace needs. Through active engagement in formal campus planning, and through the usual management oversight techniques, eventually the library culture incorporates the stakeholder-centric view of the work we do; the director at that point needs to work with new senior-level library appointees to get them on the same wavelength.

Is There a Perception among Library Staff That the Director Is the Sole Leader of the Library? Is Such a Perception Correct or Incorrect?

We have all answered the first question with a resounding "no." The director is the lightning rod, the lead advocate, the one who will take the risks and make the hard decisions. To some degree we are the ones who are rewarded financially for doing just that. However, we must also be growing the next wave of leaders who can help us and who will take our places, either at our present institution or elsewhere. The library is too complex to have only one person who understands it; so I place a lot of emphasis on professional development of AULs (assistant or associate university librarians) and department heads and in getting them involved in campus-wide and consortial work. I make sure that administrators, faculty, and donors see me together with these librarians so that they feel comfortable coming to another librarian if I am not available. Succession planning is something we always have in the backs of our minds. I am usually thinking two to three years ahead—who will be leaving, who will be ready to step in, what if so-and-so gets a new job, what if I need someone with another set of skills for a new endeavor? Some librarians naturally want this advancement; others need a little coaching to learn how to operate at the next level. There is still a perception, especially in large libraries, that "the administration" is some vast unknown inscrutable entity separate from the rest of the staff; I try to make it seem more permeable, approachable, and interactive. And yet the fact is, at the end of the day, I have to take the phone call when the chancellor demands accountability.

CONCLUSION

One way to view leadership is to examine the different communities with which the library directors in this chapter interact either formally or informally. These include boards of regents or trustees; chancellors or vice-chancellors; presidents and their assistants; presidential cabinets; provosts and their assistants; deans and assistant deans; other administrative staff, faculty members; library faculty, staff, and members of the management team; student leaders; policymakers (e.g., members of the state legislature); and members of the town or municipality. One director mentioned interaction with prospective students and, by implication, perhaps having the library play a role in student retention.

Given this complex environment in which academic libraries function, the library directors who contributed to this chapter want librarians working in the organization to be leaders and participate actively in the life of the college or university. Such activities extend the perception of how librarians contribute to campus life. Simply stated, a library's strategic planning process may envision the empowerment of the librarians to serve better the communities identified in the institutional mission, and such expectations require good communication throughout the library. Some of the directors wrote about the importance of active listening, which focuses on understanding what people are saying. The listener should be able to repeat what the speaker had said; this does not mean that the listener agrees with, but rather understands, what was said. Central to active learning is to ask good questions, listening nonjudgmentally, paraphrasing what was stated, and showing empathy.

In addition to active learning, the directors mentioned such leadership attributes as being collaborative, being politically attuned to the institution, having good communication skills (both oral and written), being engaged with others, being visible at the institutional level, a willingness to advance the library's strategic goals by working with others, empowering others, trusting in others, being an optimist (organizational institutional change leads to improvements), being willing to embrace accountability, liking people, offering a supportive environment, being observant, seeking clarity, being open with others (as much as is possible), and encouraging staff to play an institutional role. Another attribute might relate to respecting others and seeking respect in return.

As Mignon Adams noted, library directors must read widely and be aware of those readings that presidents and others might encounter. If they encounter readings such as the one about "deserted libraries" (see note 5), they must formulate an effective response and not let misperceptions go unaddressed. In effect, library directors must monitor the pulse of the institution and have other librarians help them in this endeavor. Critical to the future of academic librarianship is the hiring of librarians who can fit comfortably into this environment and who do not view work within a narrow context—staying within the library and focused on the accomplishment of daily routines. They must concentrate on strategic directions, the larger environment, and how the library helps the institution accomplish its mission.

Terrence Mech adds a critical responsibility for leaders; they need to help other librarians redefine the scope and nature of their jobs or expand their definition of their responsibilities. Other librarians need to recognize that they are not narrowly confined to a role within the library's walls. More librarians need to draw the circle to include rather than exclude others—the goal is for everyone to contribute to the success of the library and the institution.[6]

NOTES

1. Shirley K. Baker, "Leading from Below: Or, Risking Getting Fired" (St. Louis, MO: Washington University, n.d.), 1 (of 4). Available at http://www.wustl.edu/baker/leading.html (accessed November 18, 2005).

2. Ibid.

3. Ibid.

4. The term *convener* is the one that Earlham uses for the leader of a committee. It has its roots in the Quaker (Society of Friends) decision-making process from which Earlham's institutional consensus decision-making process is derived.

5. Scott Carlson, "The Deserted Library," *The Chronicle of Higher Education* 48 (November 16, 2001). Available at http://chronicle.com/weekly/v48/i12/12a03501. htm (accessed February 28, 2006).

6. E-mail message from Terrence Mech to Peter Hernon, March 7, 2006.

9

LEADERSHIP EFFECTIVENESS

Nancy Rossiter

"The quality of leadership, more than any other single factor, determines the success or failure of an organization."[1]

There are more books, articles, and dissertations on leadership than on any other topic in the field of management. The sheer volume of research and writing about leadership models indicates that leadership is neither easily defined, nor a topic where there is much consensus. Furthermore, new models and new insights continue to emerge. There is also little agreement about what makes a leader effective.[2] Effectiveness, as defined in this chapter, is the degree or extent to which leaders help an organization to achieve its mission and goals.[3] The chapter examines predominant factors that contribute to leadership effectiveness; these include punishment, communication, gender differences, personality traits, physical fitness, and emotional intelligence.

MEASURES OF LEADERSHIP EFFECTIVENESS

Many organizations realize the need for more effective leadership; however, few of them have a mechanism for systematically measuring leadership effectiveness over time.[4] This shortcoming begs the question, "If organizations do not know how to measure the success of their leadership programs, how do they know they are successful?" Leadership theories answer this question differently. For instance, trait theory suggests that successful leadership depends on personality traits such initiative and creativity, self-confidence, vision, and human relations skill. Such traits can be developed by training and practice. Situational theory proposes that leadership is a function of the situation in which the leader operates. Situational variables include, for instance, the leader's position and power, the leader-subordinate relationship, and task structure. Behavioral theory views leadership effectiveness as a function of what the leader does. The effectiveness of a particular behavior, however, depends on the situation in which it is applied.

Organizations that measure the effectiveness of their leaders might use both common measures and direct and indirect measures. Common measures include unit and/or individual performance, attitudes of followers toward leaders, and leader contribution to the quality of a group process, namely the results that the group achieves. Direct measures show the immediate impact on what is done, how it is done, or how efficiently it is done, whereas indirect measures refer to the decisions and actions that leaders take.[5]

A common measure frequently used to assess attitudes toward leaders as well as unit/individual performance is 360-degree feedback. Chapter 15 discusses this type of feedback. Direct measures can include profitability and sales revenue for leaders in for-profit organizations; indirect measures can include employee job satisfaction. Without some form of evaluation, it is difficult, if not impossible, to determine the degree to which the leader is moving the organization toward, or away from, its goals.

LEADERSHIP THEORIES

Few concepts have been the object of as much conjecture, study, and consideration as leadership and social influence, both of which focus on power or changing the actions or thoughts of individuals. For centuries, an understanding of the capacity to influence others has captured the attention of researchers, practitioners, and commentators. What makes a leader effective has also been thoroughly analyzed. Motivation is a key component of leadership: leaders motivate their teams or groups to meet the organization's mission and goals.[6]

Table 9.1 summarizes some basic components of theories related to leadership effectiveness and motivation. These theories show how leadership models or theories have evolved and changed from when Frederick W. Taylor introduced time motion studies. Subsequent models have focused on behavioral, situational, charismatic, and principle-centered leadership. These theories, as discussed in Chapter 3, explain some of the historical shifts from one leadership model to another. Clearly, the development of new leadership models is not a static process; new ones continue to gain favor and help to explain what is occurring in different work situations, as well as how to improve organizational effectiveness. At the same time, in modern society, which is stressful and highly complex, there is a critical need for leaders to renew themselves and nurture mindfulness, hope, and compassion in their lives; this is known as resonant leadership.

Table 9.1
Leadership Effectiveness and Motivational Models

Year of Publication	Theorist	Model	Basic Tenet(s)
1911	Frederick Taylor	Scientific Management	Time-motion studies, four principles of management.
1933	Elton Mayo	Hawthorne Studies	Work performance dependent on both social issues and job content.
1938	Chester Barnard	Executive Function	Organizations as systems of cooperation of human activity.
1948	Leaster Coch and John French	Michigan Studies	Job-centered versus employee-centered styles of leadership.
1948	Ralph Stogdill	Ohio State Studies	Consideration and initiating behavior.
1950	George Homans	Human Group	Evolution of groups in organizations.
1954	Abraham Maslow	Hierarchy of Needs	A hierarchy, often shown as a pyramid, reflecting the four types of needs that motivate people.
1957	Douglas McGregor	Theory X and Y	Leadership styles of managers are affected by the way they look at their subordinates.
1957	Robert Tannenbaum and Warren Schmidt	Continuum of Leader Behavior	Autocratic to democratic continuum model.
1964	Robert Blake and Jane Mouton	Managerial Grid	Situational leadership; concern for people vs. concern for task.
1965	David McClelland	Achievement Theory	Need for achievement, need for power, need for affiliation.
1966	Frederick Hertzberg	Motivation-Hygiene	Satisfaction and psychological growth result from motivation factors; dissatisfaction results from lack of hygiene factors.

Table 9.1
Leadership Effectiveness and Motivational Models (*continued*)

Year of Publication	*Theorist*	*Model*	*Basic Tenet(s)*
1967	Rensis Likert	Systems 1-4	Four different systems of organizational management; System 1–Authoritarian, System 2–Benevolent Authoritarian, System 3–Consultative, System 4–Participative.
1967	Frederick Fiedler	Contingency Model	Leadership effectiveness depends on both the leader's personality and the situation; Least Preferred Coworker Scale.
1964	Chris Argyris	Maturity-Immaturity	Mechanistic organizations following bureaucratic models lead to shallow, mistrustful relationships.
1967	Bill Reddin	3-D Management Style	Style-contingency approach; five situational elements— organization, technology, superiors, co-workers, and subordinates.
1967	Paul Hersey and Ken Blanchard	Situational Leadership	Emphasizes followers and their level of maturity. The leader must perceive the followers' maturity level and use a leadership style that fits the level.
1973	Victor Vroom and Philip Yetton	Contingency Model	The leader must chose among 5 decision making styles: Autocratic 1, Autocratic 2, Consultative 1, Consultative 2, and Group 2. The style is chosen by answering seven questions, which form a decision tree.
1974	Robert House and Terence Mitchell	Path-Goal	The leader's function is to clear the path toward the goal of the group, by meeting the needs of subordinates.

Table 9.1
Leadership Effectiveness and Motivational Models (*continued*)

Year of Publication	*Theorist*	*Model*	*Basic Tenet(s)*
1976	Victor Vroom	Expectancy Theory	Individuals have different sets of goals and can be motivated if they believe that there is a positive correlation between efforts and performance; favorable performance will result in a desirable reward, the reward will satisfy an important need, the desire to satisfy the need is strong enough to make the effort worthwhile.
1977	Robert House	Charismatic Leadership	Invoke inspirational, visionary, and symbolic behavior; transform the needs, values, preferences, and aspirations of followers; motivate followers to make significant personal sacrifices in the interest of some mission; followers become less motivated by self-interest and more motivated to serve the interests of the larger collective.
1978	James Burns	Transformational Leadership	Dynamic, two-way relationship between leaders and followers. Leaders must connect with the needs and wants of the followers and establish motivation to accomplish collective goals that satisfy the needs of both the leader and the followers.
1978	Steven Kerr and John Jermier	Substitutes for Leadership	Aspects of the environment other than the hierarchical leader can provide leadership to subordinates.

Table 9.1
Leadership Effectiveness and Motivational Models (*continued*)

Year of Publication	*Theorist*	*Model*	*Basic Tenet(s)*
1986	Noel Tichy and Mary Anne Devanna	Transformational Leadership	These leaders are agents of change, have courage; openness and faith in the followers; are led by values; believe in life-long learning; have the ability to face the complex, ambiguous, and uncertain situations, and have visionary abilities.
1989	Charles Manz	Super Leadership	Leads others to lead themselves through designing and implementing the system that allows and teaches employees to be self-leaders.
1989	Gary Yukl	Integrating Model	The subordinate's effort, skill, leader's role, resources available, and the group's cohesiveness in any particular situation determine leader behavior.
1991	Stephen Covey	Principle Centered Leadership	These leaders work on the basis of natural principles and build those principles into the center of their lives, into the center of their relationships with others, into the center of their agreements and contracts, into their management processes, and into their mission statements.

LEADERSHIP BEHAVIORS

Many leadership models focus on what a leader does or how a leader behaves, whereas much of the research considers leadership behavior and how leaders use punishment as an indicator of their effectiveness. For example, if a worker does not achieve the organization's goals, what does a leader do? Both the Path-Goal theory and Podsakoff's transactional contingent reward/punishment styles model answer this question.[7] The Path-Goal theory describes how leaders encourage and support their followers in achieving the goals they have been set by making the path that they should take clear and easy. Leaders clarify that path to guide subordinates, remove roadblocks they encounter, and increase the rewards to ensure the goals are met. Philip M. Podsakoff maintains that the quality of an employee's relationship with his or her leader counts and that a leader should use express satisfaction or appreciation for good performance.

The use of punishment or coercive power occurs in a wide variety of organizations, including the military.[8] In such settings, leaders develop stress tolerance, stamina, and self-confidence. Contingent and noncontingent punishment has been researched in relation to leader effectiveness. Contingent punishment is based on specific standards for employees' unacceptable behavior or poor performance, for example, not achieving agreed on goals. Noncontingent punishment is delivered arbitrarily. The use of noncontingent punishment promotes depression and a lower level of effort. This lower performance level is the result of learned helplessness or feelings of powerlessness. In military organizations, noncontingent punishment builds stress tolerance and self-confidence; however, it also has negative side effects on the leader, especially when an individual is seen as a "bad leader."[9]

Contingent punishment is more effective and satisfying to subordinates than noncontingent punishment. Leanne Atwater, Shelly Dionne, John Camobreco, Bruce Avolio, and Alan Laul examined individual characteristics that influence use of contingent and noncontingent punishment and thereby have an impact on leader effectiveness; these characteristics are self-esteem, moral reasoning, and physical fitness. They found that the leader's use of contingent punishment contributes positively to the leader's effectiveness. Leaders who use punishment constructively are more effective leaders. Leaders who use noncontingent punishment score lower on effectiveness. High levels of self-esteem help to minimize the use of noncontingent punishment, and leaders with low self-esteem use noncontingent punishment. Moral reasoning is positively correlated to the use of contingent punishment; this suggests that leaders with low scores may be reluctant to use contingent punishment and consequently subordinates behave less effectively. Also, high levels of physical fitness are associated with one's use of contingent punishment. Consequently, physical fitness should be encouraged because it makes leaders feel more confident in using contingent punishment when they interact with subordinates.[10]

Communication

David Clutterbuck and Sheila Hirst, who believe that communication skills are essential to leadership effectiveness, state that effective leaders are also effective communicators. (However, the reverse is not necessarily true—good communicators do not necessarily make good leaders.) They cite internal studies conducted by Microsoft and other organizations that show that effective leaders are good communicators; they:

- Set mutual expectations clearly;
- Make sure everyone has clear objectives and performance measures and check that workers understand them;
- Are good at planning and at communicating the steps between where the team is going and where it needs to be;
- Give continuous feedback; and
- Ensure that the individual and group achievements are recognized.[11,12]

Goal Setting

Identifying the fundamental nature of leadership effectiveness is no easy task given the abundance of leadership theories, approaches, and empirical findings. Through a review of recent writings, specific elements of effective leadership emerge; these include:

- Developing a collective sense of goals and objectives and how to go about achieving them;
- Instilling in others knowledge and appreciation of the importance of work activities and behaviors;
- Generating and maintaining excitement, enthusiasm, confidence, cooperation, trust, and optimism in an organization;
- Encouraging flexibility in decision making and change; and
- Establishing and maintaining a meaningful identity, such as through a strong corporate culture for the organization.[13]

Motivation, which is an important determinant of leadership performance, is a major ingredient of job satisfaction. One important method of motivating followers is through the practice of goal setting. Leaders must ensure that personal goals are aligned with the organizational goals. Further, goals should be specific, agreed on, realistic, and have a timeline. They should also frame objectives and group and individual activities. David Jacobson adds that, in addition to being achievable, goals should be inspirational and the leader should ensure that employees have a network of mentors to support them as they achieve the goals set for them.[14]

LEADERSHIP TRAITS

Some researchers focus on who a leader is, rather than what a leader does. Certainly, trait theory is one of the most popular research streams in the leadership literature, and many studies of leadership effectiveness have linked leader personality traits with leader effectiveness or performance metrics. Certain clusters of characteristics differentiate between effective and ineffective leaders. These characteristics include an individual's level of cognitive ability, conscientiousness, self-confidence, energy level, values, and tolerance for stress.[15] Robert Lord, Christy DeVader, and George Alliger, who link personality attributes to perceptions of leadership, conclude that personality traits account for an appreciable discrepancy in the perceived effectiveness of leaders.[16]

Gender

Gender is another trait discussed in the literature on leadership effectiveness. Recent meta-analyses and individual studies suggest several conclusions about male and female leaders. Although men and women are similar in behavior and effectiveness, women leaders tend to be more participative and less autocratic. Such traits appear to be well suited for many global organizations in the twenty-first century.[17]

Physical Fitness

Another trait that has been associated with leadership effectiveness is that of physical fitness. In one study, researchers looked at the effects of cognitive ability, conscientiousness, self-esteem, hardiness, moral reasoning, and physical fitness on leader emergence and effectiveness. Higher levels of physical fitness are positively correlated with both leader emergence and effectiveness.[18]

In another study, Sharon McDowell-Larson, Leigh Kearney, and David Campbell found that regular exercise is positively correlated with leadership performance. Using data collected from more than 600 top-level executives, they found that regular exercise increases leadership performance and that a regular fitness program helps executives to maintain the vigor needed to meet the demands of the job, raise the perception of leadership effectiveness among other workers, and preserve their health in the process.[19] Richard Boyatzis and Annie McKee found that resonant leaders manage their own and others' emotions in ways that make the organization successful. Rather than sacrifice themselves for workplace demands, resonant leaders avoid burnout, combat stress, and find ways to renew themselves physically, mentally, and emotionally. Therefore, being physically fit enables leaders to better manage both themselves and their organizations.[20]

OTHER LEADERSHIP BEHAVIORS

Rupert Eales-White found that five primary leadership behaviors create effective leaders. First, leaders develop their leadership role by improving self-awareness, focusing on their followers, and implementing plans to improve themselves and their organization. Second, leaders lead by example; they are honest and encourage honesty in their followers, they acknowledge their own shortcomings and mistakes, and they display confidence and commitment and create team spirit. Third, they put the work of followers into the context of the organization as a whole, so their followers know how their job fits into the big picture. Leaders develop and share a vision and values, create the big picture, set clear and agreed on goals, and monitor and review performance. Fourth, effective leaders develop their followers by providing direction and guidance, coaching, giving feedback, and providing challenging and meaningful work. And finally, they support their followers by being available and approachable, offering encouragement and praise, and listening and being receptive to ideas. In essence, effective leaders act as a safety net for their followers, providing assistance for them at many different levels.[21]

EMOTIONAL INTELLIGENCE

Emotional intelligence (EI), which is a key characteristic of leader effectiveness, is "the ability to perceive emotions, to access and generate emotions so as to assist thought, to understand emotions and emotional knowledge, and to reflectively regulate emotions so as to promote emotional and intellectual growth."[22] Leadership theories have fostered a better understanding of leadership, but how and why leaders have (or fail to have) a positive influence on their followers and organizations are still compelling issues for leadership researchers. Jennifer George found that feelings (moods and emotions) play a central role in the leadership process. By focusing one's attention on the feelings and moods of people in the organization, EI contributes to more effective leadership.[23]

In spite of the plethora of theories, those theories, as well as the leadership research, do not adequately consider leaders mood and how their emotions influence their effectiveness as leaders. When people are in positive moods, their perceptions and evaluations are more likely to be favorable, they are more prone to remember positive information, and they are more self-assured. Two preliminary studies investigated mood. First, George and Ken Bettenhausen found that the extent to which team leaders experienced positive moods was positively correlated to levels of prosocial behavior performed by group members and was negatively related to team turnover rates. This means that team leaders in positive moods tended to bring about positive reactions from their followers, making them more positive about their jobs and therefore less likely to leave the organization.[24] Second, George discovered that teams led by sales mangers who tended to have positive moods at work produced higher quality customer service than did groups that did not experience positive moods at work.[25] Both studies suggest that feelings are important factors in leading effectively.

Emotionally intelligent leaders develop a sense of goals and objectives, meaning they clearly understood the direction in which the organization is going and they have a process for achieving those goals and objectives in an effective manner. Since EI may enable leaders to develop a compelling vision for their organizations, so it requires creativity. Research linking positive moods to

Figure 9.1
Model of Leadership Effectiveness

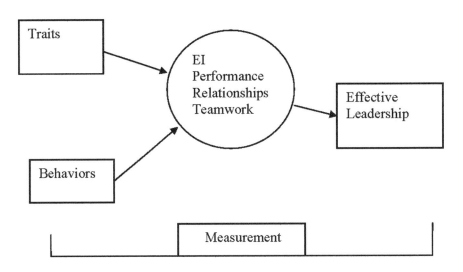

creativity shows that when leaders are in positive moods, they tend to be more creative.[26] Leaders who are emotionally intelligent can take advantage of their positive moods and envision major improvements, as well as craft a vision for the organization and communicate it effectively to the followers.

Leaders who are emotionally intelligent are more knowledgeable about and better able to manage emotions in subtle ways that may make them more effective at instilling knowledge and appreciation of work activities and behaviors. By being adept at discerning real emotions and solving problems with a minimum of stress, emotionally intelligent leaders generate and maintain excitement, enthusiasm, confidence, optimism, cooperation, and trust. Because emotionally intelligent leaders know how to manage their emotions, they may solve problems more effectively because they consider alternative scenarios and avoid rigidity in decision making.[27]

Emotionally intelligent leaders are better at maintaining a meaningful identity for the organization. An organization's identity derives from and is a consequence of its culture. An increasingly important leadership activity involves development and expression of an organization's culture. Harrison Trice and Janice Beyer suggest that cultures are infused with emotions and that organizational culture provides members with socially acceptable ways of expressing their emotions.[28] Thus management of the organizational culture involves a management of emotions. Clearly, EI should have a leading role in the communication process between leader and follower within any organizational culture.

MODEL OF LEADERSHIP EFFECTIVENESS

Figure 9.1 depicts leadership effectiveness, which might start with developing an effective measure of leadership effectiveness. This measure continues throughout the leader's evaluation. Individual organizations need to decide the best way of measuring leadership success based on their organizational goals. For example, if one organizational goals is to serve the community by providing outstanding customer service, the organization must determine how to define and measure outstanding customer service, perhaps through customer surveys and feedback. When hiring leaders, the organization should be aware of the traits and behaviors that it associates with successful leaders. The organization should also assess the EI of its leader(s) because EI accounts for up to 79 percent of leadership success.[29] If deficiencies in EI exist, the organization must develop these competencies in its leaders, through training, development opportunities, and education.

CONCLUSION

All organizations have goals; however, the degree to which they achieve them determines how successful both the leaders and the organization are. Research has shown how leaders behave as well the importance of physical fitness and EI. Such matters influence the extent to which leaders are successful. Organizations should devise ways to measure leadership effectiveness. Effective leaders generate higher employee satisfaction. Higher satisfaction saves organizations scarce resources in terms of absenteeism and turnover. Satisfied individuals also tend to be more loyal and align their own goals with those of the organization. Because leaders with high EI have followers who are more satisfied with their jobs, organizations should strive to increase the EI of their leaders through first hiring emotionally intelligent leaders and then continuing to train and develop these competencies. Furthermore, organizations should see that leaders gain the necessary renewal to continue to play significant leadership roles. As Chapter 18 explains, organizations want to be successful; they should develop emotionally intelligent leaders who are effective managers and able to change the organization's climate.

"Great leaders are almost always great simplifiers, who can cut through argument, debate, and doubt to offer a solution everybody can understand."[30]

NOTES

1. "Big Dog's Leadership Quotes." Available at http://www.nwlink.com/ ~donclark/leader/leadqot.html (accessed May 1, 2006). The quote is from Fred Fiedler and Martin Chemers, *Improving Leadership Effectiveness* (New York: John Wiley, 1984).

2. David Clutterbuck and Sheila Hirst, "Leadership Communication: A Status Re-

port," *Journal of Communication Management* 6 (2002): 351–54.

3. James Price, "Handbook of Organizational Measurement," *International Journal of Manpower* 18 (1997): 303–558.

4. Kevin McManus, "The Leadership Gap," *Industrial Engineer* 37 (2005): 20.

5. Doug Ihrkey and Larry Gates, "Leadership: What Does It Mean and How Do You Get It?," *Cacubo Annual Conference,* Milwaukee, WI, 2005. Available at http://www.cacubo.org/powerpoint/Milwaukee%20presentations/Leadership%20 Gates%20Ihrkey10%2017%202005.ppt (accessed April 27, 2006).

6. Charles Lutz, "Leading by Example," *Security Management* 49 (2005): 44–47.

7. Robert House, "A Path-Goal Theory of Leadership Effectiveness," *Administrative Science Quarterly* 16 (1971): 321–39.

8. Bernard M. Bass, *Bass and Stodgill's Handbook of Leadership* (New York: Free Press, 1990).

9. Leanne Atwater, Shelly Dionne, John Camobreco, Bruce Avolio, and Alan Lau, "Individual Attributes and Leadership Style: Predicting the Use of Punishment and Its Effects," *Journal of Organizational Behavior* 19 (1998): 559–76.

10. Ibid.

11. Clutterbuck and Hirst, "Leadership Communication."

12. Gary Yukl, *Leadership in Organizations* (Englewood Cliffs, NJ: Prentice Hall, 2002).

13. Ibid.

14. David Jacobson, *Inspiration to Perspiration: The Four Essential Steps to Achieving Your Goals* (San Diego, CA: Goal Success, 2003).

15. Bass, *Bass and Stodgill's Handbook of Leadership.*

16. Robert Lord, Christy DeVader, and George Alliger, "A Meta-Analysis of the Relation between Personality Traits and Leadership Perceptions: An Application of Validity Generalization Procedures," *Journal of Applied Psychology* 71 (1986): 402–10.

17. Peter Northouse, *Leadership Theory and Practice,* 3d ed. (Thousand Oaks, CA: Sage, 2004), 273.

18. Atwater, Dionne, Avolio, Camobreco, and Lau, "A Longitudinal Study of the Leadership Development Process."

19. Sharon McDowell-Larson, Leigh Kearney, and David Campbell, "Fitness and Leadership: Is There a Relationship?," *Journal of Managerial Psychology* 17 (2002): 316–25.

20. Richard Boyatzis and Annie McKee, *Resonant Leadership: Renewing Yourself and Connecting with Others through Mindfulness, Hope and Compassion* (Boston: Harvard Business School Press, 2005).

21. Rupert Eales-White, The COGAL Concept of Leadership," *Industrial and Commercial Training* 35 (2003): 203–207.

22. Northouse, *Leadership Theory and Practice,* 273.

23. Jennifer George, "Emotions and Leadership: The Role of Emotional Intelligence," *Human Relations* 53 (2000): 1027–56.

24. Jennifer George and Ken Bettenhausen, "Understanding Pro-Social Behavior, Sales Performance, and Turnover: A Group-Level Analysis in a Service Context," *Journal of Applied Psychology* 75 (1990): 75–109.

25. Jennifer George, "Leader Positive Mood and Group Performance: The Case of Customer Service," *Journal of Applied Psychology* 25 (1995): 778–94.

26. Alice Isen, Kimberly Daubman, and Gary Nowicki, "Positive Affect Facilitates Creative Problem Solving," *Journal of Personality and Social Psychology* 52 (1987): 1122–31.

27. Jack Mayer and Peter Salovey, "What Is Emotional Intelligence: Implications for Educators," in *Emotional Development, Emotional Literacy, and Emotional Intelligence,* ed. Peter Salovey and David Sluyter (New York: Basic Books, 1997), 5.

28. Harrison Trice and Janice Beyer, *The Cultures of Work Organizations* (Englewood Cliffs, NJ: Prentice Hall, 1993).

29. Peter Salovey and John Mayer, "Emotional Intelligence," *Imagination, Cognition and Personality* 9 (1990): 185–211.

30. Colin Powell quoted by Oren Harari, "Proven Leadership Principles," *Executive Excellence* 19 (2002): 3.

10

TEAM EFFECTIVENESS AND MEMBERS AS LEADERS[1]

Elaine Martin

"Leadership takes place every day."[2]

The use of teams in university libraries that are members of the Association of Research Libraries did not occur until the 1990s. Before then, these libraries were organized by departments and committees according to strict hierarchies. University and associate university librarians made the decisions and communicated them to supervisors who informed line staff. These managerial layers created faulty communication systems and time-consuming work processes.

The team concept emerged as a result of major budget cuts and staffing shortages, resulting in the reorganization of the entire library or one or more departments. To continue to work efficiently with fewer resources, teams composed of multilevel (supervisors and staff) and multirank (professionals and non-professionals) members were developed across departments. Staff closest to the work proposed and implemented the team decisions that upper management previously made; this eliminated the middle management layer and brought decision making to the line staff. Departmental responsibilities began to merge, and departmental lines of communication blurred. For example, reference staff began to troubleshoot computers located in the public services area and to perform responsibilities once dedicated to the staff of a systems department. Designing the online catalog for an integrated library system became a joint effort of the reference, systems, and cataloging staff rather than the sole responsibility of a technical services or systems department or unit. Joanne Euster refers to this phenomenon as "group empowerment."[3]

LIBRARY EFFECTIVENESS

Library measures of effectiveness do not extend to the use of teams. Indeed, there are disagreements over operational definitions of teams and measures of team effectiveness. As described in the library and information studies (LIS) literature, effectiveness comprises the tasks that ensure the quality of an organization's performance or the impact of that performance on the community served.[4] Considering the organization as a whole or by subunit, no single definition of effectiveness in the LIS literature has gained universal acceptance, and no definition adequately focuses on teams. Instead, perhaps the predominant view focuses on performance metrics and quantification (e.g., the number of journals per faculty or students and gate count), and comparing (benchmarking) those numbers to those in other libraries. This is not the view of organizational psychologist J. Richard Hackman and management scholar Richard E. Walton, who consider effectiveness as the degree to which the:

- Group's productive output (i.e., product or service) meets the standard of quantity, quality, and timeliness of the people who receive, review, and/or use that output (*results*);
- Process of carrying out the work enhances the capability of members to work together interdependently in the future (*socialization*); and
- Group's experience contributes to the growth and personal well-being of team members (*professional growth*).[5]

As they explain, determining how well a team performs is much more complicated than quantifying performance measures. Team effectiveness is multidimensional. It includes the continued socialization of team members and their growth as individuals. Personal, social, and systems conditions within the organization must also be addressed to measure a team's effectiveness.

In this study, a team is a group of two or more individuals working together on a defined project, task, or performance goal with a defined or expected outcome or result. The team is a recognized structure within the library but may be called team, task force, management group, work group or committee, and so on. This definition follows Hackman's view of teams, "Although some authors, such as Katzenbach and Smith . . . , take great care to distinguish between the terms *teams* and *group*, I do not. I use the terms interchangeably and make no distinction whatever between them."[6]

HACKMAN'S FRAMEWORK

In *Leading Teams,* Hackman offers a unique perspective on team effectiveness and outlines an approach for applying his concepts to different organizations.[7] He draws on his experience and on research in a variety of work team settings (e.g., orchestras, manufacturing production lines, and airline crews). According to him, a leader does not make the team great but rather facilitates the personal, social, and systems conditions that lead to team effectiveness. In his multidimensional approach to effectiveness, he identifies five key conditions that increase the likelihood of team success or effectiveness. These conditions lead to the previously mentioned three outcomes: results, socialization, and professional growth. With these conditions present, it is likely that a group will perform in ways that promote team effectiveness.

Hackman's five conditions can be divided into two groupings. The first three conditions refer to the actual design of the team, and the remaining two conditions reinforce the team's work once in place. Hackman maintains that most managers stop after the first three conditions and that, to constitute an effective team, *all* five conditions must be present:

1. *A real team:* Creating a real team is necessary for establishing the foundation for the team's future work. It involves making sure the tasks assigned to the team are clear, requires members to work together, delineates the team's authority, and ensures stable membership over time.

2. *A compelling direction:* Setting a compelling direction means someone in authority sets the direction for the team. Although the direction tells the team what is expected at the end of its work, it does not specify the means by which the team gets there.

3. *An enabling team structure:* An enabling team structure is the *shell* of the team. Structural features include designing team tasks that motivate members, specifying codes of conduct, putting the right people on the team, ensuring the size of the team is appropriate and that the mix of members is balanced for the tasks assigned to the team.

4. *A supportive organizational context:* A supportive organizational context includes aligning the reward, information, education, and technology systems so that they reinforce the team's efforts.

5. *Expert team coaching:* Expert coaching refers to facilitating group process and development. The coach motivates the team, serves as a consultant when the team has questions, and educates the team.

Hackman poses a set of questions that characterizes each condition (Figure 10.1). The answers to the questions determine the extent to which each condition is present in an organization that uses teams. Once all five conditions are in place, teams exceed expectations (performance outputs), grow more capable (work together interdependently in the future), and contribute to the learning and personal growth of individual members (promote individual well-being). Hackman claims that creating and maintaining this specific set of conditions are prerequisite to achieving multidimensional effectiveness.

Effective leaders, he maintains, use a range of personal behavioral styles and dynamic strategies to support team efficiency. Common to his view of team effectiveness are several leadership functions, namely, "the team is set up right in the first place, that it is well supported organizationally and that

Figure 10.1
Hackman's Conditions and Corresponding Questions

Condition 1 (a real team)

- How clear are the team's boundaries?
- How important is the stability of team membership?
- Are the members working in a coordinated fashion?

Condition 2 (a compelling direction)

- Did a person in authority set a direction for the team?
- Is the team's direction clear and complete?
- Did the team concept result in reduced costs, streamlined work, improved services, and/or fewer errors?

Condition 3 (an enabling team structure)

- How are the teams established? What is the mix?
- How should teams be structured? What is the appropriate size?
- Is the group well "staffed"?

Condition 4 (a supportive organizational context)

- What are the support systems in place?
- Since the adoption of the team concept, have there been any changes in the organization structure/support systems to improve the effectiveness of teams?

Condition 5 (expert team coaching)

- Has the team concept resulted in any changes in the focus of activities exhibited by the manager?
- Do members receive assistance regarding the development of effort, knowledge-based skills, and performance strategies?
- Are there certain roles, responsibilities, and tasks that teams cannot perform?

---

members have ready access to the kind of coaching that can help them exploit the team's potential to the fullest extent possible."[8] Effective leaders ensure conditions are in place for teams to be successful. Leadership behavior or personality is nonetheless an insufficient determinant of effective teams.

FOCUS OF CHAPTER

Teams are prevalent in many academic libraries, including those associated with medical schools. No study, however, has explored the transportability of Hackman's dimensions and conditions (Figure 10.2) to libraries, in this case academic medical libraries, by addressing the following questions:

- To what extent do these conditions apply to libraries?
- Is each condition essential for teams to be effective?

Figure 10.2
Conceptualization of Study

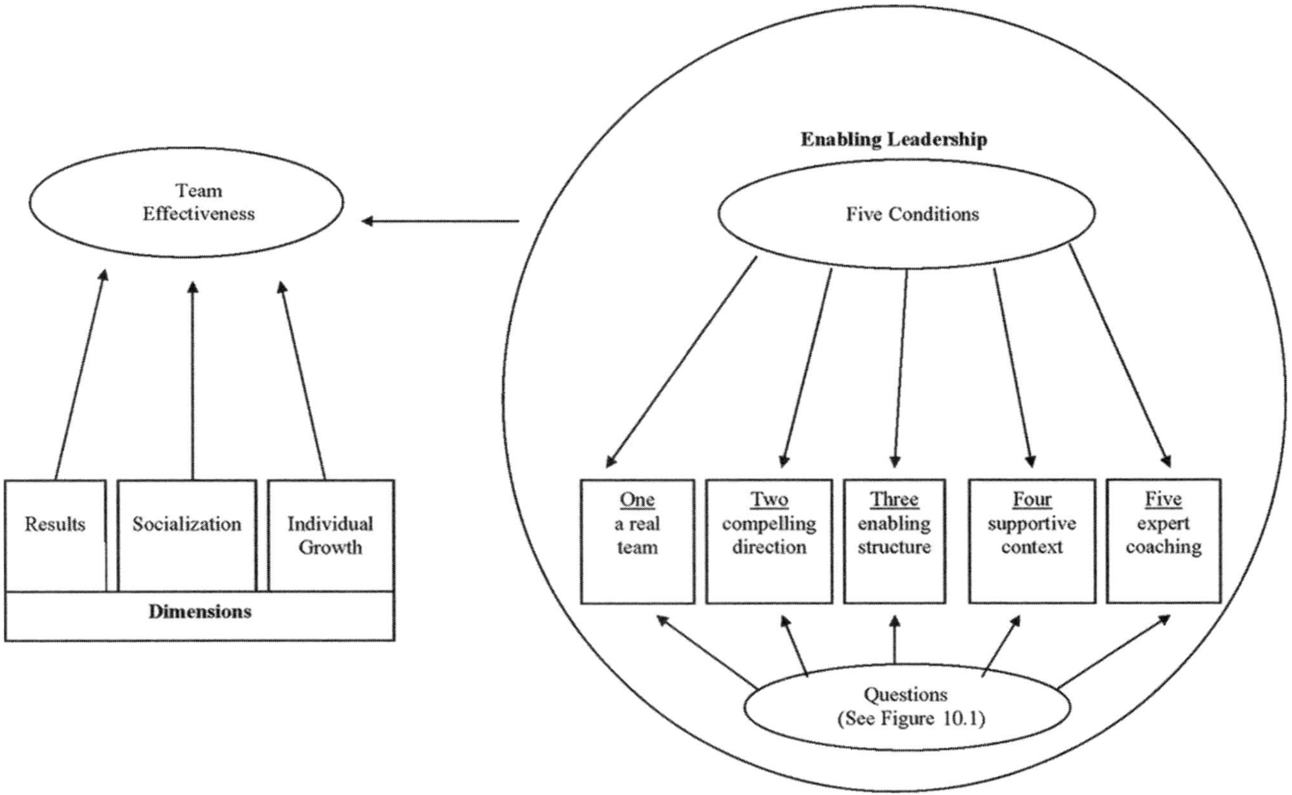

Enabling Leadership

Five Conditions

One
a real
team

Two
compelling
direction

Three
enabling
structure

Four
supportive
context

Five
expert
coaching

Questions
(See Figure 10.1)

Team
Effectiveness

Results

Socialization

Individual
Growth

Dimensions

- Might other conditions prevail?
- Does the set of questions adequately characterize a condition?
- How well do conditions/questions define library teams?
- What is the sequencing of the conditions?
- Do directors stress only the first three conditions or do they implement all five?
- How do actual teams in libraries perceive these five conditions in relation to team effectiveness?

Study findings inform academic medical library managers regarding the adoption of teams about the necessary conditions to put in place and to strengthen the effectiveness of preexisting teams. Team effectiveness is also linked to team leadership. As Hackman explains, "Anyone and everyone who clarifies a team's directions, or improves its structure, or secures organizational support for it, or provides coaching that improves its performance process is providing team leadership."[9] He continues, "The question, then, is not so much who provides team leadership but rather how much the team is getting. So long as the focus of leadership activities is on creating conditions that enhance team performance, the more leadership the better."[10]

CONTEXT

Teams may not be appropriate for every organization or project but, in certain settings, they have particular advantages, including increased operating flexibility, pooled talent and experience, more diverse resources, better information flow, and higher outputs than individual performers.[11] Daniel Goleman, Richard Boyatzis, and Annie McKee have shown that when teams work cooperatively and make decisions, their work is superior to that of even the most intelligent individuals.[12] Teams also result in higher levels of staff satisfaction and lower operating budgets.[13] Eileen Applebaum and Rosemary Batt found that teamwork yields increased efficiency (reduced cycle time) and fewer defects in products (quality).[14] David A. Nadler, Janet L. Spencer, and Associates identified advantages to teamwork, including the generation of more ideas, increased ownership of the product, increased commitment and motivation, wide range of views and perspectives, sharing risks, transfer of expertise, and social support.[15] Grounded in more than two decades of research supporting the organizational and individual benefits of groups, it is clear that the use of work teams in organizations is increasing, and many managers regard fostering teamwork as a priority.

There are many reasons *why* a group may be effective. Team cohesiveness, group composition, performance, leadership, motivation, and group goals are variables that have been identified and that can help determine whether or not a group is effective.

Research into team effectiveness has traditionally studied and identified models of work group effectiveness and developed a checklist of characteristics that guide effective teams.[16] Sharon Mickan and Sylvia Rodger describe three categories into which these characteristics fall:

- Organizational structure that includes clear purpose, appropriate culture, specified task, distinct roles, suitable leadership, relevant members, and adequate resources;
- Individual contribution defined as self-knowledge, trust, commitment, and flexibility; and
- Team processes including coordination, communication, cohesion, decision making, conflict management, social relationships, and performance feedback.[17]

Through interviews of team leaders and team members within a wide range of organizational settings, Carl E. Larson and Frank M.J. LaFasto discovered eight characteristics that consistently explained what makes teams effective: a clear, elevating goal; a results-driven structure; competent team members; unified commitment; a collaborative climate; standards of excellence; external support and recognition; and principled leadership.[18]

Much of the LIS literature regarding team effectiveness focuses on characteristics of design and development in relation to outputs or results. Increasing and fostering teamwork has become a priority for many managers. The literature focuses on how to implement teams in an effort to streamline work processes in academic research libraries. This literature cites examples of teams that have failed and succeeded. It also describes how many academic research libraries have turned away from the traditional hierarchy to adopt a more team-based approach to problem solving and decision making. For example, the reorganization and restructuring of the University of Arizona Library, which began in 1991, seem to serve as models of success;[19] conversely Michigan State University Libraries' restructuring process went much less smoothly.[20] All restructuring efforts, however, have a common thread; they reportedly take longer than expected.

Total quality management and reengineering research reported in the LIS literature suggests that the use of work teams leads to increased productivity, as well as to increased job satisfaction; the empowerment, job enrichment, and development of workers; and higher quality services.[21] Other articles describe the impact of the use of teams throughout the entire library and the issues that arise as a result of this reorganization.[22] Karen Calhoun, Zsuzsa Koltay, and Edward Weissman described the success of teams used for designing the library's Web site;[23] Alex Bloss and Don Lanier, and John Lubans discussed characteristics and responsibilities of a department head or manager in a team-based organization.[24] According to Carrie Russell, however, the development of a team-based evaluation system that rewards team performance remains a challenge.[25] Hackman concurs, suggesting that "a reward system, one that recognizes and reinforces excellence at the team level while simultaneously fostering favorable individual and organizational outcomes, can never be perfected."[26]

STUDY PROCEDURES

The multiple methods used in this case study research included in-depth, semi-structured interviews with directors; focus groups with teams; and document review of written team materials (e.g., reports and meeting minutes). Information culled from interviews and focus groups consists of direct quotations from study participants regarding the knowledge, experience, attitudes, and feelings they attribute to their roles as team members, as well as detailed descriptions of their behaviors and interactions. Document review provides quotations or entire excerpts from records, official reports, and correspondence. A combination of these data sources is necessary to validate and crosscheck case study findings. Using triangulation minimizes the weaknesses of any one approach.

For this research, a case is an academic medical library that used teams on a regular basis to solve problems or work on projects, not as a one-time solution to a problem. Those academic medical libraries in the New York/ Washington, D.C. corridor that serve the faculty, staff, and students of a medical school, as well as a hospital or clinical enterprise, became the study's population. From among them, three were selected because they had at least one team in place, expressed an interest in participating in the study, were in close proximity to the author, and represented different library sizes (according to budget and number of staff).

These libraries were a good match for Hackman's conditions and the set of questions that characterize each condition, because the directors are interested in what makes a well-run team. The directors encouraged staff development activities and were supportive of the research. The author examined whether or not the presence of all or some of these conditions in the selected libraries led to teams that perform as defined along three dimensions: results, socialization, and individual growth.

A nonacademic medical library that is active in medical librarianship served as a site for the pilot study. This library has used teams for a number of years and became an excellent site to test the study's procedures and instruments. Data collection instruments were revised based on the results of the pilot study. Figure 10.3 highlights the four libraries in the study.

Members of all teams, past and present, were invited to participate in the focus groups. There were three focus groups formed at each site; with the exception of the management team—comprising division or department heads reporting to the library director who were automatically assigned to a team based on the team's functions—focus group participants were not

Figure 10.3
Description of Pilot and Cases

Library Z

Located in the Mid-Atlantic region, it serves one of the largest biomedical research centers in the world, with a staff of approximately 18,000. The library supports the biomedical and behavioral research needs of its community with a comprehensive range of scientific, medical, administrative, information, and support services. The library provides more than 3,000 online information resources, links from database search results directly to full-text journals and provides a full array of reference, instruction and translation services to staff. A federal library, Library Z, is open to the public on a self-service basis.

Library A

This private, medium-size facility located in the Mid-Atlantic region provides services to academic health sciences faculty, staff, retired faculty/staff members and students. Individuals must present a current ID to enter the library, and persons in the biomedical or health-related professions who are not affiliated with the medical center may purchase a fee-based admission.

Library B

Located in the Mid-Atlantic region, it moved into a new state-of-the-art facility within the last decade. One of the largest health sciences libraries on the East Coast, this library serves both the general public and the faculty, staff, and students of the six professional schools housed on its campus (Medicine, Dental, Nursing, Pharmacy, Social Work and the Graduate School). The library offers a multitude of electronic resources, library instruction programs and information technology access services.

Library C

Located in a large East Coast city, it is a small, private library supporting its academic and medical center base. Its mission is to enhance learning, research and patient care by effectively managing knowledge-based resources, providing client-centered information services and education, and extending access through new initiatives in information technology. This library is closed to the general public.

predetermined by team assignment but rather by team role. There was one focus group of team leaders and two of team members; team leaders either had been or were currently leaders of working library teams, and members had never been team leaders. It did not matter if team members or leaders were new or had served on teams for a long time.

FINDINGS

This section presents general patterns that emerged across the three case studies.

Characteristics of Effective Teams

The characteristics that emerged can be divided into eight categories:

1. Team structure;
2. Accountability;
3. Communication;
4. Teaming (becoming a team);
5. Relationship to the larger organization (external leadership);
6. Team leadership behavior;
7. Support systems; and
8. Coaching.

Hackman's framework includes team structure, support systems, and coaching. Two additional conditions (a real team and a compelling direction) are subsumed under new categories. Accountability, communication, teaming, relationship to the larger organization, and leadership behavior are missing from Hackman's set of conditions and questions.

Figure 10.4 illustrates the specific characteristics of effectiveness. These characteristics were mentioned by more than one participant group in a particular library, and they were common across groups in at least two of the three cases and/or one pilot case library. The figure also defines each characteristic. Study participants neither listed these characteristics in any particular order nor weighed them in terms of importance.

Team structure includes characteristics that define what the team is asked to do, lines of authority, the decision-making process, staffing, number of teams, and limitations on size of teams. It defines how the teams will be organized and the policies and procedures for teams.

Accountability includes characteristics that help a team justify its existence over time. Examples include regular reporting to the management team and periodic review of team charges. *Communication* includes characteristics of internal and external reporting. Forms of communication include written reports, oral presentations, or postings to the library's Intranet. Liaisons or champions from the management team may also serve as a means of promoting communication and help the team ask for clarification or direction. *Teaming* includes those interpersonal characteristics of becoming a team or developing a group identity. Although Hackman limits the meaning to collaboration in his condition, participants expanded the definition to include people getting along, team members developing trust, and staff buying-in to the team's charge.

Relationship to the larger organization describes the external leadership characteristics that illustrate how teams fit into and are guided by their parent institution. Although Hackman says the team needs a compelling direction,

Figure 10.4
Characteristics of Effective Teams

Team Structure
Clearly defined charge
Minutes, agendas, etc.
Clearly defined membership
Clear lines of authority
Clear lines of decision making
Membership stability
Small number of teams
Staff limits for membership assignments
Appropriate staffing

Accountability
Regular reporting to management team
Yearly or periodic review of team charges
Minutes, agendas, etc.

Communication within Team
Regular reporting to management team
Liaisons from management to teams
Effective communication

Teaming (Becoming a Team)
Effective interpersonal skills
Group harmony
Collegiality
Noncompetitiveness
Staff buy-in
Collaborative environment
Blame-free environment
Trust
Team identity
*A real team

Team Leadership Behavior
Shared leadership
Facilitator
Self-directed leadership
Good leader
Experienced leader
Commitment to teams
Prior leadership experience

Coaching
Mentoring provided
Leadership opportunities
Development opportunities

Support Systems
Money
Training of leaders and members
Staff rewards/recognition
Technology

Relationship to the Larger Organization (External Leadership)
Strategic planning
Team goals aligned with planning
Mission consciousness
Teams mirror the institution
*A compelling direction
Engenders follower loyalty
Intervenes appropriately
Liaisons from management to teams

*One of Hackman's conditions.

he views the direction as coming from the person in authority who establishes the teams. Study participants felt that the teams needed to receive their direction from the mission of the larger institution.

Team leadership behavior includes behavioral and personal characteristics of team leaders and the library director. Hackman views leadership from a functional rather than a behavioral perspective. Study participants viewed leadership in terms of how the team leaders conducted themselves. *Support systems* include those financial, reward, education, etc. systems in place to support teams. *Coaching* includes mentoring team members and leaders.

Barriers to Effective Teams

Barriers to effective teams can be divided into the following nine categories:

1. Lack of team structure;
2. Lack of accountability;
3. Lack of communication;
4. Lack of teaming;
5. Effect of the larger organization (external leadership);
6. Ineffective team leadership behavior;
7. Lack of support systems;
8. Lack of coaching; and
9. Staffing issues.

All but one of these categories is the opposite of its corresponding characteristic. Staffing issues is the one barrier that is unique to this list, although it is related to lack of teaming.

Figure 10.5 illustrates the specific barriers to effectiveness. These barriers were mentioned by more than one participant group in a particular library and were common across at least two of the three cases and/or one pilot case library. Study participants did not list these barriers in any particular order, nor did they weigh them in terms of importance. *Lack of team structure* refers to an undefined process for forming teams. Policies and procedures for teams to follow are unclear or unavailable. A *Lack of accountability* means there is no periodic review of teams or regular reporting mechanism. Teams do not have to justify their existence or continuation. *Lack of communication* includes limited or ineffective communication mechanisms within and/or outside the team. There may not be any written reports, agendas, or minutes; if there are, they are not communicated beyond the team. *Lack of teaming* refers to those barriers that prevent groups from obtaining an *espirit de corps*. *The effect of the larger organization* covers items outside the team's control, such as poor external leadership, imposed hiring freezes, or budget cuts. Generally, these

Figure 10.5
Barriers to Effective Teams

*****Lack of Team Structure**
Unclear charge
Charge not understood
Too much rotation of membership
Too many teams
Team size (too large)
Blurred boundaries
Lack of clear decision-making process
Lack of clear team structure
Inappropriate skill mix of members

Lack of Accountability
Lack of periodic review
(especially for long-standing teams)
Lack of regular reporting to
management

Lack of Communication
No communication
Ineffective communication
Secrecy
Lack of periodic reporting to
management

Effect of the Larger Organization
Outside forces
Hiring freeze
Budget cuts
HR system
Union rules
Not enough intervention

*****Lack of Support Systems**
No leadership skills training provided
No team-based rewards system
Lack of meeting spaces
Budget cuts

Ineffective Team Leadership Behavior
Lack of leadership skills
Not enough intervention
Reluctance to confront issues
Lack of belief in shared leadership

*****Lack of Coaching**
No mentoring or coaching provided
Lack of team learning opportunities

Staffing Issues
Worker complacency
Staff work styles
Staff reluctance to serve on teams
Perceived lack of time
Lack of appropriate skills
Unclear work assignment priorities
Lack of buy-in
Competition among staff
Fear of change, especially job loss
Lack of interpersonal skills
Interpersonal conflict
Staff burnout
Concern for relationship building
Group think
Cultural differences

Lack of Teaming
Lack of trust
Lack of group identify
Lack of harmony
Group conflict

*One of Hackman's conditions.

outside forces are usually placed on the library by its parent organization and affect the ability of the teams to function because they usually limit the team's ability to obtain needed resources. *Lack of support systems* refers to ineffective or unavailable resources such as money and space. *Ineffective team leadership behavior* includes specific conduct or inaction on the part of the team leader and library director that hinders the team. *Lack of coaching* means no mentoring takes place. *Staffing issues* include staff behaviors, such as interpersonal conflicts or resistance to serving on teams, which prevent teams from functioning effectively.

Outcomes Dimensions

Study participants agreed with all three of Hackman's dimensions: the team produces results, members experience socialization, and members experience individual growth. They found that such effectiveness resulted in new services, improved services, or remodeled facilities. They thought that team members from different departments worked well together inside and outside the team, and they stated that many team members and leaders gained new skills and broader responsibilities as a result of their experience on the team.

Study participants cited another dimension of effectiveness; that is, effective teams evolve over time. They viewed teams as organic units with a life cycle; they adapt and change over time as the members and leaders became more experienced in the team process. Participants learned from the experience and changed the way teams were originally established.

View of Leadership

Hackman sees leadership as enabling rather than as behavioral. Study participants considered such a characterization as limited. They emphasized good leadership behaviors, personality, and style as characteristics of effective teams. Team members wanted leaders to do more than set the conditions in place for teams to be effective. They should intervene whenever a team struggled or whenever conflict within the team emerged. Directors, on the other hand, disagreed and wanted team members to be empowered and self-directed and to share the responsibility of leading the teams. The conflict may sometimes continue. At times, owing to their leadership philosophies, directors may let teams introduce products or services that were inferior. Nonetheless, when the director empowers a team, this should not be interpreted as giving members complete autonomy or abdicating overall responsibility.

Revisiting Hackman's Framework

Figure 10.6 revises Figure 10.3, based on study findings. Library Z, the pilot case, and Library B had used teams for at least 10 years; Library A started teams less than five years ago and Library C was in its fifth year at the time of the site visit. The longer the library had been using teams, the greater the presence of Hackman's conditions, together with the added enhancements and outcome dimensions.

Figure 10.6
Enhancements to Hackman's Framework

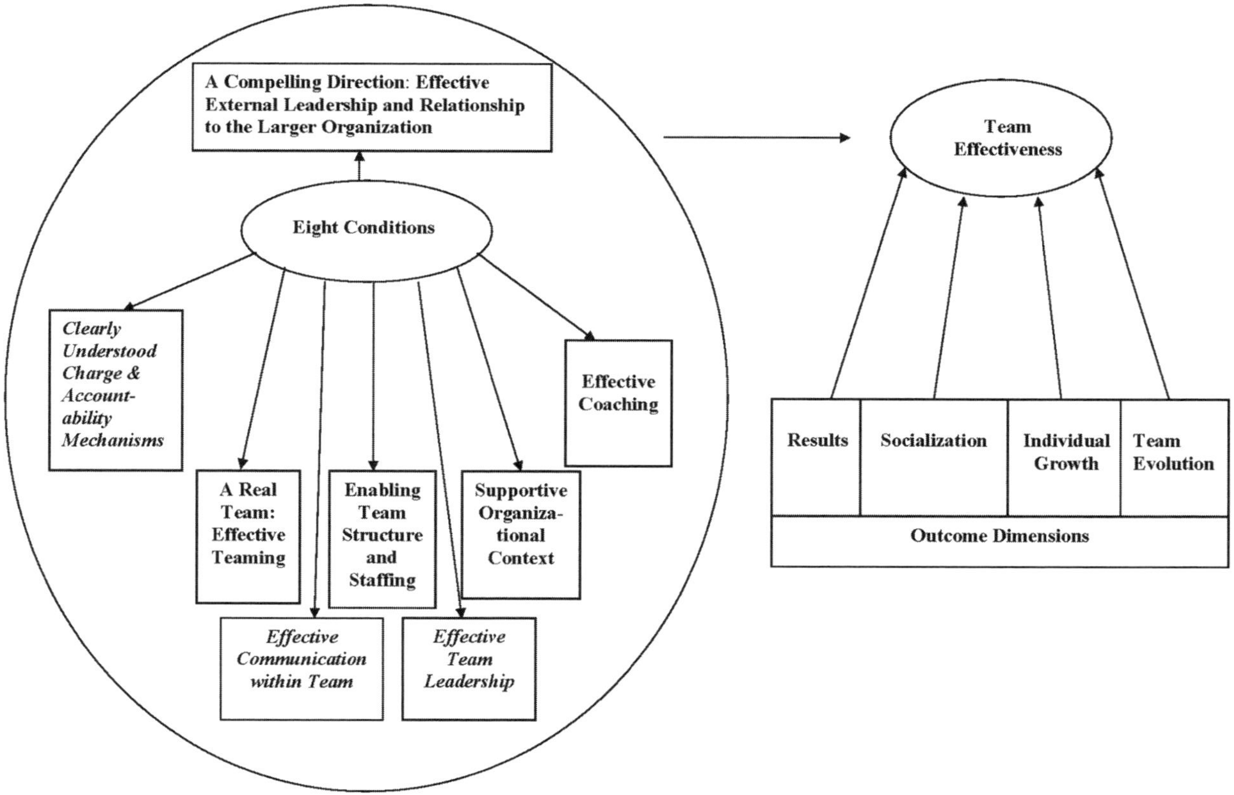

For the most part, Library Z and Library B adhere to Figure 10.5 and exhibit many characteristics of effective teams as a result. Teams in these two libraries had a compelling direction, clear charges, accountability mechanisms, effective teaming, effective modes of electronic communication, a supportive organizational context, and effective coaching. For these sites, Hackman's framework provided the teams with the necessary foundation for solving library problems by involving affected staff. Library C, on the other hand, implemented the first three of Hackman's conditions (charge, staffing, and direction) but struggled with the last two (support systems and coaching). The library director recognized these deficiencies and was investigating ways to implement them to achieve Hackman's dimensions, accountability, and effective team leadership. This director saw this investigator's visit as a good first step. Hackman says that a leader's focus on the first three conditions rather than on all five is typical of many organizations in their early stages of team development. Despite the director's commitment to a team-based organization, Library A was the least attentive to Hackman's conditions and proposed enhancements. Although teams had a compelling direction and effective electronic communication mechanisms, library managers and the director believed too much adherence to structure and process prevented team creativity and innovation. These teams, therefore, struggled to produce results and staff remained dissatisfied with the team process. The lack of foundation affected team outcomes.

CONCLUSION

The library directors participating in the study tended to struggle with when they should intervene, coach, and let teams continue independently, even if the resulting products or services were inferior. Once the directors establish teams and empower staff to make decisions, those directors cannot abandon their authority or leadership responsibilities. External leadership is situational and needs to be appropriate and to respond to the developmental needs of the teams. Directors need to know their employees, the stages of team development, the presence of team skills, and the leadership style most appropriate to the situation.

Introducing teams into an organization is not a trivial matter. Effective teams require time, patience, commitment on the part of the library director, and leadership from everyone. Figure 10.6 offers specific conditions that library leaders need to enact at both the organizational and team levels. Both leaders and team members should become active participants in the team-building process and feel that both they and the organization are committed to making Figure 10.6 a reality.

"[G]reat leaders. As you read . . . [those] words. . . . , what came to mind?"[27]

NOTES

1. This chapter is based on Elaine R. Martin, *Team Effectiveness in Academic Medical Libraries: A Multiple Case Study,* paper for the doctor of arts degree (Boston: Simmons College, 2004). Material in this chapter was first published in Elaine R. Martin, "Team Effectiveness in Academic Medical Libraries: A Multiple Case Study," *Journal of the Medical Library Association* 94, no. 3 (July 2006): 271–278.

2. Ronald A. Heifetz, *Leadership without Easy Answers* (Cambridge, MA: Belknap Press of Harvard University Press, 1994), 275.

3. Joanne R. Euster, "Teaming Up," *Wilson Library Bulletin,* 69 (January 1995): 57–59.

4. Joseph A. McDonald and Lynda Basney Micikas, *Academic Libraries: The Dimensions of Their Effectiveness* (Westport, CT: Greenwood Press, 1994). They review various definitions of effectiveness in the LIS literature and note that there is considerable disagreement in the use of the word. See also Thomas A. Childers and Nancy A. Van House, *"What's Good?" Describing Your Public Library's Effectiveness* (Chicago: American Library Association, 1993), 5.

5. J. Richard Hackman and Richard E. Walton, "Leading Groups in Organizations," in *Designing Effective Work Groups,* ed. Paul S. Goodman and Associates (San Francisco, CA: Jossey-Bass, 1986), 72–119.

6. J. Richard Hackman, *Leading Teams: Setting the Stage for Great Performances* (Boston: Harvard Business School Press, 2002), 258; Jon R. Katzenbach and Douglas K. Smith, "The Discipline of Teams," *Harvard Business Review* 71, no. 2 (March-April 1993): 111–20.

7. Hackman, *Leading Teams.*

8. Ibid., 258.

9. Ibid., 211.

10. Ibid.

11. Margaret Yancey, *Work Teams: Three Models of Effectiveness* (Denton, TX: University of North Texas Center for the Study of Work Teams, 1998). No longer available at http://www.workteams.unt.edu/reports/Yancey.html (accessed September 1, 2002).

12. Daniel Goleman, Richard Boyatzis, and Annie McKee, *Primal Leadership: Realizing the Power of Emotional Intelligence* (Boston: Harvard Business School Press, 2002).

13. Tim McAdam and Nancy M. Stanley, "Implementing Teams for Technical Services Functions," *The Serials Librarian* 28 (1996): 361–65.

14. Eileen Applebaum and Rosemary Batt, *The New American Workplace: Transforming Work Systems in the United States* (Ithaca, NY: ILR Press, 1994).

15. David A. Nadler, Janet L. Spencer, & Associates, *Executive Teams* (San Francisco, CA: Jossey-Bass, 1998).

16. Sharon Mickan and Sylvia Rodger, "Characteristics of Effective Teams: A Literature Review," *Australian Health Review* 23, no. 3 (July 2000): 201–208.

17. Ibid.

18. Carl E. Larson and Frank M. J. LaFasto, *Teamwork: What Must Go Right/What Can Go Wrong* (Newbury Park, CA: Sage Publications, 1989).

19. Joseph R. Diaz and Chestalene Pintozzi, "Helping Teams Work: Lessons Learned from the University of Arizona Library Reorganization," *Library Administration & Management* 13 (Winter 1999): 27–36.

20. Rita Echt, "The Realities of Teams in Technical Services at Michigan State University Libraries," *Library Acquisitions: Practice and Theory* 21 (Summer 1997): 179–87.

21. G. J. J. deJager and Adeline S. A. duToit, "Self Directed Work Teams in Information Services: An Exploratory Study," *South African Journal of Library & Information Science* 65 (December 1997): 194–98.

22. See Laura Bender, "Team Organization-Learning Organization: The University of Arizona Four Years into It," *Information Outlook* 1 (1997): 19–22; Matthew Bowers, Linda DeBeau-Melting, John DeVries, and Merry Schellinger, "Organizational Restructuring in Academic Libraries: A Case Study," *Journal of Library Administration* 22 (1996): 33–44; Diaz and Pintozzi, "Helping Teams Work;" George R. Jaramillo, "Utilization of Teams in an Academic Library Environment," *Colorado Libraries* 22 (1996): 17–23; Thomas W. Shaughnessy, "Lessons from Restructuring the Library," *The Journal of Academic Librarianship* 22 (July 1996): 251–57; Mary J. Stanley, "Taking Time for the Organization," *College & Research Libraries News* 62 (October 2001): 900–902, 908.

23. Karen Calhoun, Zsuzsa Koltay, and Edward Weissman, "Library Gateway: Project Design, Teams and Cycle Time," *Library Resources and Technical Services* 43 (1999): 114–22.

24. Alex Bloss and Don Lanier, "The Library Department Head in the Context of Matrix Management and Reengineering," *College & Research Libraries* 58 (1997): 499–508; John Lubans, "'I Ain't No Cowboy, I Just Found This Hat:' Confessions of an Administrator in an Organization of Self-managing Teams," *Library Administration & Management* 10 (1996): 28–40.

25. Carrie Russell, "Using Performance Measurement to Evaluate Teams and Organizational Effectiveness at the University of Arizona," *Library Administration & Management* 12 (Summer 1998): 159–65.

26. Hackman, *Leading Teams*, 146.

27. Ibid., 211.

11

GEN-XERS AND MILLENNIALS JOIN THE LIBRARY EXPRESS

Arthur P. Young

"There is a mysterious cycle in human events. To some generations much is given. Of other generations much is expected. This generation has a rendezvous with destiny."[1]

Generational studies, the analysis of traits and their workplace implications, have not received much attention in the library and information science community until the last decade. We neglect the study of generational differences and leadership attributes at our own peril. A fuller understanding of the differences inherent in the various generations is necessary for the continuing vitality of the library profession, particularly in the areas of recruiting, workplace dynamics, and leadership development. This chapter addresses the various generations in the workplace, with particular emphasis on gen-Xers (born 1965–1979) and millennials (born 1980–1999). Studies related to these generations, both directly related to the library profession and others, are introduced. A personal perspective on some of the issues raised by the research, derived from more than three decades in library administration, rounds out this chapter.

Before examining generational perceptions of leadership attributes, it is important to provide a framework of context, concerns, and aspirations for each of the age cohorts. Traditionalists (born 1900–1945) constitute a still important segment of the senior workforce. Prominent influences on the traditionalists include Joe DiMaggio, Joe Lewis, Joe McCarthy, Alfred Hitchcock, Duke Ellington, Charles Lindbergh, John Wayne, Bob Hope,

Elizabeth Taylor, and Tarzan.[2] There are about 75 million traditionalists. Many of those who grew up during the Depression era did not have an abundance of material goods, and economic well-being was never taken for granted. Teamwork, loyalty, and striving toward a common goal are particularly strong traits of this group. These attributes are not surprising, given the fact that more than half of the males in this group are veterans and tend to look at organizations from a chain-of-command perspective.

Baby boomers, born between 1946 and 1964, constitute a cohort of 80 million. Notable baby boomer contemporaries include Martin Luther King, Jr., the Kingston Trio, Richard Nixon, John Kennedy, Rosa Parks, John McEnroe and Jimmy Connors, Gloria Steinem, Barbra Streisand, Janis Joplin, Captain Kirk, the Beatles, and the Rolling Stones. The greatest invention of the boomer generation was television, a new medium that accelerated communication and heightened the impact of many events on such divisive issues as Vietnam, Watergate, and civil rights. If traditionalists could be described as loyal, the baby boomer generation could best be personified as optimistic. The postwar economy, GI loans, and the availability of jobs translated into a new level of well-being for this group. Along with optimism, boomers are often fiercely competitive.[3]

Gen-Xers, a cohort of 46 million, are becoming an influential generation that is climbing the rungs of corporate America and public service on many fronts. Personalities who have influenced this generation include Bill Clinton, Monica Lewinsky, Quentin Tarantino, Clarence Thomas, Newt Gingrich, O. J. Simpson, George Lucas, Madonna, and Michael Jordan. Products of 24/7 media, generation X matured during a period of great skepticism about individuals and institutions.[4]

Perhaps the most insightful commentator on the gen-X group, particularly the elite or the top 15 percent of the gen-Xer cohort, is Bernard Carl Rosen, author of the protean book, *Masks and Mirrors: Generation X and the Chameleon Personality*.[5] Rosen's psychologically oriented analysis adds much depth to our understanding of the gen-X environment and behavior traits. Generation X is riding the crest of the information revolution and the global appearance of service economies. This generation believes in meritocracy and competition, and has little patience with failure. They must compete for favor and jobs in a setting that has many new groups that aspire to the same levels of attainment. This level of competition can obviously lead to serious anxiety and frustration. Rosen presents a rather stark portrait:

Perhaps most important of all, many Xers feel they're losing control over their lives. Why is that? Is it only because the pitiless competitive milieu in which they work, its hectic pace of life, its buzzing, strepitous clamor, is making elite Xers anxious? This surely adds to the Xers' sense of a world careening out of control, but there is another factor: the economy has undergone fundamental change—it has become global—and this is complicating the Xers' lives. No generation before the Xers knew with such thundering explicitness that America was dependent upon the good will, resources, and trade of other countries. No other generation was so "globalized," was so exposed to the competition, moods, mistakes, demands, and follies of other nations.[6]

Competition, anxiety, fear of failure, and clashes with the boomer generation have led to a chameleon persona among many gen-Xers. Rather than confrontation and resolution, they have opted for dissimulation, simulation, feinting, and manipulation. This mindset is both a tactic and another way to ward off potential failure. Colloquially put, chameleonism is a bob-and-weave relationship with both peers and superiors.

Another perceptive commentator on generation X, Diana Schaub, explores intergenerational conflicts between baby boomers and gen-Xers, with perceptive comments from a wide range of individuals, from the founding fathers to political philosophers and literary authorities. Each generation has within it the duality of conservative and progressive tendencies, and one generation becomes the seed bed for the succeeding generation. She invokes Abraham Lincoln as both a quintessential traditionalist and transformational figure in American history, leading to the insight that transformation in every generation begins as an embedded and conservative value in an earlier generation. This insight makes it clear that no generation can be considered *sui generis,* and that adjacent generations must always be examined for a full portrait.[7]

An excellent new research-based book on gen-X women focuses on what women want at work and how their boomer bosses can help them achieve their goals. The authors are best heard in their own voices:

We can't create X-friendly workplaces using traditional management skills. To do so would be like trying to build a quantum computer with 1950s technology. It's simply impossible! An old room-sized IBM was designed using transistors; quantum computers use atomic encoding. It's an entirely new ball game. The same idea applies to re-creating organizations. It is impossible to plan, organize, direct, or control a complex revolution. Old skills are inadequate. New skills are needed—skills that expand our current capacity for leading change. We call these Quantum Skills because they draw heavily from recent research in quantum physics, complexity science, and positive psychology; and using them will enable twenty-first-century revolutionaries to help their organizations take a quantum leap into new ways of being at work. The skills are:

- *Quantum Seeing:* the ability to *see* intentionally;
- *Quantum Thinking:* the ability to *think* paradoxically;
- *Quantum Feeling:* the ability to *feel* vitally alive;
- *Quantum Knowing:* the ability to *know* intuitively;
- *Quantum Acting:* the ability to *act* responsibly;
- *Quantum Trusting:* the ability to trust life; and
- *Quantum Being:* The ability to *be* in relationships.[8]

Millennials, 76 million in number, are starting to graduate from college in expanding numbers. It is still early to make judgments about this newest generation, but some speculative evidence is already appearing. The millennials grew up with information technology and embrace the interconnected global community. People influencing millennials include Prince William, Chelsea Clinton, Ricky Martin, Leonardo DiCaprio, Courtney Love, Mark McGuire, Sammy Sosa, and Serena Williams. Millennials are very concerned about workplace safety and security. Realistic may be the adjective of choice to describe the outlook of millennials. Neil Howe and William Strauss, in their pathbreaking book, *Millennials Rising,* characterize the Millennial generation as possessing seven distinguishing traits: (1) special, a sense of their importance to the nation's future as inculcated by their parents; (2) sheltered, beneficiaries of a sweeping youth safety movement in the country; (3) confident, a collective sense of their own generation's potential; (4) team-oriented, an indication of a strong instinct for peer-based activities; (5) achieving, beneficiaries of much-needed revision of school standards; (6) pressured, to hit the books and avoid risky behavior; and (7) conventional, the notion that social rules are important to a society's well-being.[9]

Lynne C. Lancaster and David Stillman nicely capture the differences between the generations on some key issues and values. Under the rubric of intergenerational clash points, Figure 11.1 summarizes those differences.

Figure 11.1
Intergenerational Clash Points

Generation	Career Goals	Rewards	Balancing the Generations	Retirement
Traditionalists	Build a legacy	Job well done	Support me in shifting the balance	Reward
Baby boomers	Build a career	Money, title and recognition	Help me balance everyone else and find meaning myself	Retool
Generation Xers	Build a portable career	Freedom as the ultimate reward	Give me balance now	Renew
Millennials	Build parallel careers	Meaningful work	Need flexibility to balance my activities	Recycle

Source: Lynne C. Lancaster and David Stillman, *When Generations Collide* (New York, HarperCollins Publishers, 2002), 55–140.

Knowledge of the attitudes and behavior traits of gen-Xers and millennials will enable us to better adapt organizational structures and to initiate more innovative service. Expanding our knowledge base to determine perceptions of needed leadership skills for preceding, current, and future generations will add measurably to our capability to respond and to reorient. Peter Hernon, Ronald Powell, and Arthur Young are engaged in a multiyear investigative project to assess academic library leadership attributes within several different populations. They surveyed directors of libraries in the Association of Research Libraries (ARL) and the Association of College and Research Libraries, and gen-X cohorts.[10] The articles in *College & Research Libraries* and the larger coverage found in our book received polite notice and several compliments, but it was not until an article appeared in *American Libraries* that a more strident reaction took place.[11] Our findings on ARL and non-ARL library director attributes were based on the perceptions of those directors currently in place and did not reflect prioritization or commentary from the authors of the study. As indicated, the May 2004 *American Libraries* article provoked quite a loud response, revealing a different value system than some library directors, a belief that their role and opinions in the library had been undervalued, and for some a misunderstanding of the research process for the study reported in the article. This negative reaction certainly indicated the need for further research, and the results of that exploratory study are now furnished.

During spring and summer 2005, we contacted gen-Xers from academic libraries, all born between 1965 and 1979. The process started with one of the critics of our article in *American Libraries*. He happily decided to participate in the study and to recommend other academic librarians to participate. The Delphi technique, a research tool that requires successive rounds or iterations involving lists that subjects add to, subtract from, and rank, was used for the study. Ten gen-X academic librarians were ultimately selected for the project. They worked in all sections of the country. There were six female and four male participants, and one minority. Participants received an initial list, provided by the authors, of gen-X qualities as derived from the literature: build work relationships with others; comfortable with change; commitment to explaining decisions; encourage participation and task completion at all levels; flexible; good interpersonal skills; sensitivity to diversity; and show initiative. Participants were then asked to examine the list and to reword any of the attributes, add some additional traits, and remove any attributes that were considered inappropriate. Everyone was asked to focus on attributes as they contribute to effective academic library leaders, regardless of their professional positions. The modified list was then submitted to everyone for a second vetting. For this round, participants were asked to assign a value of 1 to 10 for each attribute, thereby indicating its importance to leaders for the present and next 10 years. One means "no importance," five represents "modest importance," and 10 equals "maximum importance." Again, respondents had the opportunity to recommend attribute(s) for deletion. If two or more participants recommended deletion of an attribute, the attribute was removed.

There were 80 total attributes, and the top 10, as ranked by the gen-X cohort, are these: successful in securing resources—funds, technology, staffing, etc.; good interpersonal skills; honest; articulated vision that inspires others; build partnerships within the library or across campus; a passion for libraries and librarianship; build working relationships with others; comfortable with change; strong communication skills—verbal and written; recognize interpersonal communication skills at all levels—personally approachable—provide paths—communicate directly when appropriate. Most of the favorably scored attributes related to communications and interpersonal skills, not a surprise finding for this group. Interestingly, the very highest rated attribute is the overall health of the library organization, an outcome benchmark for success.

Conversely, the bottom-ranked attributes are these: enjoy challenges and learning new skills; reward excellence performance with praise, choice assignments, salary increases, and bonus; technology driven (does not like to be left behind when it comes to new technologies); encourage librarians to self-appoint task forces to work on projects rather than make executive decisions about who works on what; encourage participation and task completion at all levels of the organization; sense of humor; courageous; charismatic; willing to "get your hands dirty;" consensus building; discover and explore new, radical, unconventional and/or even controversial means for achieving desired ends; and willing to sit at a reference desk from time to time. These attributes are somewhat of a mixed bag, but do suggest that the traditional decision-making executive model is not one that gen-Xers fully endorse.

As further context for the gen-X responses, it is useful to review the leadership attributes as espoused by ARL and non-ARL library directors in our earlier studies. Their responses were broken down and ranked within the three broad categories of *Managerial Attributes, Personal Attributes,* and *Areas of Knowledge.* Tables 11.1 and 11.2 identify the desirable attributes of ARL directors and non-ARL directors grouped by quartile within the three major categories.

Table 11.3 presents gen-X attributes by quartile. In all, 51 (63.8%) of the 80 gen-X leadership attributes appeared in the list of attributes for ARL library directors. Only 20 (25%) of the attributes that respondents identified appeared among those attributes mentioned by directors of non-ARL libraries. Table 11.4 further analyzes the gen-X attributes, and indicates whether the attributes fall into the same quartile in either the ARL or non-ARL list as they did in the gen-X list, whether they occurred in one or both of the other lists, or whether they were in neither list in any quartile and thus represented new attributes unique to the gen-X study.[12] A total of 14 (17.5%) of the gen-X attributes appeared in the same quartile as one or both of the other lists of attributes as they did in the gen-X list, 38 (47.5%) appeared in one of the other lists but not

Table 11.1
Attributes for ARL Library Directors—Combined Quartiles

Managerial attributes

First quartile
  Committed to service
  Results-oriented
  Communicate effectively with staff
  Delegate authority
  Build a shared vision for the library
  Manage/shape change
  Able to function in a political environment
  Develop a campus visibility for the library
  Set priorities
  Plan for life cycles of information technologies and services

Second quartile
  Facilitate a productive work environment
  Willing to make tough decisions
  Promote professional growth in staff
  Manage fiscal resources/budgets
  Advocate for the librarian's role in higher education
  Think outside the box (in new and creative ways applicable to the problem)
  Build consensus in carrying out strategic directions
  Lead and participates in consortia and cooperative endeavors
  Respond to needs of various constituencies

Third quartile
  Engage in fundraising and donor relations
  Nurture the development of new programs and services/refines existing ones as needed
  Develop various sources of funds (grants, gifts, contracts, and fee-based services)
  Committed to staff diversity
  Collaborative
  Entrepreneurial
  Bring issues of broad importance to the university community, for steering wide discussion and action, when appropriate
  Demonstrate effective networking skills
  Create and implement systems that assess the library's value to its users

Fourth quartile
  Ensure that planned action is implemented and evaluated
  Facilitate the group process
  Resolve conflicts
  Keep the library focused on its mission
  Change/shape the library's culture
  Develop and foster partnerships with groups and organizations on/off campus
  Lead in a shared decision-making environment
  Create an environment that fosters accountability

Personal Attributes

First quartile

Credible (trustworthiness, keeps commitments, and follow-through)
Even-handed
Self-confident
Accessible
Committed to a set of values (integrity)
Able to handle stress
Work on multiple tasks simultaneously
Comfortable with ambiguity
Committed to job and profession
Focused on change
Exercise good judgment
Articulate direction for the library
Inspire trust

Second quartile

Treat people with dignity/respect
Able to work effectively in groups
Articulate (good oral/written/presentation skills)
Sense of perspective
Self-awareness of strengths and weaknesses
Honest
Energetic
Resilient
Innovative
Organizational agility
Persuasive
Reasonable risk-taking skills

Third quartile

Diplomatic
Open minded
Good listener
Intelligent
Analyze and solve problems
Have a variety of work experiences
Able to think on his/her feet, or "wing it"
Optimistic
Understand that one does not have all of the answers
Enthusiastic
An enabler and facilitator

Fourth quartile

Able to compromise
Sense of humor

Personal Attributes (continued)

Fourth quartile (continued)

Good interpersonal/people skills
Intuitive
Broad knowledge of issues
Able to ask the right question
Manage time effectively
Committed to learning from mistakes
Take initiative
Have team-building skills
Committed to explaining decisions

Areas of Knowledge

First quartile

Scholarly communication
Complex environment in which the library functions
Financial management
Facilities planning (including remote storage and multiuse buildings)
Digital libraries
Planning (strategic, long-term) skills

Second quartile

Trends in higher education
Information technology
Collection management and development (e.g., all formats, preservation, and
  acquisitions)
Outcomes (and accreditation) assessment
User expectations/information needs
Intellectual property rights

Third quartile

Management issues
Fundraising skills
Community's view of the library
Public relations
Service quality measurement
Goals (educational, research, and service) of the parent institution

Fourth quartile

Information delivery systems
Publishing industry
Resource sharing
Information literacy
Teaching and learning theory

Source: Peter Hernon, Ronald R. Powell, and Arthur P. Young, "University Library Directors in the Association of Research Libraries: The Next Generation, Part Two." *College & Research Libraries* 63 (January 2002), 85–87.

Table 11.2
Attributes for Non-ARL Academic Library Directors: Quartiles Based on Average Scores

Managerial Attributes

First quartile
Supervisory experience
Proven managerial ability in personnel, fiscal, budgetary, and program matters
Ability to plan, implement, and assess strategic goals
Ability to work in collegial, networked environment
Understanding of and commitment to institutional mission

Second quartile
Proven facilitative leadership skills
Proven ability to foster team building and participatory management
A record of innovative and effective leadership
Firm commitment to quality
Vision in formulating programs and implementing strategies to integrate print and electronic resources

Third quartile
Experience in positions of increasing responsibility
Commitment to diversity

Fourth quartile
Demonstrated ability to identify trends
Experience developing digital libraries

Personal Attributes

First quartile
Integrity
Strong interpersonal skills
Ability to serve as an advocate for library
Excellent oral and written communication skills
Ability to work collaboratively with campus colleagues

Second quartile
Ability to articulate vision for library within the institution
Demonstrated ability to exercise mature judgment
Have MLS
Flexible
Good listening skills
Commitment to professional development of library personnel
Respect for scholarship and learning

Third quartile
Strong service orientation
Enthusiasm for work in an educational environment
Sense of humor
Documented record of problem solving

Table 11.2
**Attributes for Non-ARL Academic Library Directors: Quartiles Based on
Average Scores (continued)**

Personal Attributes (continued)

Fourth quartile
Creative
High energy level
Dynamic
Second advanced degree

Areas of Knowledge

First quartile
Knowledge of library operations
Experience with change management
Experience with current technology and information systems as they apply to
libraries
Experience with program assessment and evaluation

Second quartile
Experience with information technology
Experience with long-range planning
Experience with collaborative arrangements between/among multicampus and
    statewide settings, and other institutions
Experience with scholarly communication
Experience with public relations
Knowledge of collection development
Experience with marketing of services and resources
Record of scholarly achievement

Third quartile
Experience with facilities planning
Proven fundraising capabilities and success in securing funding support
Experience with information literacy
Knowledge of bibliographic control
Experience managing or planning digital libraries

Fourth quartile
Experience with grant writing
Experience in planning or coordinating new library building projects
Expertise with distance education

Source: Peter Hernon, Ronald R. Powell, and Arthur P. Young, *The Next Library Leadership*
(Westport, CT: Libraries Unlimited, 2003), 70–71.

Table 11.3
Gen-X Attributes by Quartile

Managerial Attributes

First quartile
Successful in securing resources—funds, technology, staffing, etc.
Build partnerships within the library or across campus
Build working relationships with others
Acknowledge the work and contributions of others
Committed to development of staff
Listen and reflect on the needs and desires of the library community
Supportive of employees' work/life balance
Aware of his/her own limitations and seeks the advice and assistance of others

Second quartile
Ability to see the impact of decisions, five days, five months, and five years down the road
Follow through on initiatives
Promote the success of others
Delegate tasks to others
Deeply committed to their institution and its mission
Give regular feedback on job performance (before formal reviews)
Realistic about gen-X workplace attitudes; willing to provide professional development support and other so-called extras to encourage and retain newer librarians
Supportive of librarians' workplace issues (workload, benefits, meeting requirements for promotion and tenure, and union/collective bargaining status)
Commitment to involving others and explaining decisions
Sensitivity to diversity issues

Third quartile
Recognize employees'/team members' accomplishments
Address the performance issues of subordinates
Leveraging resources
Create and share a vision
Explain decisions and involves others in them
Politically savvy
Embrace new technology. Comfortable with incorporating innovative technology to enhance and add to current library services
Fully aware of the organization/team, the individuals in the organization/on the team, and all functions of the organization/team

Fourth quartile
Awareness of library paraprofessionals' workplace issues; supportive of their work, especially in the area of access and circulation
Aware of importance of library as place; takes lead in creating a welcoming environment for college community
Reward excellent performance with praise, choice of assignments, salary increases and bonuses

Table 11.3
Gen-X Attributes by Quartile (continued)

<hr>

Managerial Attributes (continued)

Fourth quartile (continued)

Encourage librarians to self-appoint task forces to work on projects rather than make executive decisions about who works on what

Encourage participation in task completion at all levels of the organization

Willing to sit at reference desk from time to time, even if not a public service team leader or coordinator

Personal Attributes

First quartile

Good interpersonal skills

Honest

Articulate a vision that inspires others

A passion for libraries and librarianship

Comfortable with change

Strong communication skills—verbal and written

Recognize interpersonal communication essential on all levels; personally approachable; provide paths; communicate directly when appropriate

Capable and dependable

Strong listening skills

Trustworthy

Fair

Show initiative

Second quartile

Flexible

Motivated to succeed

Open—will share information and will incorporate good feedback into decisionmaking. (Keep people informed and listen well.)

Candid, trusting of staff

Recognize own bad decisions/willing to admit mistakes

Admit mistakes and learn from them

Deliver on promises

Accessible

Aware of his/her own strengths and plays to them

Confront problems and accepts criticism willingly and thoughtfully

More often than not enthusiastic and positive about others' ideas

Enthusiastic

Inclusive

Loyal to staff

Set high standards

Acknowledge the prerogative to be autocratic under certain circumstances and own those decisions when they are made

Third quartile

Able to coach and reassure staff through changes

Make effective use of meeting time

Table 11.3
Gen-X Attributes by Quartile (continued)

Personal Attributes (continued)
Third quartile (continued)
   User-oriented—understand the importance of teaching (both staff and patrons)
   Sense of purpose/goal oriented
   Unafraid to buck regional or national trends if it is right for their institution
   Acknowledge director's role as a coach, teacher, and mentor
   Willingness to share credit, even on individual efforts
   Communicate frequently
   Persuasive

Fourth quartile
   Enjoy challenges and learning new skills
   Technology driven (does not like to be left behind when it comes to new technologies)
   Sense of humor
   Courageous
   Charismatic
   Willing to "get your hands dirty"
   Consensus building
   Discover and explore new, radical, unconventional, and/or even controversial means for achieving desired ends

Areas of Knowledge
Second quartile
   Understand budgeting and fiscal processes

Third quartile
   Understand new technology, how it relates and will impact libraries

Fourth (and Third) quartile
   Understand marketing concepts

Source: Arthur P. Young, Peter Hernon, Ronald R. Powell, "Attributes of Academic Library Leadership: An Exploratory Study of Some Gen-Xers," *The Journal of Academic Librarianship* 32, no. 5 (September 2006): 495–96.

Table 11.4
Analysis of Gen-X Attributes by Quartile

Managerial Attributes
First quartile
   First quartile of either list: 1 (12.5%)
   Either list: 5 (62.5%)
   Neither list: 2 (25%)

Second quartile
   Second quartile of either list: 1 (10%)

Table 11.4
Analysis of Gen-X Attributes by Quartile (continued)

Managerial Attributes (continued)

Second quartile (continued)
Either list: 5 (50%)
Neither list: 4 (40%)

Third quartile
Third quartile of either list: 1 (12.5%)
Either list: 4 (50%)
Neither list: 3 (37.5%)

Fourth quartile
Fourth quartile of either list: 0
Either list: 4 (66.7%)
Neither list: 2 (33.3%)

Personal Attributes

First quartile
First quartile of either list: 8 (66.7%)
Either list: 3 (25%)
Neither list: 1 (8.3%)

Second quartile
Second quartile of either list: 2 (12.5%)
Either list: 9 (56.3%)
Neither list: 5 (31.3%)

Third quartile
Third quartile of either list: 0
Either list: 3 (33.3%)
Neither list: 6 (66.7%)

Fourth quartile
Fourth quartile of either list: 1 (12.5%)
Either list: 2 (25%)
Neither list: 5 (62.5%)

Areas of Knowledge

First quartile
None

Second quartile
Either list: 1 (100%)

Third quartile
Either list: 1 (100%)

Fourth quartile
Either list: 1 (100%)

Source: Arthur P. Young, Peter Hernon, Ronald R. Powell, "Attributes of Academic Library Leadership: An Exploratory Study of Some Gen-Xers," *The Journal of Academic Librarianship* 32, no. 5 (September 2006): 500.

in the same quartile, and 28 (35%) did not appear in either of the other lists. In other words, 51 (63.8%) of the gen-X attributes matched an attribute occurring somewhere in at least one of the lists of attributes of ARL and non-ARL library directors. There were 28 new, or differently worded, attributes:

Managerial Attributes

- Acknowledge the work and contributions of others;
- Supportive of employee work/life balance;
- Promote the success of others;
- Give regular feedback on job performance (before formal reviews);
- Realistic about Gen-X workplace attitudes; willing to provide professional development support and other "extras" to encourage and retain newer librarians;
- Supportive of librarians' workplace issues (workload, benefits, meeting requirements for promotion and tenure, and union/collective bargaining status);
- Recognize employees'/team members' accomplishments;
- Address the performance issues of subordinates;
- Embrace new technology. Comfortable with incorporating innovative technology to enhance and add to current library services;
- Awareness of library paraprofessionals' workplace issues; supportive of their work, especially in the area of access and circulation; and
- Reward excellent performance with praise, choice of assignments, salary increases, and bonuses.

Personal Attributes

- Capable and dependable;
- Motivated to succeed;
- Inclusive;
- Loyal to staff;
- Set high standards;
- Acknowledge the prerogative to be autocratic under certain circumstances and own those decisions when they are made;
- Able to coach and reassure staff through changes;
- User-oriented—understand the importance of teaching (both staff and patrons);
- Sense of purpose/goal oriented;
- Acknowledge director's role as a coach, teacher, and mentor;
- Willingness to share credit, even on individual efforts;
- Communicate frequently;
- Technology driven (does not like to be left behind when it comes to new technologies);
- Courageous;

- Charismatic;
- Willing to "get your hands dirty;" and
- Discover and explore new, radical, unconventional, and/or even controversial means for achieving desired ends.

No new attributes related to areas of knowledge emerged.

When examining the new attributes as identified by the gen-Xers, it should be noted that the library directors were asked to identify attributes for directors of libraries, whereas those in the gen-X study were given a somewhat broader charge—to identify attributes or traits that *effective* academic library *leaders,* regardless of their professional positions, should possess (Table 11.5). The new attributes in the managerial category largely reflect the perspective of nondirectors. They emphasize the importance of acknowledging and rewarding the work of others, and they address workplace issues. Several of the personal attributes indicate the importance attached to being supportive of staff. They suggest that leadership be strong, but fair. Competency with new technology appears in both categories. These findings reveal that there are significant differences between the attributes most highly valued by a number of academic library directors and by the gen-X librarians. The latter appear to place more value on maintaining a balance between one's job and personal life, and they frequently stress the importance of an employee-oriented workplace that values teamwork, fairness, and loyalty. Work/life balance is a key aspiration for gen-Xers. To date, there is no published library research on the leadership perceptions of the millennial generation.

This review of generational traits, and perception of desired leadership attributes, forms a larger canvas against which certain observations can be made about the future design of organizations, ongoing organizational climates, and the nature of future leadership directions.

Figure 11.2 identifies for both gen-Xers and millennials some key organizational and leadership qualities to consider under the rubrics of recruitment, retention, and leadership. The issues under recruitment and retention are based on trait studies of the cohorts; the leadership column under the gen-X row is derived from high-ranking leadership qualities as specified by gen-Xers; the leadership column under the millennial row is derived from a consideration of the traits of this group. Recruitment will continue to be a top managerial responsibility in all libraries, and the challenges for the creative attraction of high-quality candidates will intensify. Gen-Xers value job freedom above all, and often construct their careers to facilitate portability. For this group, flexible schedules and meaningful assignments are paramount recruiting tools. Those employers that operate within an information-rich context, both technology and personnel, will enter the recruiting sweepstakes with an advantage.

Job security, perhaps somewhat paradoxically, still rates very high as a requirement for gen-Xers, and employers must be able to convey that sense

Table 11.5
Gen-X Leadership Attributes Compared with Attributes for ARL and Non-ARL Library Directors

	ARL	*Non-ARL*
Managerial Attributes—Gen-X		
First quartile		
Successful in securing resources—funds, technology, staffing, etc.	3	1
Build partnerships within the library or across campus	4	
Build working relationships with others	3	2
Acknowledge the work and contributions of others		
Committed to development of staff	2	
Listen and reflect on the needs and desires of the library community	2	
Supportive of employees' work/life balance		
Aware of his/her own limitations and seeks the advice and assistance of others	4	
Second quartile		
Ability to see the impact of decisions, five days, five months, and five years down the road	4	
Follow through on initiatives	4	
Promote the success of others		
Delegate tasks to others	1	2
Deeply committed to their institution and its mission		1
Give regular feedback on job performance (before formal reviews)		
Realistic about gen-X workplace attitudes; willing to provide professional development support and other so-called extras to encourage and retain newer librarians		
Supportive of librarians' workplace issues (workload, benefits, meeting requirements for promotion and tenure, union/collective bargaining status)		
Commitment to involving others and explaining decisions	3	1
Sensitivity to diversity issues	3	3
Third quartile		
Recognize employees'/team members' accomplishments		
Address the performance issues of subordinates		
Leveraging resources	3	
Create and share a vision	1	
Explain decisions and involves others in them	1	1
Politically savvy	1	

Table 11.5
Gen-X Leadership Attributes Compared with Attributes for ARL and Non-ARL Library Directors (continued)

	ARL	Non-ARL
Personal Attributes—Gen-X (continued)		
Third quartile (continued)		
Embrace new technology. Comfortable with incorporating innovative technology to enhance and add to current library services		
Fully aware of the organization/team, the individuals in the organization/on the team, and all functions of the organization/team	4	
Fourth quartile		
Awareness of library paraprofessionals' workplace issues; supportive of their work, especially in the area of access and circulation		
Aware of importance of library as place; takes lead in creating a welcoming environment for college community	1	
Reward excellent performance with praise, choice of assignments, salary increases and bonuses		
Encourage librarians to self-appoint task forces to work on projects rather than make executive decisions about who works on what	1	
Encourage participation in task completion at all levels of the organization	1	2
Willing to sit at reference desk from time to time, even if not a public service team leader or coordinator	1	
Good interpersonal skills	4	1
Honest	2	1
Articulate a vision that inspires others	1	2
A passion for libraries and librarianship	1	
Comfortable with change	1	2
Strong communication skills—verbal and written	2	1
Recognize interpersonal communication essential on all levels; personally approachable; provide paths; communicate directly when appropriate	1	
Capable and dependable		
Strong listening skills	3	2
Trustworthy	1	
Fair	4	
Show initiative	4	
Second quartile		
Flexible	2	2
Motivated to succeed		

161

Table 11.5
**Gen-X Leadership Attributes Compared with Attributes for ARL and
Non-ARL Library Directors (continued)**

	ARL	Non-ARL
Personal Attributes—Gen-X (continued)		
Second quartile (continued)		
Open—will share information and will incorporate good feedback into decision making. (Keep people informed and listen well.)	3	
Candid, trusting of staff	1	
Recognize own bad decisions/willing to admit mistakes	4	
Admit mistakes and learn from them	4	
Deliver on promises	1	
Accessible	1	
Aware of his/her own strengths and plays to them	2	
Confront problems and accepts criticism willingly and thoughtfully	3	
More often than not enthusiastic and positive about others' ideas	3	3
Enthusiastic	3	3
Inclusive		
Loyal to staff		
Set high standards		
Acknowledge the prerogative to be autocratic under certain circumstances and own those decisions when they're made		
Able to coach and reassure staff through changes		
Make effective use of meeting time	4	
User-oriented—understand the importance of teaching (both staff and patrons)		
Sense of purpose/goal oriented		
Unafraid to buck regional or national trends if it is right for their institution	2	
Acknowledge director's role as a coach, teacher and mentor		
Willingness to share credit, even on individual efforts		
Communicate frequently		
Persuasive	2	
Fourth quartile		
Enjoy challenges and learning new skills	2	
Technology driven (does not like to be left behind when it comes to new technologies)		
Sense of humor	4	3
Courageous		

Table 11.5
Gen-X Leadership Attributes Compared with Attributes for ARL and Non-ARL Library Directors (continued)

	ARL	Non-ARL
Personal Attributes—Gen-X (continued)		
Fourth quartile (continued)		
Charismatic		
Willing to get his/her hands dirty		
Consensus building	2	
Discover and explore new, radical, unconventional, and/or even controversial means for achieving desired ends		
Knowledge—Gen-X		
Second quartile		
Understand budgeting and fiscal processes	1	
Understand new technology, how it relates and will impact libraries	2	1
Fourth (and Third) quartile		
Understand marketing concepts	3	2

Note: If a number appears in the ARL or non-ARL column, it signifies that the Gen-X attribute appeared in the corresponding list and the number indicates in which ARL or non-ARL quartile the Gen-X attribute appeared. If the ARL or non-ARL column is blank, then the Gen-X attribute did not appear in the corresponding list.

Source: Arthur P. Young, Peter Hernon, Ronald R. Powell, "Attributes of Academic Library Leadership: An Exploratory Study of Some Gen-Xers," *The Journal of Academic Librarianship* 32, no. 5 (September 2006): 497–99.

of security to attract them to the workplace. The retention of gen-Xers will require that they be accorded the opportunity for new digital roles within library organizations so that they can amass career skills that are beyond just those related to the particular job. Mentoring and peer interaction are valued assets for the gen-Xer and are sometimes decisive in retention decisions. Learner-centered library workplaces will become an increasingly attractive part of the retention picture. For gen-Xers, top management positions are often not a career goal, and this decision must be understood and not become a source of automatic expectation.

The highest ranking leadership attributes, as expressed by the gen-X cohort, are to secure resources, to build partnerships, to promote good interpersonal skills and to exhibit integrity at all levels, and to develop solid budgeting skills. The recruitment of millennials will likewise involve flexible hours, opportunity for telecommuting, and particularly strong orientation programs. Millennials brought up in a totally information-driven environment will know much more about prospective employers and have many more questions to ask than

Figure 11.2
New Generational Climate/Leadership Imperatives

	Recruitment	Retention	Leadership
Gen-X	• Flexible schedules • Meaningful assignments • Information-rich organization	• New digital roles • Career (skills not job predominant) • Mentoring • Learner centered buildings • Senior management not always the goal	• Secure resources • Build partnerships • Honest • Good interpersonal skills • Knowledge of budgeting
Millennial	• Flexible hours • Telecommuting • Strong orientation programs	• Job sharing • Support multitasking • Feedback whenever requested	• Participative • Team building • Experiential workplace

previous generations. Retention for millennials will involve job sharing, support for multitasking, and the availability of feedback whenever it is requested. Millennials like to know where they stand at any given time. It is too early to have a list of leadership attributes directly from this cohort, but the already known behavioral characteristics suggest that leadership from the evolving millennial cohort will emphasize participative organizations, team building, and the availability of experiential activities within the workplace.

REFLECTIONS

There are clearly some different aspirations and leadership attributes that can be identified that separate the generations, sometimes sharply. At the same time, it has always been so, and it is wise to remember that each generation carries forward some traits from the prior one and breaks new ground, sometimes in rebellion, from its predecessor. There is a little something to the "enemy is us" comment when thinking about intergenerational similarities and differences. So, be of good cheer, your great-grandchildren will be perfect!

Neither traits nor attributes can be researched, discussed, or implemented independent of the organizational milieu. Libraries have historically adapted new technologies while maintaining the earlier ones, an ongoing layered environment, if you will, but there is increasing evidence that more cosmic shifts may be in our future. The Internet, Google™, digital repositories, intelligent query systems, and 24/7 access to information may well change both the basic mission and physical workplace of the future. Learner-centered workspaces, approachable and minimal information desk profiles, absence of massive circulation desks, and increasing reliance on digital over print will surely dominate our futures. Library organizational structures, frequently unchanged for decades, will be flattened and streamlined. Staff will be redeployed. I cannot imagine building a library from scratch that would have the same bifurcated divisions and departments as most libraries have today. The new library will require agile management that is comfortable with a participative approach. "Idea teams" will emerge and newer staff will be encouraged and supported to show their stuff. There will be partnerships, both within and without academe, and a commitment to collaborative communication.[13]

Sustainable and successful academic libraries may be best realized through adherence to two core concepts. First, library supervisors at all levels must be receptive, responsive, and nurturing toward the younger staff. If new entrants into the profession do not perceive a welcoming climate, they will not hesitate to move on. Much has been written about partnerships and collaboration between and among libraries, but these relationships must first apply to the library staff and be present throughout the organization.[14]

The second core element for sustainable and successful academic libraries involves the way we perceive the relationship between libraries and users. Libraries are inherently complex organisms, and we have devoted a great deal of time and attention to orienting users toward the library through bibliographic instruction, information literacy programs, and other initiatives. This approach is limited and only partially successful. A more even-handed and lasting approach involves what Robert S. Taylor suggested more than three decades ago, namely to orient the library toward the user rather than the other way around. Orienting the library toward the user places the facility and all that it does through the filters of simplicity, removal of barriers, and timeliness. Forms, signage, homepages, and everything else should be vetted through the conceptual notion of orienting the library toward the user. A simple idea with powerful ramifications![15]

CONCLUSION

This chapter has focused on leadership attributes as perceived by gen-X librarians and compared those perceptions with those of both ARL and non-ARL library directors. Despite some very real differences, it should be emphasized that nearly two-thirds of the leadership attributes as articulated by gen-X librarians may be found on the lists generated by ARL and non-ARL library directors. This amount of overlap clearly suggests that an accommodation of the varying perceptions is certainly possible. The newest generational cohort to appear in the workplace, the millennials, is too young to have received systematic research on its perceptions of leadership traits, but its own behavior patterns are beginning to be documented. This group appears team-oriented, participative, interested in immediate feedback on progress and in opportunities for multiple workplace experiences. Comparison of the gen-X and millennial cohorts does not suggest a divergence that cannot be bridged and molded into a coherent and responsive organization. It is certainly worthwhile to continue the exploration of the various mindsets of the generations in the workplace, but there are transcending issues that should also be addressed.

Responsive and respectful supervisory echelons at all levels will be required for the recruiting and retention of bright and innovative young librarians. The library as an entity needs to reinvent its core values, especially the notion of whether to orient the user toward the library or to orient the library toward the user. The latter option would seem to have a much better chance for success with its emphasis on efficiencies, effectiveness, and encouragement of long-term relationships between the organization and its clients. Libraries have faced challenges for millennia, but the consideration and adoption of these propositions are all the more imperative in view of the momentous questions now facing academic libraries. Our capacity to respond will be truly consequential, as we face the landscape that Jerry Campbell defines for us:

Academic libraries today are complex institutions with multiple roles and a host of related operations and services developed over the years. Yet their fundamental purpose has remained the same: to provide access to trustworthy, authoritative knowledge. Consequently, academic libraries—along with their private and governmental counterparts—have long stood unchallenged throughout the world as the primary providers of recorded knowledge and historical records. Within the context of higher education especially, when users wanted dependable information, they turned to academic libraries. Today, however, the library is relinquishing its place as the top source of inquiry. The reason that the library is losing its supremacy in carrying out this fundamental role is due, of course, to the impact of digital technology. As digital technology has pervaded every aspect of our civilization, it has set forth a revolution not only in how we store and transmit recorded knowledge, historical records, and a host of other kinds of communication but also in how we seek and gain access to these materials.[16]

"Gen Xers also seek balance in their lives now—not when they retire."[17]

NOTES

1. The introductory quotation from Franklin Delano Roosevelt pertains to the prewar generation of the 1930s; however, it distills the cyclical nature of generations throughout history and their different and overlapping characteristics. Franklin D. Roosevelt quoted in Frank Freidel, *Franklin D. Roosevelt: A Rendezvous with Destiny* (Boston: Little, Brown & Co., 1990), 202.

2. Lynne C. Lancaster and David Stillman, *When Generations Collide* (New York: HarperCollins Publishers, 2002), 18–20.

3. Ibid., 20–22.

4. Ibid., 24–27.

5. Bernard Carl Rosen, *Masks and Mirrors: Generation X and the Chameleon Personality* (Westport, CT: Praeger, 2001).

6. Ibid., 37.

7. Diana Schaub, "On the Character of Generation X," *Public Interest* 137 (Fall 1999): 3–24.

8. Charlotte Shelton and Laura Shelton, *The NeXt Revolution: What Gen X Women Want at Work and How Their Boomer Bosses Can Help Them Get It* (Mountain View, CA: Davies-Black Publishing, 2005), 196.

9. Neil Howe and William Strauss, *Millennials Rising: The Next Great Generation* (New York: Random House, 2000): 43–46.

10. Peter Hernon, Ronald Powell, and Arthur Young, "Academic Library Directors: What Do They Do?," *College & Research Libraries* 65 (November 2004): 538–63; *The Next Library Leadership: Attributes of Academic and Public Library Directors.* (Westport, CT: Libraries Unlimited, 2003); "University Library Directors in the Association of Research Libraries: The Next Generation, Part Two," *College & Research Libraries* 63 (January 2002): 73–90; "University Library Directors in the Association of Research Libraries: The Next Generation, Part One," *College & Research Libraries* 62 (March 2001): 116–45.

11. Arthur Young, Ronald Powell, and Peter Hernon, "What Will Gen Next Need to Lead?," *American Libraries* 35 (May 2004): 31–35; "Gen X Bites Back," *American Libraries* 35 (September 2004): 43–45.

12. Arthur P. Young, Peter Hernon, Ronald R. Powell, "Attributes of Academic Library Leadership: An Exploratory Study of Some Gen-Xers," *The Journal of Academic Librarianship* 32, no. 5 (September 2006): 482–502.

13. For an incisive portrait of the "new age" academic library, see Jerry D. Campbell, "The Academic Library as a Virtual Destination," *Educause Review* 41 (January/February 2006): 16–30.

14. A recently conducted survey of Gen-X librarians is replete with responses that underscore this point. See Rachael Singer Gordon, *The Nextgen Librarian's Survival Guide* (Medford, NJ: Information Today, Inc., 2006).

15. Robert S. Taylor, *The Making of a Library: The Academic Library in Transition* (New York: John Wiley, 1972), 92–111.

16. Campbell, "Changing a Cultural Icon," 16.

17. Susan M. Heathfield, "You Guide to Human Resources: Generation X." Available at http://humanresources.about.com/od/glossaryg/g/gen_x.htm (accessed May 17, 2006).

12

DIVERSITY AND LEADERSHIP

Camila A. Alire

"Managerial leadership . . . focuses on the knowledge, abilities, and skills of middle to senior managers in the information profession to help an organization establish and accomplish its purpose and direction."[1]

The library profession should consider questions such as "What role does diversity have on the managerial leadership style?" "Do managerial leaders need to value diversity to lead and/or transform their library organizations successfully?" "How does the managerial leadership style affect minority leaders and followers?" When answering these questions, the focus should be on transforming libraries to accomplish a mission, vision, and goals relevant to the direction that the parent institution is going.

Within this context, this chapter centers on transformational leadership and a managerial leadership model that is a derivative of that style. It is also about how that model might have some bearing on diversity and leadership in our information profession. The model, the Simmons College Managerial Leadership Model (see Figure 17.3), guides a new PhD program in managerial leadership in the information professions.

If transformational leadership could be characterized in several words, it would be about *affecting change*. Webster's dictionary defines transformation as "the process of changing."[2] Effective transformational leaders are those who embrace change because it is necessary to move library organizations forward. They can motivate and/or empower their followers in the organization to work on a shared vision and implement that vision. They can mentor/coach followers to deal successfully with the change process. To do all of this successfully requires strong leadership competencies.

WHAT IS TRANSFORMATIONAL LEADERSHIP?

Much has been written since the early 1990s about transformational leadership, which is about leaders developing the leadership capabilities of an organization. Bernard M. Bass and Ronald E. Riggio distinguish between leader development and leadership development. Leader development, which prepares a person for leadership, focuses on how the leader and the followers develop "shared leadership capacity."[3]

Transformational leadership is also about people's behaviors and values. How we look at leadership and diversity can affect the library's organizational culture. To change that organizational culture where minorities are valued as employees and potential leaders, the library's core values must include accepting and promoting diversity.

If leaders do not value diversity or embrace people who are different from them, then they are not transformational leaders. According to Bass and Riggio, an important component of transformational leadership is the ability to stimulate and inspire followers to achieve extraordinary outcomes; and by doing so, they develop their own leadership capacity. This important component is the key to developing the leadership capabilities of minorities within the library organization. Transformational leadership should be colorblind.

In transformational relationships, the followers' attitudes should mirror those of the leaders. This makes it easier for library leaders to develop their followers' commitment to the libraries and to the leaders. There is a major disconnect when leaders do not value diversity yet they have minorities in their organizations. This disconnect or incongruity within the organization adversely affects the organizational culture.

Transformational leadership is about empowering followers. It is difficult, however, for minorities within organizations to be followers if they are neither valued nor empowered by the leaders. They could become dissatisfied with the organization and most likely have minimal commitment to the library, its values and mission. An organizational culture characterized by dissatisfaction, a lack of commitment, and a sense of value can start to change if transformational leaders empower not only the minority staff but also the entire staff and pay attention to their personal development needs. In essence, the leaders help them to realize their leadership potential.

The whole concept of teamwork is essential in transformational leadership; however, library leaders need to ensure that minority staffs are engaged on these teams. Empowering followers leads to teamwork and organizational effectiveness. When minority staffs are disenfranchised, that could affect their performance, the performance of their teams, and the overall performance of the entire organization.

It is not enough for leaders to empower the minorities in their organizations; they also have to develop them as leaders. It takes leaders who are very self-confident, who truly value diversity, who respond to minorities' needs and concerns, and who put the organizational mission and goals above their personal ones. It is not sufficient for leaders to be committed to diversity; they must turn that commitment into effective action and develop a record of success—nurturing the development of the minority and other staff members.

LIBRARIES AND TRANSFORMATIONAL LEADERSHIP

As Bass and Riggio write, "problems, rapid changes, and uncertainties call for a flexible organization with determined leaders who can inspire employees to participate enthusiastically in team efforts and share organizational goals."[4] The key phrases in this quotation about transformational leadership are *flexible organization* and *leaders who can inspire* others to meet organizational expectations. Based on the author's administrative experience, transformational leadership is the most effective leadership style for anyone working in the library profession. When done correctly, it facilitates successful change and adaptation in library organizations.

Libraries are experiencing rapid change as a result of the technological transformation of society, higher education, and service delivery. Furthermore, the information market is very competitive. Libraries are not the only information provider in town. With Google™, Amazon.com, and other commercial information providers, there is a need to transform libraries into customer-service organizations that make people want to use them. The information-seeking behaviors of current and potential library customers are drastically changing. This is particularly influenced by younger generations such as the millennials/netGens and the gen-Xers, and the change is manifested in information technology. These generations are more technology savvy than many of the library staffs. Libraries must adapt their services and types of resources (print to electronic) to meet those generational needs. They need to modify what they do to fit these new conditions. All of this is dealing with change. A successful, transformed library organization is one that has the "flexibility to forecast, meet new demands and changes as they occur."[5] A library leader with transformational leadership characteristics can lead through these changes.

Another reason for the transformation of libraries is the challenge of library funding. Librarians can no longer sit passively and ignore the role of effective marketing strategies in promoting library resources and services. They need to be actively and aggressively involved in library advocacy. Library marketing and advocacy play a critical role in positioning the library for successful, future funding. Although these concepts have been around the library profession for the past 25 years, it is only more recently that librarians have been more involved in these strategies. The author contends that libraries that have embraced effective marketing and advocacy practices most likely have transformational leaders at the helm.

Our country's changing demographics can affect the transformation of any type of library. The change realized here is not only understanding the diversity of this country but also changing how we operate to meet the information needs of those diverse populations. Transformational leaders understand that strong organizational development requires successful management of a diverse workforce.

It is this last effect—the country's changing demographics—which is the diversity focus of this chapter. Recognizing that diversity encompasses a myriad of areas such as gender, religion, sexual orientation, and creed, the author concentrates on ethnic/racial diversity and managerial leadership.

DIVERSITY AND TRANSFORMATIONAL LEADERSHIP

Transformational leadership must be promoted as the leadership style of choice to librarians of color, because it facilitates successful change and adaptation in library organizations. It is one thing to serve as minority leaders in mostly white organizations; it is another thing to try to effect change in those organizations. And, for minority managerial leaders to be successful, they need to be prepared for that.

In an article about diversity and leadership, Alire basically took the leadership skills and attributes she possesses and uses as a minority leader on a daily basis and categorized them into five categories (Figure 12.1).[6] The majority of the attributes are predominant ones found within transformation leadership, which is all about empowering followers to excel beyond expectations with a common goal of making the library or organization better than it was before.

For the most part, leadership traits and skills of minority leaders are no different than those of white leaders. American Indians, however, are adamant that their leadership styles are not traditionally *Western*. Their styles are indigenous to their culture realizing that there is no Indian way of leading. "The indigenous leadership styles encompass a continuum of styles that defy any simple reduction."[7] Nonetheless, Native American leadership is strongly based on the art of persuasion using factors like the spoken word, tradition, and spirituality to persuade others to do something they had not planned on.

Linda Sue Warner and Keith Grint provide four variables that build the foundation of persuasion leadership: tradition, narration, experience, and observation.

Figure 12.1
Categories of Leadership Qualities, Traits, and Skills

Charismatic

Collaborative

Communicating effectively

Empowering

Enthusiastic

Inspirational

Motivational

Optimistic

Team–building

Visionary

Adaptable

Advocating for change

Ambiguity—tolerant

Creative

Delegating

Flexible

Implementing

Innovative

Risk-taking

Versatile

Personal

Ambitious

Culturally sensitive

Integrity

Respectful

Self-confident

Sense of humor

Sense of self-worth

Organizational

Decision making

Politically savvy

Leadership Development

Mentoring

Network

Role modeling

They also share the four leadership styles from the Tahdooahnippah/Warner model (social scientist, elder, role model, and author) that correspond with their four variables.[8]

When comparing some of the American Indian leadership variables with those from Figure 12.1, there are key similarities:

- Persuasive;
- Culturally sensitive;
- Communicating effectively (particularly through oral tradition);
- Respectful;
- Human interacting;
- Networking;
- Strong sense of values; and
- Charismatic

Probably the biggest difference is that in American Indian culture, leadership is embedded in their strong spirituality and is distributed among the entire community.

Putting leadership differences aside, minority leaders bring an additional trait to their organizations and that is strong cultural competencies. "Emerging leaders need to know how to market their own cultural competencies and their sensitivity to other cultural differences and how to make them strong leadership qualities."[9] Those competencies include ethnic history and culture, language skills, and experience in serving and/or working with minorities. Not to be minimized is the experience of living and working as a minority employee.

Also, minority leaders are key in diversifying their library organizations. They are best at leading efforts to find obstacles to achieving diversity within the organizations, especially within organizational policies and procedures. They have the natural awareness and sensitivity to know what to look for. Part of changing a library for the better and for the future is leading the dynamics of change that diversity would bring.

THE SIMMONS LEADERSHIP MODEL FOR THE INFORMATION PROFESSIONS

As discussed in Chapter 17, the Simmons College, Graduate School of Library and Information Science, Leadership model (the Simmons model) was adapted from the National Center for Healthcare Leadership (NCHL) Leadership Competency model. The center developed a model around the recognition that the healthcare profession is mission- and values-driven and that these professionals must focus on their customers because of their competitive market. The NCHL model was designed to assist in the leadership development of health care providers. The model focuses on competencies such as the art of influencing and consensus- and coalition-building. Most specifically, it incorporates transformational leadership throughout the model.[10]

The Simmons model was adapted to be the focus of its new doctoral program on managerial leadership in the information professions (MLIP; see Chapter 17). This program, unlike traditional PhD programs in library and information studies (LIS), which primarily prepares students as educators, focuses on preparing middle to senior library managers to lead their library organizations in their ever-changing environments. There are three inter-related leadership components in the Simmons model (see Figure 17.3): transformation, accomplishments, and people. The transformation component covers some of the major variables in transformational leadership: vision, implementing a successful change process, and building community support around the new model. The accomplishment component encompasses implementing the vision and accompanying strategies and, in that process, allows library staffs to excel in organizational performance. The third component, people, deals with the library leader providing an organizational environment that values library staff and helps them not only to reach their potential but also to surpass it.

A test of the application and viability of the model is to view it from the perspective of diversity and leadership. The leadership competencies under the transformation component include achievement orientation, problem solving, community orientation, financial skills, information discovery, innovative thinking, and strategic orientation. Some of these competencies are more relevant than others, and they will be the focus.

Achievement orientation can be realized by minority staff only when the leader recognizes and values their racial/ethnic differences. Achievement orientation relates to how minority library staff can assist in the transformation of the organization. The author contends that minority staff can be successful if validated by the library managerial leader and encouraged to be innovative, results oriented, competitive, and constantly improving. This validation should be no different than that of the white staff, but it becomes a major difference if the validation is not provided.

Problem solving is another transformational competency. In most cases, effective problem solving requires teamwork. Again, minority library staff need to be expected and encouraged to be part of the team. This will not happen if the leader's values are incongruent with diversity values. A managerial leader ensures that all staff are engaged in the problem-solving activities that are critical in transforming the library to meet the changing needs of the library customers.

In today's environment, the community orientation competency should be a strength cultivated by minority staff because it includes aligning the library's needs with the values of the community "including its cultural and ethnocentric values and to move managerial leadership forward."[11] A managerial leader would understand the important role that minority staff can play with this competency.

Innovative thinking as a transformational competency allows for the "what if" staff to take risks. This can be very challenging for minority staff if they have grown up in environments (social, educational, professional/vocational) where they are marginalized and rejected repeatedly. Risk-taking is not necessarily a leadership trait that is as prominent among minorities as it is among white staff. Therefore the managerial leader must provide an encouraging atmosphere for minorities to take risks and an atmosphere that does not punish them for innovation setbacks.

Part of the strategic orientation competency includes the ethnocultural implications related to the library organization's success. The managerial leader who values diversity needs to empower minority staff to help keep the pulse on these implications. The managerial leader needs to be self-confident enough to let this happen.

The second component in Figure 17.3 is accomplishments. Communication skills, organizational awareness, LIS domain knowledge, accountability, change leadership, collaboration, initiative, performance measurement, and project management are all competencies that fall under accomplishments. Again, relative to diversity and leadership, some of these competencies are more relevant than others.

Excellent communication skills (written and oral) are necessary for minorities to lead. The challenge for some minorities who are managerial leaders in their own right is the stereotype that accompanies tentative speech patterns and/or strong accents. There is a strong tendency for nonminorities to equate those speech patterns/accents with lack of education and ignorance. This could not be further from the truth. People need to get beyond those stereotypes and accept minorities as the leaders they are. The white managerial leaders set the tone for their staff regarding stereotypes. They need to be aware of this kind of insensitivity and lead by example.

Oral communication skills are solid competencies used by Native American leaders. They develop those skills early on because oral traditions and storytelling are part of their core values. Managerial leaders who understand these values should be able to empower Native American employees. They can encourage them to use those communication skills to help move the organization forward.

Minority managerial leaders need to develop a communications skills package that can make them even more successful. Part of the package includes building strong skills in impression management, which is a transformational leadership competency in which they learn how to use "exemplary behavior, appearance, body language and verbal skills" to their advantage.[12]

Organizational awareness refers to "the ability to understand and learn the power relationships in one's own organization and in other organizations."[13]

The implications for diversity are evident in this competency. Minority managerial leaders in mostly white library organizations need to understand that they must have their eyes and ears opened constantly. Information can be viewed as power, and those who withhold information abuse that power. Consequently, minority managerial leaders, especially in a new environment, cannot wait and assume that people are going tell them who the informal and formal power brokers are. They need to figure it out on their own. By the same token, white managerial leaders need to look for, pay attention to, and work with the minorities who are the influencers internal and external to their library organizations. These minority power brokers should not be dismissed. A managerial leader who values diversity will know to do this.

The LIS domain knowledge competency is definitely affected by diversity. The concept of diversity, implicit or explicit, should be integrated in every element of LIS education and is critical in the curriculum that prepares managerial leaders.

Another accomplishment competency is change leadership. Managerial leaders need to engage and energize all their staff to deal successfully with change. How does change leadership affect diversity? It will not be a problem where all employees are empowered to be involved in the design and implementation of change. It will be a challenge in library environments where minority staff are particularly disenfranchised within the organization. Managerial leaders need to appreciate and incorporate the ethnocultural characteristics minority followers bring to organization.

The collaboration competency is really about team leadership, and diversity should play a big role here. When building teams, managerial leaders need to recognize everyone's individual differences and diverse backgrounds. This also requires them to be culturally sensitive so that minority staff become bona fide members on the appropriate teams. There cannot be successful team leadership when people in the organization are disenfranchised for whatever reasons.

The third area of the figure is the people component. Human resource management as a competency is the key to diversity. Managerial leaders should be aggressive in using techniques that will diversify their library workforces. They should not leave this totally up to their human resources managers; instead they should take the lead in finding and encouraging minorities to apply for positions in their library organizations.

Within their libraries, managerial leaders should also work with minority individuals and help them in their professional development. This should include supporting staff development programs that will allow minority staff to move up within their organizations. The managerial leaders should not wait for the minority employees to approach them. Leaders have a sense of who have great potential for leadership development. Consequently, they should be proactive and encourage/support minority employees to consider leadership development possibilities. More specifically, they should nominate them for leadership development programs.

Ambition is not a trait with which most minorities grow up. In fact, being ambitious is usually frowned upon by minority family members. Managerial leaders who are culturally sensitive will know this and will design a course of action that will encourage minorities to become leaders while still saving face.

Relationship building is another variable in the people component. This is one of the most critical components for minority staff and minority managerial leaders. As long as library staffs are predominantly white, the whole concept of building networks could be a challenge for minorities. That is, it is easier to network with colleagues that look like you and speak like you. When a new minority staff member joins a mostly white library organization, it is easy to allow institutional racism to predominate. "Institutional racism denotes that the values, beliefs, and traditions of one race are so imbedded in the institution that minorities who come in with a different set are not accepted because of those differences."[14] Managerial leaders need to recognize this possibility and guard against it.

Managerial leaders also have to help minorities build their networks. This can be done through introductions, inclusion, and development. Again, the leader must lead by example.

Are minority managerial leaders affected by relationship building? If they are functioning as leaders, they have already developed a strong network. Networking is fundamental to successful transformational leadership. And it is not enough for the minority managerial leaders to deal only with their network; as role models they have to help other minorities to build their networks.

Another factor in the people component is self-confidence. This is directly tied to diversity. One aspect that managerial leaders need to understand about minority followers is that many may have experienced patterns of marginalization and/or rejection. For the leaders, part of dealing successfully with people is assessing their level of self-confidence and then working with them to develop more confidence.

In summary, the three components of Figure 17.3 have competencies that link directly to diversity. It is important, however, to note that these competencies link well with everyone. Nonetheless, managerial leaders need to understand, embrace, and infuse diversity in their library organizations.

CONCLUSION

The responses to the questions posed at the beginning of this chapter relative to managerial leadership and Figure 17.3 are clear. Diversity does have a role in the managerial leadership style. Managerial leaders do need to value diversity to lead and/or transform their library organizations successfully. And the managerial leadership style affects minority leaders and followers in all three components of the Simmons model: transformation, accomplishment, and people.

The components of that model and their competencies as reviewed in this chapter apply to all staff and leaders—be they white or minority. Still, the discussion in this chapter was not about white managerial leaders and/or white followers; it focused on diversity and managerial leadership. One of the criteria for the transition from being managers to being *inspirational managerial leaders* is how skilled they are in valuing and incorporating diversity in all aspects of their library organizations. The Simmons model (Figure 17.3) provides for diversity to be very prevalent in managerial leadership.

"Everyone benefits from diverse leadership and leadership styles. Thus, those in the library profession need to act aggressively to increase the numbers of minority leaders in order to affect dramatic change in libraries, other library organizations, and the respective communities."[15]

NOTES

1. Simmons College, Graduate School of Library and Information Science, *Ph.D. Managerial Leadership in the Information Profession—Program Description,* unpublished (Boston, MA: Simmons College, 2006).

2. Victoria Neufelt, ed., *Webster's New World Dictionary of American English,* 3d ed. (New York: Webster's New World. 1988), 2427.

3. Bernard M. Bass and Ronald E. Riggio, *Transformational Leadership,* 2d ed. (Mahwah, NJ: Lawrence Erlbaum Associates, Publishers, 2006), 143.

4. Ibid., 138.

5. Ibid., 137.

6. Camila A. Alire, "Diversity and Leadership: The Color of Leadership," *Journal of Library Administration*™ 32, no. 2/4 (2001): 95–109.

7. Linda Sue Warner and Keith Grint, "American Indian Ways of Leading and Knowing," *Leadership* 2, no. 2 (May 2006): 225–44.

8. Ibid., 236–37.

9. Alire, "Diversity and Leadership," 102.

10. National Center for Healthcare Leadership, "NCHL Leadership Competency Model, Version 2.0" (Chicago: National Center for Healthcare Leadership, 2004).

11. Ibid., 6.

12. Bass and Riggio, *Transformational Leadership,* 151.

13. National Center for Healthcare Leadership, "NCHL Leadership Competency Model," 7.

14. Alire, "Diversity and Leadership," 99.

15. Ibid., 106.

13

INEFFECTIVE (BAD!) LEADERSHIP

Donald E. Riggs

"Sweet are the uses of adversity."[1]

Library leadership is an interesting phenomenon. Until about 20 years ago, the word *leadership* could not be found in major library indexing tools. Does this mean that there was no leadership in libraries from 1636 (founding of Harvard College) to 1980? Absolutely not! For some unexplainable reasons, the library profession has been slow to embrace leadership. One of the reasons may have been that leadership implies a "business approach" to operating libraries, and such an approach was not endorsed by library administrators. Schools of library and information studies (LIS) are also responsible for the slow acceptance of leadership. Schools of LIS were teaching administration courses, whereas business schools were teaching management courses. Now business schools are teaching leadership courses and LIS schools are teaching management. Only a few LIS schools now offer a course on leadership. In some schools, the management course is taught by a person who has not served as a library manager, or has little interest in the topic. We all need to take the responsibility of preparing future library leaders more seriously.

DIFFERENCES BETWEEN LEADERSHIP AND MANAGEMENT

Unfortunately, the words *leadership* and *management* are thought by some as being the same. This is a serious error. Notwithstanding the interdependence of the two, they are far apart in intent and meaning. Leaders and managers are both required for effective and efficient libraries. It is not uncommon to learn of libraries that are underled and overmanaged, and vice versa. In sum, leadership *and* management are both necessary.

Warren Bennis believes that leaders "master the context" rather than surrender to it. Leaders are people who take charge, energize, and motivate colleagues (followers), and translate dreams into reality. He draws the following distinction between managers and leaders:

- The manager administrates; the leader innovates.
- The manager is a copy; the leader is an original.
- The manager focuses on systems and structure; the leader focuses on people.
- The manager relies on control; the leader inspires trust.
- The manager has a short-range view; the leader has a long-range perspective.
- The manager asks how and when; the leader asks what and why.
- The manager always has an eye on the bottom line; the leader has an eye on the horizon.
- The manager imitates; the leader originates.
- The manager accepts the status quo; the leader challenges it.
- The manager is the classic good soldier; the leader is her/his own person.
- The manager does things right; the leader does the right things.[2]

Managers focus on efficiency, whereas leaders give more attention to effectiveness. Without much difficulty, it is easy to ascertain why the management of libraries is less complex to write about and discuss than leadership. If leadership is discussed in the broadest context, then several intangibles must be addressed; for example, values of the libraries, the library's mission, the trust factor, and staff development and growth.

ESSENTIALS OF EFFECTIVE (GOOD) LEADERSHIP

An effective library leader is normally perceived as someone who makes things happen that managers cannot. An effective leader is more of a transformational leader than a transactional one. As the words imply, a transformational leader is a change agent, finds day-to-day boring and routine, and enjoys inspiring followers to achieve shared goals and objectives. The transactional leader functions best in a strict rules/policies environment. The leader is one step above the manager. Both types of leaders are necessary in an effective library environment. We frequently hear that a library is overled, but undermanaged, and vice versa.

The obvious characteristics of effective leaders include:

- *Vision.* Burt Nanus, a prolific author on visionary leadership, describes a vision as a realistic, attractive future for an organization.[3] A good vision reflects high ideals, clarifies a library's purpose, and encourages commitment, and it reveals the uniqueness of the respective library. Developing and articulating a compelling vision of the library are perhaps the most responsible roles of the effective leader.

- *Planning.* Numerous surveys have been conducted on the importance of planning by presidents/chief executive officers (CEOs). Planning is ranked as one of the top priorities for these executives. Strategic planning has proven to be a successful management technique in libraries. Being the chief strategist for the library, the director should not delegate this responsibility. Unlike traditional planning, the strategies (ways to achieve goals and objectives) are the cat's meow of strategic planning.

- *Human elements.* The effective library leader is first and foremost a humanist. This leader is effective in large part because of the emphasis placed on the human dimension. An effective leader gives high priority to the growth and development of the staff. Decisions affecting the future of the staff are made openly and fairly.

- *Change agent.* The LIS profession and libraries are enjoying unprecedented change. Libraries that are adapting to the rapid rate of change are led by good leaders. They are leaders who know how to introduce change, nurture it, and understand/appreciate the staff's concerns about how their work is modifying.

- *Agenda setter.* Libraries deserve long- and short-term agendas. They should be created with library-wide participation; there should not be any surprises. A good leader must be knowledgeable of all major aspects of the respective library. Whenever budget decision makers inquire about any aspect of the library, the director should be ready with answers and a future-driven agenda.

- *Honesty and the truth.* A few years ago an assistant director of a large academic library asked me how frequently I lied to my staff. My response was "never!" I went on to explain that if I know a piece of sensitive information and was asked a question pertaining to the issue, I would say something to the effect that I could not discuss it. Apparently, this person's director made a practice of lying to the staff. My policy/practice is to be honest, tell the truth, and if I cannot discuss the issue, then explain such to the questioner. Regardless of the leadership style involved, we should seek the truth. Followers respect leaders who are open, honest, and truthful.

- *Courage.* Mark Twain is noted as saying, "do what is right, you will please some and astonish the rest." An effective library leader must accept the blame for failures, assume responsibility for lack of planning/budgeting, and have the courage to call the shots during an unpopular but correct decision.

- *Representing the library.* We have known library leaders who have been effective, but have not represented their respective libraries at state, regional, or national conferences/meetings. Moreover, it is difficult to gauge a leader's effectiveness by attending conferences/meetings. Participation in these conferences, however, serves as a good role model for developing leaders. The leader's visibility at library associations has proven to pay dividends in recruitment and retention of staff. One can contribute to the profession and represent one's library in a variety of ways (e.g., writing).

- *Fundraising.* Fundraising is certainly an art, not a science. Many variables determine the success of a fund/capital campaign. For example, are there several potential wealthy donors in the community, who are the library's competitors, and are the fundraising goals realistic? Depending on the size of the library, a good strategy may be the employment of a full-time development officer. Nevertheless, fundraising is a major responsibility of the effective leader.

The preceding characteristics are not intended to be inclusive, but they lend examples that one normally finds with effective leaders. They also are one or more of the reasons that some leaders are considered ineffective.

LACK OF LITERATURE CITINGS

The phenomenon of not finding much in the literature on library leadership is joined by the fact that little has been written on ineffective leadership. If there is effective leadership, then is there not ineffective leadership? In the perfect world we would find effective leadership, but the human condition does not exist in a "good/effective" leadership environment only.

George R. Goethals, Georgia J. Sorenson, and James MacGregor Burns edited the most comprehensive and inclusive four-volume *Encyclopedia of Leadership*.[4] This definitive work does not discuss ineffective (bad) leadership directly. There are some implications of poor leadership, but the reader has to read "between the lines" to discover them.

WHY ARE WE RELUCTANT TO ADDRESS/ DISCUSS BAD LEADERSHIP?

Bad leadership and ineffective leadership, for the intent of this chapter, are interchangeable. Ineffective may be a more politically correct term. Nevertheless, there is a scarcity on the topic in the literature. Humans tend to favor the positive, rosy aspects of most endeavors. Bad leadership could be perceived as being closely associated with dishonestly and the criminal element. Thus we tend to depict others in a more positive light. This is not to say that the media go easy on criminals and other wrongdoers. Bad leadership encompasses immorality, unethical behavior, and incompetence.

LEADERSHIP GROUPS

Leadership, including that of libraries, is a complex topic including many intangibles. Intellectually, we would do a major disservice to the subject if the focus is on the good elements only. Barbara Kellerman has placed bad leadership in the following seven groups:

1. Incompetent
2. Rigid
3. Intemperate
4. Callous
5. Corrupt
6. Insular
7. Evil[5]

When one thinks of the bad leaders with whom they have worked or known, the leaders will likely fall into one of the preceding groups. The groups are independent of one another.

DYSFUNCTIONAL PATTERNS

Dysfunctional patterns in leadership contribute to bad leadership; examples include:

- Conflict avoidance. Library leaders who want to be popular will avoid making decisions or taking action on issues that will tarnish their image.
- Mistreatment of staff/subordinates. Library leaders who do not know how to use power correctly will abuse subordinates by assigning them unpleasant tasks, not giving them credit for their work, and throwing road blocks in the staff's growth and development.
- Micromanagement. Some library leaders cannot delegate tasks and are perceived as not trusting staff. These types of leaders are certainly misplaced. They should have been detected early their career as transactional managers, and are not effective leaders.
- Inaccessibility. The expression, "our library leader has an open door policy," is generally well received. Library staff expect access to their leaders. If one does not try to be available to the staff, then that leader will have difficulty in establishing "buy in" to their vision and mission. A library director or department head should meet regularly and meet often with staff.
- Noncommunicator. Communication is the "language" of leadership. An effective library functions with open communication. The success of the programs and services offered by a library depends on such communication, on the other hand, poor communication can contribute to bad leadership.
- Passive-aggressive. Library leaders who are perceived as passive-aggressive are headed for a disaster. They want to be loved by all, but do little to earn this respect. Being nice while talking with another, then later unfairly demeaning this person shows poor judgment by the leader.
- Irrational behavior. A leader whose behavior is unbecoming should be removed as soon as possible. Leaders who are irrational are a "poison" in the library construct. Such behavior is too serious to be forgiven or overlooked. Good employees will leave their positions for another position at a library led by rational leaders.

PICKING A NEW LIBRARY LEADER

Much of the responsibility of choosing a new library leader (including directors, department heads, and coordinators) can be tracked back to the work/recommendations of search committees. Based on serving on numerous search committees, being interviewed by search committees, and assisting executive search firms, I genuinely conclude that the search process is undertaken as a serious endeavor by all involved.

Based on the complexities of the human dimensions of search committees, it is remarkable how well these committees do in getting the right person for the right job. All search committees are not perfect, and some of their imperfections are given here. These imperfections contribute to ineffective (bad) leadership.

Search committees normally have members from areas served by the library (e.g., community, faculty, and students); the members prepare a job announcement, update the job description, and do other tasks expected of them. The committee discusses what the library needs in a new leader. It meets and reviews the applications. Expectations of the committee/home institution and qualifications of the candidates are reviewed. Here is when the potential problem of getting a bad leader begins. Individual search committee members begin thinking about their respective areas and the candidates' potential impact on the area (e.g., department of history). Too frequently the new library leader is selected on the basis of subjective data. The committee and home institution are known, notwithstanding the work/investigations of candidates' past performance records, for recommending the next leader based on a short-term view. A candidate, for example, could be selected on the basis of one's successful experience in constructing new library buildings. What about the other qualifications and leadership skills deemed necessary for success?

Libraries are increasing the use of search firms to assist them in selecting leaders. Why is this the case? The search firm has more time to do a systematic search, it will aggressively seek out and pursue leaders who have proven themselves in other libraries, and it will not be bias. Moreover, search firms bring experience to the search endeavor; they are not learning on the job.

SITUATIONAL LEADERSHIP

It is not uncommon to think that a leader in one environment will be successful in another environment. In some cases, nothing could be further from the truth. A successful university football coach will not necessarily be a successful coach of a National Football League (NFL) team. Some coaches become highly successful in the NFL, and others fail. One should not assume that an effective leader in one library would transfer that success to another library. This is not true. The situation determines, along with the characteristics of the library leader, whether the new leader will be effective or ineffective.

FOLLOWERS

Can one be a leader without followers? In most instances followership is part of the leadership equation. Bad followers reflect bad leaders. If a library leader is incompetent, some of the followers may be part of the problem.

Followers can serve a fundamental role in improving the image of the leader from bad to better. If the leader is of a paranoid disposition, then the followers must not be drawn into the trap of viewing colleagues in a pervasive, unwarranted suspicion of others. Bad leaders have a tendency of wanting to *control* all library operations, services, and programs; this type of leadership disposition plays havoc with the follower's daily work. Librarians will likely leave this type of environment that does not encourage trust and confidence. Ineffective leaders tend to blame others when goals and objectives are not met. Followers become the scapegoats of unfinished projects, missed deadlines, and other endeavors normally overseen and completed by an effective leader. Empowerment is not encouraged by bad leaders.

WHAT CAN BAD LEADERS DO TO BECOME BETTER LEADERS?

A bad library leader may never become a good leader. Some people are not destined to become good leaders; this observation is based on the hard reality of human shortcomings. To paraphrase Kellerman's self-help for leaders, bad library leaders may find some benefit/improvement by:

- Limiting their tenure. If a library leader finds oneself in a "fail-fail" situation, one should leave the leadership position. Such action is normally better for all parties concerned.
- Sharing power. Ineffective library leaders have to learn how to delegate responsibility, authority, and power. It is unhealthy for a library to leave all power in the hands of the director only.
- Getting and staying real. Losing touch with reality is a common complaint leveled at bad leaders. Dreams and vision must be based on the ability to achieve them.
- Compensating for your weaknesses. Each leader has weaknesses; these soft spots should be acknowledged and strategies put into place to compensate for them.
- Staying balanced. Library leaders should learn how to live the balanced life. Workaholics tend to be one dimensional; they should enjoy their family, a hobby, or participation in service organization.
- Remembering the mission. The mission of the library should be reviewed regularly and modified when necessary. It is a cornerstone to the library's strategic plan.[6]

CONCLUSION

The spectrum of leadership includes the good and bad. Little on bad leadership can be found in the literature; a possible rationale for this omission is based on the "immaturity" of the study of leadership. It is predicted that ineffective (bad) leadership will become part of our repertoire during the next few years. An intellectual approach to library leadership requires an understanding of both effective and ineffective leaders. We are witnessing some approaches that will strengthen library leadership (e.g., institutes and senior fellow programs), and more emphasis on development of library leaders is yet to come. Making ineffective library leaders more effective will improve current and future services of libraries.

"I'd follow that person—anywhere—blindfolded!"[7]

NOTES

1. William Shakespeare. Available at brainyquote.com, http://www.brainyquote.com/quotes/quotes/w/williamsha155070/html (accessed September 23, 2006).

2. Warren Bennis, *On Becoming a Leader* (Reading, MA: Addison-Wesley, 1989), 34.

3. Burt Nanus, *Visionary Leadership: Creating a Compelling Sense of Direction for Your Organization* (San Francisco: Jossey-Bass Publishers, 1992).

4. George R. Goethals, Georgia J. Sorenson, and James MacGregor Burns, eds., *Encyclopedia of Leadership,* four volumes (Thousand Oaks, CA: Sage, 2004).

5. Barbara Kellerman, *Bad Leadership: What It Is, How It Happens, Why It Happens* (Boston, MA: Harvard Business School, 2004).

6. Ibid., 233–34.

7. Author unknown.

14

ASSESSING LEADERSHIP SKILLS

Nancy Rossiter

"The growth and development of people are the highest calling of leadership."[1]

Because leaders have an enormous impact on organizations and the realization of their mission, vision, and goals, many organizations have created programs to enhance and nurture the performance of their leader. As these programs are costly in terms of time and money, the question arises, "Are they really helping to develop the leadership skills and abilities that those organizations need?" The predominant development models used for leadership evaluation include skills-based, competency-based, maturity-based, and Situational Leadership II. This chapter explains these models and discusses their practical implications.

DEVELOPMENT OF LEADERSHIP SKILLS

Ellen Van Velsor, director of the Center for Creative Leadership, headquartered in Greensboro, North Carolina, considers assessment, challenge, and support as critical components in developing leadership skills. Leadership assessment is information, presented formally or informally, that evaluates leaders. It reveals strengths, development needs, and how effective leaders are. Assessments at the Center for Creative Leadership include personality inventories and 360-degree leadership assessments (see Chapter 15 for more information), as well as feedback from simulations, program staff, and fellow participants.[2]

To accelerate leadership development, leaders should seek appropriate challenges and stretch beyond their current capabilities. Challenge calls for new skills and perspectives not currently available to leaders. These elements create an imbalance and question the established ways of thinking and acting. Challenge can come from a new promotion, a merger, or restructuring.[3]

Support means creating experiences that enhance self-confidence and provides reassurance about strengths, skills, and ways of thinking and acting. Building support in the face of challenges is a key skill in developing competence and confidence. This is often accomplished through coaching and mentoring. According to Van Velsor, balancing challenges with assessment and support allows leaders to contribute to their own growth while remaining creatively engaged with work.[4] This concept is similar to Richard Boyatzis and Annie McKee's concept of "resonant leadership," where leaders manage their own emotions and others in ways that drive the success of the organization.[5]

SKILLS-BASED ASSESSMENT MODEL

As leaders develop, they acquire skills that make them more effective. Research on leadership skills development has progressed in two distinct paths. One of them focuses on the structure of skill acquisition as certain tasks are practiced, and the other concentrates on the processes involved as people acquire knowledge and skills in different domains of experience. Studies that focus on skill acquisition seek to understand how performance improves over time as a function of practice.[6]

The research concentrating on processes focuses on how people acquire expertise in different educational settings. These studies indicate that leadership expertise develops slowly for more than a decade. Expert leaders can draw on different concepts and styles, organize information on the basis of identifying principles, and are capable of applying concepts in a way that is flexible and contingent on the situation.[7]

Both research paths have different goals; however, when taken together, they reveal a more complete picture of the skill acquisition process. First, people must acquire the basic concepts, learn what is expected, and apply them in specific situations. Then they must apply the concepts in more complex problem-solving situations and in different settings. Finally, the knowledge drawn from multiple sources must be rapidly integrated, allowing leaders to address rapidly unfolding, complex problems.[8]

Michael Mumford, Michelle Marks, Mary Shane Connelly, Stephen Zaccaro, and Roni Reiter-Palmon assessed differences in leadership skills across six grade levels of officers in the U.S. Army. They found that certain skills and experiences were critical at certain phases of the leaders' careers. These findings led the

Table 14.1
Measures of Leadership Skills

Measure	Targeted Constructs	Description	Scoring Procedures
Complex problem solving (cued)	Problem construction, information encoding, category search, best fitting categories, combination and reorganization, idea evaluation, solution implementation, monitoring.	Presents a complex ill-defined leadership problem. Probes questions and cues used to elicit responses on different creative problem-solving skills.	Three judges rate responses to appropriate questions to access effective application of the problem-solving skills. Scores obtained for each skill by averaging judges' ratings.
Solution construction	Time frame of goals, attention to restrictions, self-orientated goals, organizational goals.	Presents two novel ill-defined leadership problems. Respondents asked to indicate most important problem to address, key information needed to resolve the problem, and other problems that would need to be considered.	Three judges read through the responses to all questions and rate responses for key solution characteristics. Scores obtained by averaging ratings across the two problems.
Social judgment	Self-reflectivity, self-objectivity, judgment under uncertainty, solution fit, systems perception, systems commitment.	Presents two scenarios of organizational problems. Respondents asked to indicate why situation occurred, central mistake made by the person in situation, and what respondent would have done in the situation.	Three judges read through responses to all questions and rate on social judgment dimensions for each problem. Scores obtained by averaging the judges' ratings across the two problems.

Table 14.1
Measures of Leadership Skills (continued)

Measure	Targeted Constructs	Description	Scoring Procedures
Creative thinking	Realism of consequences, complexity time span, positive and negative consequences, principle-based positive outcome sensitivity, negative outcome sensitivity.	Presents a string of "what if" events. Respondents asked to list the likely consequences or the outcomes of this event.	Three judges read through responses to each "what if" event and rate each on leader-based creative thinking characteristics. Scores obtained by averaging judges' responses across all problems.
Leadership expertise	Principle-based knowledge structures, organization, coherence of knowledge categories, consistence with existing leader activity taxonomy, and number of categories.	Respondents presented wit a list of leadership tasks. After reading though tasks, they are asked to create a set of categories and then assign tasks to those categories.	Number of categories is counted. Categories and task assignments reviewed by three judges who rate on all constructs. Scores obtained by averaging judges' ratings.

Source: Michael Mumford, Michelle Marks, Mary Shane Connelly, Stephen Zaccaro, and Roni Reiter-Palmon, "Development of Leadership Skills: Experience and Timing," *Leadership Quarterly* 11 (2000): 87–114.

researchers to develop an organization-based model of skill development. They also found that it may take leaders up to 20 years to acquire all the skills needed to solve novel, poorly defined organizational problems. Also, their development is progressive, moving from simple knowledge involving social skills, to complex, integrated solutions.[9]

Table 14.1 describes measures by which Mumford et al. assesses leadership performance. Each measure presented is composed of one or more tasks designed to elicit certain skills. These measures were found to assess leadership skills effectively.

The measure *cued complex problem solving* involves eight problem-solving processing skills associated with high-level creative problem solving. These skills are problem constriction, information encoding, category search, category specification, category combination and reorganization, idea evaluation, solution implementation, and solution monitoring. In a predetermined exercise, the participants read a scenario and are asked questions intended to guide their responses and address the eight skill areas. The measure *uncued problem solving* likewise involves a scenario for evaluation, but it is less structured and assesses problem-solving skills; however, no cues are provided for the participant's approach to the problem. Solution construction skills target skills and expertise in structuring complex, ill-defined problems while considering constraints and the broader context of the problem. Examples include considering resource capacities, organizational versus personal goals, and the degree of risk allowed by the problem approach. Social judgment skills reflect an understanding of people and social systems. Participants again were evaluated on their responses to complex organizational scenarios.[10]

COMPETENCY-BASED ASSESSMENT MODELS

Competency models of leadership assessment determine and quantify skill sets necessary for accomplishing specific tasks by providing feedback from multiple raters. The competencies are agreed upon skills that help organizations identify top performers. According to James Armitage, Nancy Brooks, Matthew Carlen, and Scott Schultz, these models and their associated assessments provide a limited view of what is required for effective leadership. Competency models measure only the gaps in skills and attributes. After obtaining this information, organizations try to bridge the gap between their leader's areas of incompetence identified by the assessments and the best practices of leadership. To do this, organizations send their leaders to training programs and may follow up such programs with coaching, mentoring, or both. Even with the best training programs, leader effectiveness can be severely undermined if the organization focuses only on individual skill gaps; the context of the organization should also be taken into account. Other factors that contribute to leader effectiveness include organizational culture, industry, stage of growth, and process maturity. One environment in which an individual achieves a high score on a 360-degree feedback assessment does not guarantee the same high score for the same individual when he or she is assessed in a different environment. For example, the mix of skills and attributes needed to lead an entrepreneurial venture successfully is very different form those needed to run a large, bureaucratic, multinational organization. Hence, focusing solely on individual does not give a clear picture of the leadership competencies necessary within the organizational context.[11]

Figure 14.1 illustrates how the competency model focuses on the individual after a 360-degree assessment and development process has been implemented. It shows how individuals are selected for training once skill gaps are detected, going to the training "of the day," measuring the improvement (usually through self-reports) and finally performing a 360-degree feedback evaluation, where skill gaps may again be found, perpetuating the circle.

Figure 14.1
Competency Model Decision Cycle

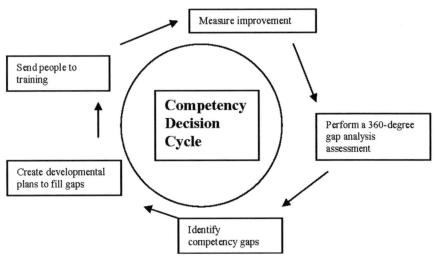

Source: James W. Armitage, Nancy Brooks, Matthew Carlen, and Scott Schulz, "Remodeling Leadership," *Performance Improvement* 45 (2006): 40, www.ispi.org. Reprinted with permission.

MATURITY-BASED ASSESSMENT MODELS

Implicit in the name "maturity model" is the notion that the organization has gone through some sort of transformation from an initial state to a more advanced state acquired through active learning by way of meaningful experience on the job.[12] Some of these leadership development experiences are the result of job assignments, hardship or adversity, and personal relationships. Job assignments are a major influence on leadership development as leaders cope with new tasks and unfamiliar situations. Hardship experiences, such as being fired, making business mistakes, or being responsible for downsizing, also play a role in leadership development. Personal relationships have also been found to influence leader's development. This influence comes in the form of a relationship with a boss who acted as a role model and influenced their leadership development. Another influence is organizational context, which links leadership development to compensation plans and rewards. Further, the extent to which the organization supports leadership development impacts future leaders.[13]

Through the process of leadership development, a number of transformations have occurred along the way to maturation. Maturity models involve more than just competent individual leaders; it requires leadership maturity

Figure 14.2
Leadership Maturity Model

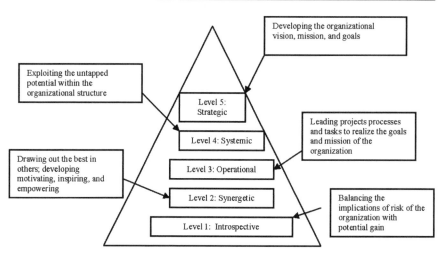

Source: James W. Armitage, Nancy Brooks, Matthew Carlen, and Scott Schulz, "Remodeling Leadership," *Performance Improvement* 45 (2006): 40, www.ispi.org. Reprinted with permission.

at both the individual and organizational levels. *Leadership maturity* implies effective performance of the organization's leaders and the leadership system. Organizations enable their leaders to produce desired results by providing resources and training. For this to occur, organizations themselves need to achieve mature organizational leadership; competency models, however, are not designed to address this.[14]

Armitage et al. proposed the Leadership Maturity model (LMM), which is superior to competency models in that it goes beyond looking at the abilities and attributes of the leader. It addresses the capacity and capability of the organization, the context in which the leader leads, and the organizational infrastructure that either supports or inhibits performance. The LMM takes a systemic view of the individual and the organizational variables that determine effectiveness, growth, and maturation as they relate to leadership. The leader is only one part of the organization's leadership system.[15]

Figure 14.2, which illustrates the LMM, shows that leadership consists of internalizing and practicing certain principles. There is an inherit progression in mastering the principles that is often overlooked: supporting principles must be mastered before other principles can be applied effectively. These supporting principles function as the base of the pyramid, and they allow for stability of the apex. The order and interdependence of these principles are the foundation of the five-level LMM.[16]

SITUATIONAL LEADERSHIP II ASSESSMENT MODEL

The Situational Leadership II Assessment, developed by Kenneth Blanchard, measures and provides feedback on four leadership styles: directing, coaching, supporting, and delegating. It also measures the leader's skills on setting goals, observing and monitoring team performance, and providing team members with positive and negative feedback on results.[17] (Chapter 10 elaborates on team leadership.)

Leaders using a directing style provide specific direction about what, how, and when things need to be done. The feedback from this part of the assessment tells leaders how well goals are set as team members learn a new task, as well as if they are monitoring teams closely enough when they are learning a new task. Low scores indicate that leaders should focus on developing team members' confidence, competence, and motivation.

The coaching style of leadership provides direction and support. The feedback on this area of the assessment explains the extent to which the leader's team perceives that the choice of leadership style matches their needs for direction and support. Leaders who score low in this area should make more of an effort to praise the progress of the team.

Leaders who use the supporting style provide support and encouragement to those who need support and encouragement. Feedback on this area of the assessment shows the extent to which team members perceive the leader as matching their choice of leadership to their need for support. This area of the assessment asks leaders to think of a specific example of when they provided support when it was needed, and what the outcome was. Then those leaders are asked what they could have done differently to improve the outcome. Leaders scoring low on this area of the assessment may want to ask more questions of their followers and encourage team members to solve their own problems.

The delegating style of leadership allows team members to manage their own performance. Feedback on this area of the assessment reveals the extent to which team members perceive that the leaders match the choice of a leadership style to their need for autonomy. Leaders scoring low on this area of the assessment should ask their team members to inform them about resources they need to excel and then secure those resources for them.[18]

The Situational Leadership II Skills Assessment also assesses the skills of goal setting as well as observing and monitoring feedback. Blanchard explains that goals should follow the SMART criteria; they are specific, measurable, attainable, relevant, and trackable. Feedback on this area of the assessment shows the extent to which team members perceive that the leader effectively uses the leadership skill of goal setting. The observing and monitoring skills analyze how frequently the leader observes and monitors team performance. Feedback in this area shows the extent to which team members perceive that they are appropriately monitored and observed. The feedback assesses the extent to which the leader lets people know directly or indirectly how well they are achieving organizational goals.[19]

According to Blanchard, the major benefit of this assessment is that it makes leaders read through an objective analysis of behaviors and take time to reflect on the consequences of their leadership style and management skills on the people whom they manage.[20]

LIBRARY LEADERSHIP DEVELOPMENT ASSESSMENT

The library profession has numerous management and leadership development programs. In one study of library leadership programs, Florence Mason and Louella Wetherbee examined 31 library leadership programs that focused on leadership development. They found that, since 1966, there has been an increased emphasis on leadership in librarianship and that more leadership programs have emerged. (These programs are briefly described in Chapter 16.) Mason and Wetherbee found that, despite the growing number of leadership development programs, very little research—independent assessment—has been published on the programs and their success. They note that the influence of the training relies on participant retrospective accounts and there is a need for a more thorough examination of the impact of the training programs. They state the "self-reports do little to address the question of whether the participants actually learned anything new, whether the training was applied in the workplace and whether that knowledge and these skills improved the individual or improved the workplace performance."[21] Most programs use evaluation forms that the participants fill out at the conclusion of the program, whereas longitudinal studies involving an experimental design would illuminate the results of the programs more clearly.[22]

Mason and Wetherbee note several problems with the assessment of library leadership programs. First, there are few published evaluations of training programs, and the results that are published rely heavily on self-reports. Second, there is a lack of a clearly agreed upon definition of what constitutes "leadership skills" in libraries. Third, even where longitudinal studies have been conducted, problems remain with the interpretation of the data; for example, in one study it was unclear if the control and the experimental groups were really independent groups that could be compared with each other. Finally, the experimental design of using a control group may not be useful for detecting differences in the groups as a result of leadership training.[23]

Mason and Wetherbee also examined programs hosted by library schools. They noted problems with library school curricula in the sense that the package of skills required for leadership skills in librarians and staff is not a "one-size-fits-all" list; there is considerable variety in library leadership competencies. The library profession does not have an accepted set of core leadership competencies for the profession and its subsets (e.g., academic and public librarianship). Because of this lack of agreed upon competencies, training programs may be worthwhile and beneficial to participants, but there is no way to determine of the most effective skills are being taught.[24] Another complication is that most leadership development programs are short term and do not seek to development leadership abilities, skills, and understanding of theory over time.

IMPLICATIONS

The models discussed in this chapter serve as a basis for extending current theories and have practical applications. Leader behavior inevitably varies from one situation to another. At times, the behavior changes significantly. Therefore it is difficult to distinguish the kinds of assessments likely to be useful across a wide range of situations. This problem is not unique to leadership; it is one that educators who create assessment grapple with as they develop development programs and evaluate them on a formative basis.[25]

Typically, the research on leader assessment has focused on various skills that underlie leadership performance. The research examines the leader's decision making, intelligence, and communication abilities and then uses the information gathered to create assessment center exercises. An assessment center defines a process of using multiple assessment techniques (e.g., situational exercises and job simulations) to evaluate library workers.[26] Assessment centers, however, have come under much criticism in recent years because of the limited behavioral applications and expense. Research conducted by Mumford et al. has found that structured, focused exercises produce an effective prediction of leader abilities and that these exercises provide a potentially useful new approach to leader assessment.[27]

One of the problems noted by Mumford et al. is that the current assessment centers focus on observable performance, paying little attention to some key capabilities, principle-based knowledge, mental models, and identification of consequences, which are more difficult to ascertain with the conventional observation techniques. Thus exercises should be developed to provide viable assessments of these hidden capabilities that could offer some insight into effective organizational leadership.[28]

Mumford et al. also stated that training programs should be devised using case studies or other instructional techniques to look at alternative definitions of problems or multiple consequences of an event.[29] Leadership programs based on this type of pedagogy could, over time, develop key leadership capabilities.

CONCLUSION

Leadership skill assessment is a difficult process. Challenges with assessment and evaluation of leadership programs in the library profession come about as a result of the lack of a common vocabulary in what constitutes leadership skills and the lack of agreed upon leadership competencies. When leaders in a library and the profession can agree on what these skills are, assessment of programs will become much easier.

When choosing or developing an assessment model, it is also necessary to consider the organizational context. This can be a tricky process, as different skills are required in different library settings. Furthermore, library leaders should take a long-term approach to their training and development programs, as some models have found that it takes up to 20 years to acquire the skills needed to be an effective leader.

"The task of the leader is to get his people from where they are to where they have not been."[30]

NOTES

1. "Harvey S. Firestone Quotes." Thinkexist.com. Available at http://en.thinkexist.com/quotes/harvey_s._firestone/ (accessed April 18, 2006).

2. Ellen Van Velsor, "Assess, Challenge, and Support," *Executive Excellence* 17, no. 6 (June 2000): 19.

3. Ibid.

4. Ibid.

5. Richard Boyatzis and Annie McKee, *Resonant Leadership: Renewing Yourself and Connecting with Others through Mindfulness, Hope, and Compassion* (Boston: Harvard Business School Press, 2005).

6. Michael Mumford, Michelle Marks, Mary Shane Connelly, Stephen Zaccaro, and Roni Reiter-Palmon, "Development of Leadership Skills: Experience and Timing," *Leadership Quarterly* 11 (2000): 87–114.

7. Ibid.

8. Ibid.

9. Ibid.

10. Stephen Zaccaro, Michael Mumford, Mary Shane Connelly, Michelle Marks, and Janelle Gilbert, "Assessment of Leader Problem-Solving Capabilities," *Leadership Quarterly* 11 (2000): 37–64.

11. James W. Armitage, Nancy Brooks, Matthew Carlen, and Scott Schulz, "Remodeling Leadership," *Performance Improvement* 45, no. 2 (February 2006): 40.

12. Ibid.

13. Florence Mason and Louella Wetherbee, "Learning to Lead: An Analysis of Current Training Programs for Library Leadership," *Library Trends* 53 (Summer 2004): 187–217.

14. Armitage et al. "Remodeling Leadership," 40.

15. Ibid.

16. Ibid.

17. Kenneth Blanchard, "Assessing Your Leadership Skills," *Executive Excellence* 7, no. 5 (May 1990): 21.

18. Ibid.

19. Ibid.

20. Ibid.

21. Mason and Wetherbee, "Learning to Lead: An Analysis of Current Training Programs for Library Leadership."

22. Ibid.

23. Ibid.

24. Ibid.

25. Mumford, Marks, Connelly, Zaccaro, and Reiter-Palmon, "Development of Leadership Skills."

26. Mason and Wetherbee, "Learning to Lead: An Analysis of Current Training Programs for Library Leadership."

27. Mumford, Marks, Connelly, Zaccaro, and Reiter-Palmon, "Development of Leadership Skills."

28. Ibid.

29. Ibid.

30. Henry Kissinger. Available at Big Dog's Leadership Quotes, http://www.nwlink.com/~donclark/leader/leadqot.html (accessed September 23, 2006).

15

———

360-ASSESSMENT

Peter Hernon and Nancy Rossiter

"Feedback is a part of our lives, and we receive it frequently from friends, family, co-workers, strangers on elevators, or drivers passing us on the highway."[1]

As Charles B. Lowry, dean of libraries at the University of Maryland, pointed out, for a few years in the mid-1990s, some libraries adopted a 360-assessment but called it "'upward evaluation.' However, there's no data on the experience." Today, "peer evaluations of a library faculty (including the managers) and a five-year review of all managers (university mandated for me and my direct reports) have taken place."[2] Given that directors tend to go through such periodic reviews, this chapter discusses 360-assessment as one method to review the experiences, knowledge, and development of those seeking senior management positions (or those already in such positions). The instrument highlighted in this chapter might become part of either formal evaluation or professional development.

Feedback might come from the library director, others on the senior management team, others throughout the organization or institution, editors of peer-reviewed journals, colleagues on professional committees, and others. Many organizations other than libraries have conducted 360-assessments, which is also known as multirater, multilevel, or full-circle feedback, to provide senior executives with constructive feedback on their professional growth and self-awareness for either development or performance appraisal. Assessments for both functions, however, should be kept separate. This chapter focuses mainly on assessing personal and professional development.[3]

The principal strengths of 360-assessments are that the results include the multiple perspectives and the alignment of self-perception with the perceptions of such others as co-workers, managers in higher positions, and perhaps the public. The purpose is to identify gaps in those perceptions and what needs to be done to align performance goals with the perceptions of others. In the process, those subject to such assessment gain a realistic understanding of themselves and how others perceive them, and, it is expected, they continue their professional growth. Because those evaluated must be able to apply the feedback to specific contexts, what they learn from the assessment must be contextual and capable of application to specific situations.

In a 360-assessment, the process of evidence gathering might be either formal or informal. The evidence might be gathered anonymously from 3 to 15 individuals who are in a position to observe someone's behavior, skills, and actions. Developmental feedback occurs in an environment in which those providing their perceptions feel comfortable offering sensitive commentaries, and the recipient realizes that the results will not be used for performance appraisal. The individual also must be receptive to benefiting from the comments. Feedback for performance appraisals lets the individual know if he or she is reaching expected levels of job performance. The feedback takes the form of a discussion between the employee and the manager, and that discussion could contribute to decisions such as those regarding promotion or a salary increase.

For self-improvement, the first step is to seek a self-assessment (completion of the 360-assessment survey by the individual(s) under review). The next step is to involve others in providing evidence, and the third step is to compare the two results. Finally, a decision is made about the areas of self-improvement and strategies are offered. The library director must invest in helping those assessed to learn and mature.

If the intent is to conduct performance appraisal, there is a need for a baseline of evidence against which to compare the subsequent feedback. Some three to six months before the formal appraisal, a 360-assessment might be conducted and, in cooperation with the library director, each evaluated individual might produce a developmental plan. Once the actual performance appraisal is conducted, the results can be compared against that plan. Then, say, a year later, the 360-assessment might be replicated and any changes noted. The central question is, "How have the individual's skills and behaviors improved over time?" If there was no or insignificant improvement, why is this so?

STANDARDIZED INSTRUMENTS AND SOFTWARE

Jane L. Wilson points out that:

The important question to ask before selecting an instrument for use is what is the purpose of the feedback? Is the instrument I am using appropriate for the setting? For what purpose was the instrument designed? Is it for developmental feedback or performance appraisal? Will it give me the feedback I need?[4]

Ellen Van Velsor, Jean B. Leslie, and John W. Fleenor, who expand on these questions, present a step-by-step process "to evaluate any 360-degree-feedback instrument intended for management or leadership development."[5]

A search of the Internet (using search engines such as Google) points to numerous software packages for conducting and analyzing 360-assessments. Although the work by Velsor, Leslie, and Fleenor was published in 1997, their discussion of issues such as measurement scales, reliability, internal validity (whether the instrument measures what it claims to measure), and face validity (whether the instrument looks appropriate for your managers) is relevant.[6]

FREQUENCY OF EXAMINING MANAGERS

Robert E. Kaplan and Charles J. Palus insert an important reminder when considering the frequency of such assessment: Do the staff subject to review and the reviewers have experience in completing a 360-assessment?[7] For this reason, they recommend gathering feedback annually. Realistically, it is probably too time-consuming for libraries to invest in intensive data collection, review, and synthesize annually. The review process might be done once every three to five years or if the staff subject to evaluation requests a substantial internal position elevation (e.g., from assistant to associate or deputy university librarian). For anyone receiving a 360-assessment for the first time, there might be a simulation of the experience or some other detailed introduction to the process.

Still, 360-assessments are not one-time events. Even if they are fully implemented every several years, there might be annual data collection in one or two areas. The organization must link such assessments to its strategic plan and overall goals and integrate the evidence collected with other (objectively) gathered data.

DEVELOPING A 360-ASSESSMENT FOR LIBRARY LEADERSHIP

Daniel Goleman, who popularized the term emotional intelligence (EI), showed that its possession is directly linked to leadership effectiveness.[8] He characterized EI as managing the mood of the organization and as the "sine qua non of leadership."[9] The five components of emotional intelligence that he identified are self-awareness, self-regulation, motivation, empathy, and social skill. The first three components relate to "self-management," whereas the other two address "managing relationships with others."[10]

Peter Hernon, Ronald R. Powell, and Arthur P. Young identified leadership traits and Goleman depicted those for EI. Hernon and Nancy Rossiter then took the traits from both studies and examined more fully the assorted traits for EI.[11] EI therefore becomes a way to organize a 360-assessment. The directors who participated in the Hernon and Rossiter study stressed that difficulty in selecting only a few of the traits as most important for each of the five categories.

They also mentioned that priorities might shift given particular situations and which traits the senior management team as a whole possessed. Consequently, it is impossible to select a generic subset of traits for each and all tables.

As a general guide, the respondents did rate "cognitive ability to deal with complex scenarios/situations" as most important trait for *self-awareness* (Table 15.1A) followed by "a realistic understanding of oneself: emotions, strengths, weaknesses, needs, and drives"; "know where he or she is going— taking the organization"; "a sense of humor"; and "respect for individuality and diversity."

Of the 25 items listed for *self-regulation* (Table 15.1B), "stable temperament and ability to maintain an emotional balance under constant tensions" was *ranked* as most important" followed by "integrity." Both "comfortable in making judgment calls" and "comfortable with ambiguity" tied for third position. "Flexible in adapting to change or overcoming obstacles" was ranked fourth and "skill at diagnostic, strategic, and tactical reasoning" achieved fifth place.

For *motivation* (Table 15.1C), the most important trait is "visionary—able to build a shared vision and rally others around it," followed by "motivate people to develop and adhere to a shared vision," "commitment to job, organization, institution, and profession," "articulate direction for the library," and "optimism (even in the face of failure)."

The fourth component of EI, *empathy,* contained 14 items, 6 of which were among those identified as most important (Table 15.1D). There was widespread consensus that "treat people with dignity/respect" was the first choice, followed by "attract, build, and retain talent" and "good interpersonal/people skills," which tied for second position. Rounding out the other most important choices were "keep organization focused on high-quality service," "exercises good judgment," and being a "good listener."

Social skill, the final component of EI (Table 15.1E), as the respondents rated, emphasized the "ability to function in a political environment." Of less importance were "effective in leading change," "develop and foster partnerships," "collaborative," "build rapport with a wide circle of people," and "resonance (inspiring people to work together to solve problems, inspiring excellence)."

For *self-management* (Tables 15.1A-C), "visionary—able to build a shared vision and rally others around it" was most frequently identified as most important. "Stable temperament and ability to maintain an emotional balance under constant tensions" (see Table 9.1B) was second followed by "cognitive ability to deal with complex scenarios/situations" (Table 15.1A). Turning *managing relationships with others* (Table 15.1D-E), all of the previously mentioned traits were considered most important. Taking all five tables into account, the greatest consensus was about the importance of "visionary—able to build a shared vision and rally others around it" (Table 15.1C) and "ability to function in a political environment" (Table 15.1E).

In summary, instead of examining all of the traits identified in the table, individual libraries can (and probably should) select a small subset from all

Table 15.1
The Components of Emotional Intelligence

Self-awareness (A)

Able to hone one's ability
Absence of ego (or ego is not a barrier)
Articulate
Assertive
Challenge assumptions
Cognitive ability to deal with complex scenarios/situations
Drive for task completion
Enthusiastic
Intuitive
Know where he or she is going—taking the organization
Narcissism (an acceptable level)
Realistic understanding of oneself: emotions, strengths, weaknesses, needs, and drives
Recognize how one's feelings affect others and one's job performance
Resilient
Respect individuality and diversity
Respect scholarship, learning, and teaching
Self-confident
Sense of humor
Sense of personal identity
Show initiative
Tenacity
Willingness to tolerate frustration and delay
Record of proven leadership

Self-regulation (B)

Ability to figure out what is going on without having to be told
Ability to compromise
Ask the "right"/ "tough" question
Broad knowledge of issues
Comfortable in making judgment calls
Comfortable with ambiguity
Comfortable with change
Demonstrates endurance
Diplomatic
Evenhanded
Flexible in adapting to change or overcoming obstacles
Good listening skills
Handle stress well
Honesty
Initiative
Innovative, seeks out, and acts on challenges and new opportunities
Integrity

Table 15.1
The Components of Emotional Intelligence (continued)

Self-regulation (continued)

Open-minded
Propensity for reflection
Realistic organizational awareness
Receptivity to change
Sense of perspective
Skill at diagnostic, strategic, and tactical reasoning
Stable temperament and ability to maintain an emotional balance under constant tensions
Think "outside the box"(in new and creative ways applicable to the problem)
Trustworthy

Motivation (C)

Articulate direction for the library
Accessible to others
Change/shape the library's culture
Commitment to job, organization, institution, and profession
Create an environment that fosters accountability
Creative
Driven to achieve beyond expectations
Encourage risk taking
Genuine belief in the abilities of, and good faith in, others in the organization to advance the mission
Figure out what is going on without having to be told
Good oral and written presentation skills
High energy level
Mobilize individual commitment
Motivate people to develop and adhere to a shared vision
Nurture staff
Optimism (even in the face of failure)
Tolerate some mistakes
Treat others as an equal
Understand small group dynamics
Visionary—able to build a shared vision and rally others around it

Empathy (D)

Attract, build, and retain talent
Be open-minded
Comfortable with team culture
Cross-cultural sensitivity and record of achievement
Exercises good judgment
Give praise generously
Good interpersonal/people skills
Good listener
Have integrity

Table 15.1
The Components of Emotional Intelligence (continued)

Empathy (continued)

Interested in others
Keep organization focused on high-quality service
Thoughtfully consider the feelings of others
Treat people with dignity/ respect
Trust others

Social Skill (E)

Ability to function in a political environment
Ability to gather outside resources
Advocate for librarians' role in higher education
Bring issues of broad importance to the academic community, fostering wide discussion and action, when appropriate
Build rapport with a wide circle of people
Collaborative
Consensus building in carrying out strategic direction
Develop and foster partnerships
Effective in leading change
Enabler and facilitator
Entrepreneurial
Establish credibility with colleagues
Expertise in building and leading teams
Friendly (with a purpose)
Good people networking skills
Help participants in meetings, consortia, and cooperative endeavors to be results-oriented
Lead in a shared decision-making environment
Persuasiveness
Resonance (inspiring people to work together to solve problems, inspiring excellence)
Serve as a role model of the desired behavior

Source: Peter Hernon and Nancy Rossiter, "Emotional Intelligence: Which Traits Are Most Prized," *College & Research Libraries* 67 (May 2006): 260–275.

For alternative forms of 360-degree assessment, see Marilyn K. Gowing, "Measurement of Individual Emotional Competence," in *The Emotional Intelligent Workplace: How to Select for, Measure, and Improve Emotional Intelligence in Individuals, Groups, and Organizations,* edited by Cary Cherniss and Daniel Goleman (San Francisco: Jossey-Bass, 2001), pp. 83–131.

five sections of the table or focus on either self-management or managing relationships with others. Either way, it is important to recognize that the possession of EI means an ability to demonstrate competence in all of the traits listed in the table. External validity refers to EI as a whole, but it might also be associated with the characterization of any of EI's components (broadly at the level of self-management or managing relationships with others, or more narrowly by addressing self-awareness, self-regulation, motivation, empathy,

and social skill). For example, how well does the evaluated individual manage relationships with others or demonstrate social skill? External validity is
likely of less importance than is internal validity. Still, 360-assessment needs
to focus on a subset of traits.

Once the library has settled on the relevant performance dimensions (the
components and the traits), the various groups involved identify the behaviors
related to these dimensions. There is a standardized process for interpreting
those complex behaviors and showing the extent to which they encompass
the dimensions. Although 360-assessments depend on self-perceptions and
self-reflection, it is critical not to rely on them too much. The insights gained
are indicative, not absolute. Fabio Sala of the McClelland Center for Research
and Innovation of the Hay Group in Boston administrated a 360-assessment
survey to more than 1,000 individuals from different organizations. He found
"that higher level employees (e.g., senior executives) had greater discrepancy
between self- and other-ratings than lower level individuals (e.g., managers
and individual contributors)."[12] In effect, self-awareness may perhaps be less
important than the other components of EI.

Reliability, which refers to consistency and accuracy of interpretation, encompasses issues such as the training of feedback givers for the purpose of either
development or performance appraisal, the scoring of individual traits through
an observation process, and the linkage of traits to a given leadership style. If
the purpose of having 360- feedback is unclear, if the evidence is not integrated
with the other data, and if there is mistrust because of abuse or poor communication, the value of having such an assessment declines appreciatively.

THE INSTRUMENT

Each of the items on the Emotional Intelligence Assessment Survey (Table
15.2) is ratable and can be judged objectively. The traits covered are all ones
that the feedback recipient can develop. Some of the traits, however, might
not have value within a given organization (e.g., entrepreneurial ability) and
others (e.g., articulate direction for the library) might be confined to the
director. Thus each item on the draft instrument should be reviewed for local
relevance. John E. Jones and William L. Bearley note:

It is tempting to measure too many things in multirater feedback instruments. Brevity
is a critical requirement for such assessments, because of two primary factors: (1) the
need for raters to complete the task quickly, and (2) the necessity that the feedback
be completely understandable to the feedback recipients. We recommend that 360°
assessment instruments contain less than 50 items.[13]

In addition to developing the set of traits to study, it is important to settle
on an appropriate and relevant rating scale. Jones and Bearley offer different
recommendations for a scale, but they "favor the use of [either] a 6- and
10-point" scale.[14]

Table 15.2
Emotional Intelligence Assessment Survey

	1	[2	3	4]	[5	6]	[7	8	9]	10
	↓				↓				↓	
	Low				*Medium*			*High*		
Self-awareness										
Able to hone one's ability	1	[2	3	4]	[5	6]	[7	8	9]	10
Absence of ego (or ego is not a barrier)	1	[2	3	4]	[5	6]	[7	8	9]	10
Articulate	1	[2	3	4]	[5	6]	[7	8	9]	10
Assertive	1	[2	3	4]	[5	6]	[7	8	9]	10
Challenge assumptions	1	[2	3	4]	[5	6]	[7	8	9]	10
Cognitive ability to deal with complex scenarios/situations	1	[2	3	4]	[5	6]	[7	8	9]	10
Drive for task completion	1	[2	3	4]	[5	6]	[7	8	9]	10
Enthusiastic	1	[2	3	4]	[5	6]	[7	8	9]	10
Intuitive	1	[2	3	4]	[5	6]	[7	8	9]	10
Know where he or she is going—taking the organization	1	[2	3	4]	[5	6]	[7	8	9]	10
Narcissism (an acceptable level)	1	[2	3	4]	[5	6]	[7	8	9]	10
Realistic understanding of oneself: emotions, strengths, weaknesses, needs, and drives	1	[2	3	4]	[5	6]	[7	8	9]	10
Recognize how one's feelings affect others and one's job performance	1	[2	3	4]	[5	6]	[7	8	9]	10
Resilient	1	[2	3	4]	[5	6]	[7	8	9]	10
Respect individuality and diversity	1	[2	3	4]	[5	6]	[7	8	9]	10
Respect scholarship, learning, and teaching	1	[2	3	4]	[5	6]	[7	8	9]	10
Self-confident	1	[2	3	4]	[5	6]	[7	8	9]	10
Sense of humor	1	[2	3	4]	[5	6]	[7	8	9]	10
Sense of personal identity	1	[2	3	4]	[5	6]	[7	8	9]	10
Show initiative	1	[2	3	4]	[5	6]	[7	8	9]	10
Tenacity	1	[2	3	4]	[5	6]	[7	8	9]	10
Willingness to tolerate frustration and delay	1	[2	3	4]	[5	6]	[7	8	9]	10
Record of proven leadership	1	[2	3	4]	[5	6]	[7	8	9]	10

Table 15.2
Emotional Intelligence Assessment Survey (continued)

Self-regulation

Ability to figure out what is going on without having to be told	1	[2	3	4]	[5	6]	[7	8	9]	10
Ability to compromise	1	[2	3	4]	[5	6]	[7	8	9]	10
Ask the "right"/ "tough" question	1	[2	3	4]	[5	6]	[7	8	9]	10
Broad knowledge of issues	1	[2	3	4]	[5	6]	[7	8	9]	10
Comfortable in making judgment calls	1	[2	3	4]	[5	6]	[7	8	9]	10
Comfortable with ambiguity	1	[2	3	4]	[5	6]	[7	8	9]	10
Comfortable with change	1	[2	3	4]	[5	6]	[7	8	9]	10
Demonstrates endurance	1	[2	3	4]	[5	6]	[7	8	9]	10
Diplomatic	1	[2	3	4]	[5	6]	[7	8	9]	10
Evenhanded	1	[2	3	4]	[5	6]	[7	8	9]	10
Flexible in adapting to change or overcoming obstacles	1	[2	3	4]	[5	6]	[7	8	9]	10
Good listening skills	1	[2	3	4]	[5	6]	[7	8	9]	10
Handle stress well	1	[2	3	4]	[5	6]	[7	8	9]	10
Honesty	1	[2	3	4]	[5	6]	[7	8	9]	10
Initiative	1	[2	3	4]	[5	6]	[7	8	9]	10
Innovative, seeks out, and acts on challenges and new opportunities	1	[2	3	4]	[5	6]	[7	8	9]	10
Integrity	1	[2	3	4]	[5	6]	[7	8	9]	10
Open-minded	1	[2	3	4]	[5	6]	[7	8	9]	10
Propensity for reflection	1	[2	3	4]	[5	6]	[7	8	9]	10
Realistic organizational awareness	1	[2	3	4]	[5	6]	[7	8	9]	10
Receptivity to change	1	[2	3	4]	[5	6]	[7	8	9]	10
Sense of perspective	1	[2	3	4]	[5	6]	[7	8	9]	10
Skill at diagnostic, strategic, and tactical reasoning	1	[2	3	4]	[5	6]	[7	8	9]	10
Stable temperament and ability to maintain an emotional balance under constant tensions	1	[2	3	4]	[5	6]	[7	8	9]	10
Think "outside the box"(in new and creative ways applicable to the problem)	1	[2	3	4]	[5	6]	[7	8	9]	10
Trustworthy	1	[2	3	4]	[5	6]	[7	8	9]	10

Table 15.2
Emotional Intelligence Assessment Survey (continued)

Motivation

Articulate direction for the library	1	[2	3	4]	[5	6]	[7	8	9]	10
Accessible to others	1	[2	3	4]	[5	6]	[7	8	9]	10
Change/shape the library's culture	1	[2	3	4]	[5	6]	[7	8	9]	10
Commitment to job, organization, institution, and profession	1	[2	3	4]	[5	6]	[7	8	9]	10
Create an environment that fosters accountability	1	[2	3	4]	[5	6]	[7	8	9]	10
Creative	1	[2	3	4]	[5	6]	[7	8	9]	10
Driven to achieve beyond expectations	1	[2	3	4]	[5	6]	[7	8	9]	10
Encourage risk taking	1	[2	3	4]	[5	6]	[7	8	9]	10
Genuine belief in the abilities of, and good faith in, others in the organization to advance the mission	1	[2	3	4]	[5	6]	[7	8	9]	10
Figure out what is going on without having to be told	1	[2	3	4]	[5	6]	[7	8	9]	10
Good oral and written presentation skills	1	[2	3	4]	[5	6]	[7	8	9]	10
High energy level	1	[2	3	4]	[5	6]	[7	8	9]	10
Mobilize individual commitment	1	[2	3	4]	[5	6]	[7	8	9]	10
Motivate people to develop and adhere to a shared vision	1	[2	3	4]	[5	6]	[7	8	9]	10
Nurture staff	1	[2	3	4]	[5	6]	[7	8	9]	10
Optimism (even in the face of failure)	1	[2	3	4]	[5	6]	[7	8	9]	10
Tolerate some mistakes	1	[2	3	4]	[5	6]	[7	8	9]	10
Treat others as an equal	1	[2	3	4]	[5	6]	[7	8	9]	10
Understand small group dynamics	1	[2	3	4]	[5	6]	[7	8	9]	10
Visionary—able to build a shared vision and rally others around it	1	[2	3	4]	[5	6]	[7	8	9]	10

Empathy

Attract, build, and retain talent	1	[2	3	4]	[5	6]	[7	8	9]	10
Be open-minded	1	[2	3	4]	[5	6]	[7	8	9]	10
Comfortable with team culture	1	[2	3	4]	[5	6]	[7	8	9]	10
Cross-cultural sensitivity and record of achievement	1	[2	3	4]	[5	6]	[7	8	9]	10

Table 15.2
Emotional Intelligence Assessment Survey (continued)

Empathy (continued)

Exercises good judgment	1	[2	3	4]	[5	6]	[7	8	9]	10
Give praise generously	1	[2	3	4]	[5	6]	[7	8	9]	10
Good interpersonal/people skills	1	[2	3	4]	[5	6]	[7	8	9]	10
Good listener	1	[2	3	4]	[5	6]	[7	8	9]	10
Have integrity	1	[2	3	4]	[5	6]	[7	8	9]	10
Interested in others	1	[2	3	4]	[5	6]	[7	8	9]	10
Keep organization focused on high-quality service	1	[2	3	4]	[5	6]	[7	8	9]	10
Thoughtfully consider the feelings of others	1	[2	3	4]	[5	6]	[7	8	9]	10
Treat people with dignity/ respect	1	[2	3	4]	[5	6]	[7	8	9]	10
Trust others	1	[2	3	4]	[5	6]	[7	8	9]	10

Social Skill

Ability to function in a political environment	1	[2	3	4]	[5	6]	[7	8	9]	10
Ability to gather outside resources	1	[2	3	4]	[5	6]	[7	8	9]	10
Advocate for librarians' role in higher education	1	[2	3	4]	[5	6]	[7	8	9]	10
Bring issues of broad importance to the academic community, fostering wide discussion and action, when appropriate	1	[2	3	4]	[5	6]	[7	8	9]	10
Build rapport with a wide circle of people	1	[2	3	4]	[5	6]	[7	8	9]	10
Collaborative	1	[2	3	4]	[5	6]	[7	8	9]	10
Consensus building in carrying out strategic direction	1	[2	3	4]	[5	6]	[7	8	9]	10
Develop and foster partnerships	1	[2	3	4]	[5	6]	[7	8	9]	10
Effective in leading change Enabler and facilitator	1	[2	3	4]	[5	6]	[7	8	9]	10
Entrepreneurial	1	[2	3	4]	[5	6]	[7	8	9]	10
Establish credibility with colleagues	1	[2	3	4]	[5	6]	[7	8	9]	10
Expertise in building and leading teams	1	[2	3	4]	[5	6]	[7	8	9]	10
Friendly (with a purpose)	1	[2	3	4]	[5	6]	[7	8	9]	10

Table 15.2
Emotional Intelligence Assessment Survey (continued)

Social Skill (continued)										
Good people networking skills	1	[2	3	4]	[5	6]	[7	8	9]	10
Help participants in meetings, con-sortia, and cooperative endeavors to be results-oriented	1	[2	3	4]	[5	6]	[7	8	9]	10
Lead in a shared decision-making environment	1	[2	3	4]	[5	6]	[7	8	9]	10
Persuasiveness	1	[2	3	4]	[5	6]	[7	8	9]	10
Resonance (inspiring people to work together to solve problems, inspiring excellence)	1	[2	3	4]	[5	6]	[7	8	9]	10
Serve as a role model of the desired behavior	1	[2	3	4]	[5	6]	[7	8	9]	10

A 10-point scale is easily understood and avoids a numeric midpoint. The following bracketed scale is based on the familiar 10-point rating scale but is broken by brackets into five important sections that aid its interpretation. (Brackets are not necessary in the questionnaire, however.)

1 [2 3 4] [5 6] [7 8 9] 10

A respondent will focus on either the lower or upper half of the scale. The 10-point scale, in effect, becomes a 5-point scale at either end, with the [7 8 9] grouping offering the rater a way to fine-tune a nonextreme score. That is, a score of 5 or 6 indicates that the person demonstrates the trait at a *medium* level or perhaps *it is somewhat like this person [to demonstrate this trait]*.

Scores of 1 and 10 indicate that the person demonstrates the trait at either a *low* (1) or *high* (10) level; as an alternative, 1 might represent *definitely unlike this person,* and 10 becomes *definitely like this person.* Such scores are extremes—there is no worse or better. Therefore most raters probably do not choose either of these scores. As an alternative, the range [7 8 9] might represent something between *medium* and *high,* or *it is like this person.* On the other hand, [2 3 4] represents a quality between *medium* and *low,* or it is *unlike this person.*

Selecting the 5 or 6 forces an inclination in one direction or the other. If someone feels strongly about an exact midpoint, he or she will write it in, mark the center point, or circle both the 5 and 6 together. (Similarly, a small number of people may mark positions between the other scores as well.) In such case, someone compiling the scores might enter the decimal midpoint (e.g., 5.5). In any case, such matters must be discussed and resolved before data collection to ensure a high level in inter-rater reliability.

The numbers between 1 and [5 6] or [5 6] and 10 represent a certain degree (or lack thereof) of demonstrating a particular trait. Presumably, most raters will respond in these ranges. The particular usefulness of these ranges is that they allow raters to indicate degrees to which a trait is demonstrated. The 3 and 8 are midpoints within these ranges. Raters who score an 8 indicate that there is still room for improvement. An average score of at least 8 is very good, whereas raters who score a 7 are at the lowest range of that bracket.

Scores below 7 should cause concern, but of greatest and most immediate concern are those whose score falls below [5 6]. These responses clearly signal a need for significant improvement in mastering that trait.

IMPLEMENTATION PROCEDURES

The Emotional Intelligence Assessment Survey is a 360-multirater instrument for managers in academic and public libraries. With testing in other countries, it might become an international instrument for diagnosing a manager's leadership skills and traits and providing a foundation for improving leadership potential. In addition to self-ratings, a panel (library director, fellow members of the senior management team, and perhaps a member or two from the larger community) rates the participant on different aspects of his or her work behavior and offers examples to support the ratings. Any outside rater must be carefully selected to provide objective and relevant insights. In those instances in which the senior management team is small, the review process is either limited or others are brought into the process. Managers in more than one library might participate, assuming they have an adequate knowledge to render an informed, objective judgment.

A most critical part of 360-assessments is the procedure for collecting evidence anonymously from all participants, ensuring confidentiality in data collection, and interpreting and applying the results in an objective manner. Dave Ulrich and Norm Smallwood maintain that once those assessed received the written feedback report, "the best approach is to acknowledge the feedback, thank those who provided it, focus on one or two specific behavioral changes that will be based on the data, then build in a follow-up method to monitor progress on the behavioral changes."[15]

The Steps

The first step is to choose the survey instrument and then decide how the process will be implemented. Likewise, the organization should determine the scope of the assessment: Will it be used organization wide or just for certain departments or individuals? As with any large project, it may be necessary to perform a pilot test to see whether the preliminary results meet the goals of the assessment process. Procedures should be put in place to ensure that the results remain anonymous. It is unfortunate to note that one organization hid a code number underneath the staple on an assessment instrument to track the individuals who answered the questions. This procedure was noticed by an individual taking the assessment when she went to make a copy of the instrument. She then informed others that the process was not credible.

Other procedures include determining how many and which individuals will participate in the 360-assessment process. These assessments typically start with the individual performing a self-evaluation, then usually includes the individual's boss, any subordinates that report to the individual, and co-workers. This process can extend to other supervisors, customers, and in some cases, suppliers or other people with whom the individual has contact.

Many problems are associated with this type of assessment process. Some people report instances of "back scratching"; for example, when co-workers are involved in this process, they may rate each other favorably because of the alliance they have with each other. Other problems arise from the fear associated with rating one's own boss (echoing the confidentiality issue). The amount of time and money needed to perform this type of assessment may be a problem. Generally, it takes several months (and some have reported over a year) to tabulate and return the report to the individual.

THE FEEDBACK REPORT

The information gathered from the individual's circle of influence is tabulated and summarized and generally put into a report format. As indicated previously, the individual does not know who made the comments in the report, although in practice, many are able to figure this out through their interpersonal relationships. In most processes, the information obtained is separated out, and strategies for improvement correlate to each major section. In performance appraisal situations, how an individual does on specific sections of the appraisal can directly influence compensation.

RESONANT LEADERSHIP

Although the focus of this chapter has been on self-awareness and self-improvement to gain more mastery of the components of EI, or one characterization of leadership (see Chapter 3), leaders should be reminded that renewal, "or developing practices—habits of mind, body, and behavior—that enable us to create and sustain resonance in the face of unending challenges, year in and year out," is crucial to sustained, high-quality leadership.[16] Richard Boyatzis, professor in the departments of organizational behavior and psychology at Case Western Reserve University, and Annie McKee, co-chair of the Telcos Leadership Institute and instructor at the University of Pennsylvania Graduate School of Education, note:

leaders today face unprecedented challenges that can result in a vicious cycle of stress, pressure, sacrifice, and dissonance. To counter the inevitable challenges of leadership roles, we need to engage in a conscious process of renewal both on a daily basis and over time.[17]

When 360-assessment focuses on personal development, those reviewing the results should remind those being evaluated about the importance of renewal and should discuss the methods most effective for the individual. Renewal focuses on *mindfulness* ("live in full consciousness of self, others, nature, and society"), *hope* ("inspire through clarity of vision, optimism, and a profound belief in their—and their people's—ability to turn dreams into reality"), and *compassion*.[18] Renewal might come from activities and roles related to work or personal lives.

CONCLUSION

The process of a 360-assessment has been applied and used effectively in different work settings, but its success is no indicator that such an assessment is applicable everywhere. Walter W. Tornow and Manuel London discuss how organizations can determine if they will find such feedback relevant. They also identify how to implement such a review and note challenges "to be aware of from the perspective of the individual and the organization."[19] According to them, "360-degree feedback processes may encourage an organizational climate where people feel free to ask, give, and receive feedback in person as part of the normal day-to-day course of doing business rather than waiting for formal ratings."[20] The result helps change organizational culture and makes the staff more receptive to professional and personal development and growth.

If libraries want to include the instrument highlighted in this chapter as part of peer review or a mandated five-year review, the senior management and upper administration in the university should review and refine the instrument and its interpretation. This chapter presents only an initial instrument and encourages others to make the effort to create a library-oriented assessment tool for gauging emotional intelligence. Perhaps those in upper administration might also be interested in reviewing their skills with EI on an informal basis.

"Leaders who effectively receive informal and formal feedback will put themselves in a position to give persuasive feedback to others."[21]

NOTES

1. Jane L. Wilson, "360 Appraisals," *Training & Development* 51 (June 1997): 44.

2. E-mail message from Charles B. Lowry to Peter Hernon, dated October 6, 2005.

3. See D. W. Bracken, M. A. Dalton, R. A. Jako, C. D. McCauley, and V. A. Pollman, *Should 360-degree Feedback Be Used Only for Developmental Purposes* (Greensboro, NC: Center for Creative Leadership, 1997; Norwood, MA: Books24X7.com [electronic resource]). They argue that 360-assessments are best used for employee development.

See also Peter Ward, *360-Degree Feedback* (London: Institute of Personnel and Development, 1997; Norwood, MA: Books24x7.com [electronic resource]).

4. Wilson, "360 Appraisals," 44.

5. Ellen Van Velsor, Jean Brittain Leslie, and John W. Fleenor, *Choosing 360: A Guide to Evaluating Multi-rater Feedback Instruments for Management Development* (Greensboro, NC: Center for Creative Leadership, 1997; Norwood, MA: Books24X7.com [electronic resource]).

6. Ibid., see introduction to step nine.

7. Robert E. Kaplan and Charles J. Palus, *Enhancing 360-degree Feedback for Senior Executives: How to Maximize the Benefits and Minimize the Risks* (Greensboro, NC: Center for Creative Leadership, 1994; Norwood, MA: Books24X7.com [electronic resource]).

8. Daniel Goleman, *Emotional Intelligence* (New York: Bantam Books, 1995).

9. Daniel Goleman, "What Makes a Leader?," *Harvard Business Review* 82 (January 2004): 82.

10. Ibid., 88.

11. See Peter Hernon, Ronald R. Powell, and Arthur P. Young, *The Next Library Leadership: Attributes of Academic and Public Library Directors* (Westport, CT: Libraries Unlimited, 2003); Goleman, "What Makes a Leader?;" Peter Hernon and Nancy Rossiter, "Emotional Intelligence: Which Traits Are Most Prized," *College & Research Libraries* 67 (May 2006): 260–275.

12. Fabio Sala, "Executive Blind Spots: Discrepancies between Self- and Other-Ratings," *Consulting Psychology Journal: Practice & Research* 55 (Fall 2003): 222.

13. John E. Jones and William Bearley, *360 Feedback: Strategies, Tactics, and Techniques for Developing Leaders* (Amherst, MA: HRD Press; Minneapolis, MN: Lakewood Publications, 1996; Norwood, MA: Books24x7.com [electronic resource]).

14. Ibid., Chapter 14.

15. Dave Ulrich and Norm Smallwood, *Why the Bottom Line Isn't! How to Build Value through People and Organization* (New York: John Wiley & Sons, 2003), 197.

16. Richard Boyatzis and Annie McKee, *Resonant Leadership: Renewing Yourself and Connecting with Others through Mindfulness, Hope, and Compassion* (Boston: Harvard Business School Press, 2005), 5.

17. Ibid., 9.

18. Ibid., 3.

19. Walter W. Tornow and Manuel London, *Maximizing the Value of 360-degree Feedback: A Process for Successful Individual and Organizational Development* (San Francisco: Jossey Bass, 1998; Norwood, MA: Books24X7.com [electronic resource]). See, for instance, the "Conclusion," 1.

20. Ibid. See "Conclusion: 360-Degree Feedback: A Fad or a Fit?"

21. Ulrich and Smallwood, *Why the Bottom Line Isn't!*, 197.

16

•◦•∙•◦•

PREPARING THE NEXT
GENERATION OF DIRECTORS
AND LEADERS

Nancy Rossiter

"A leader's job is the recruitment, development, and retention of talent. Talent is the brand."[1]

As we think about the future and the role that academic libraries will play, a critical question is, "How do we ensure they will continue to be lead successfully?" Conventional leadership wisdom suggests that library directors hire people for managerial positions who have vision and strategy. Jim Collins, however, found these are not necessarily the key qualities to make organizations successful. Instead, leaders of great organizations, he explained in *Good to Great*, focus first on "who" and then "what"; in other words, great leaders attended to their people first and strategy second. They put the right people on "the bus," move the wrong people off, usher the right people into the right seats, and then figure out where to drive the bus.[2] This chapter looks at various ways library leaders can ensure the future success of new leaders in the library through hiring practices, intern programs, development, mentoring, and supporting new leaders.

WHO WILL LEAD LIBRARIES?

Much has been written recently in library literature about the "graying" of the library profession. Statistics that support this viewpoint include 25 percent of today's librarians will be 65 by 2009 and 58 percent will reach that age by 2019.[3] Many of the positions that older librarians fill will be at the upper levels of the organization. Peter Hernon, Ronald Powell, and Arthur Young found that turnover has been high in university library leadership positions and is expected to continue in the near future.[4] For instance, in any one year beginning with 2000, there are anywhere between 10 and 20 directorships open in the Association of Research Libraries. One library system in Ft. Lauderdale, Florida, reported that out of 270 librarian positions, it had 40 vacancies in the 2004/2005 fiscal year and expected to have the need for 45 additional librarians to staff expanded libraries that were opening in the system.[5] With examples such as these, it appears that recruiting the next generation of library leaders is of critical importance. One roadblock to this recruitment effort is the negative perception of leadership positions from Generation X and Y librarians and the unwillingness of many librarians to aspire to positions of middle management.

Several recent studies have explored how individuals belonging to generations X and Y differ from the traditionalist and baby boomer generations in their attitudes toward library management (see Chapter 11). Rachel Singer Gordon found that Generation X and Generation Y librarians, ages 18–30, tend to have a negative view of management. The results indicated that this view is due to the perception that upper-level library managers are more courteous to patrons than to staff, particularly younger staff, as well as to people outside of leadership positions. Also, she discovered that the amount of time that a library director devotes to the position is potentially a turn-off; younger librarians do not want to detract from time spent with family and friends, as well as time to pursue other interests. One of Gordon's respondents stated: "There is no amount of money or prestige that would entice us to sacrifice our families, our home lives, and our sanity for the long hours and Sisyphean ordeal of a directorship. . . . It's not that we are reluctant to assume leadership roles, it is just that no one has shown us a good enough reason why we should."[6] Clearly, if this attitude toward library managerial positions is prevalent, those in leadership positions need to address the problem and make leadership positions more attractive to nascent library leaders.

HIRING NEW LIBRARY LEADERS

A critical factor in preparing the next generation of leaders is to know what qualities to look for and how to convert these key people into leaders. Jack and Suzy Welch suggest looking for the four traits when hiring future leaders: positive energy, the ability to energize, edge, and execute. Energy refers to the ability of leaders to start and end the day with enthusiasm and never seeming to tire in the middle. Energize is the ability of future leaders to get others revved up—inspiring others to do what was not thought to be possible. Edge refers to the ability to make tough decisions. People with edge know when to make critical decisions, even if they have not assembled all the relevant information needed to make the decision. Execute means the ability to get the job done. Leaders can have energy, can energize others, and have edge, but still not have the ability to follow through with organizational goals and plans. Execution is the ability to persevere through unexpected obstacles, resistance, and chaos.[7] By looking for these qualities in the hiring process, library leaders will have a good starting point for future development.

SELF-ASSESSMENT

Leadership development generally starts with leaders performing some kind of self-assessment. It involves looking at one's leadership skills from several different perspectives. Many self-assessments fall into three parts: the skills one is good at, what one likes to do, and what the market values. Self-assessments include an evaluation of four different skill areas: technical, process, managerial leadership, and industry and business knowledge. In the technical and process sections the topics of improving business processes are evaluated. The managerial leadership area looks at how well one communicates, analyzes, negotiates, and leads projects. In the industry and business knowledge section, how one listens, learns, relates, and contributes to organizational outcomes is examined.[8] By performing self-assessments, future library leaders can better understand their strengths and weaknesses. Areas of weakness can be addressed through training and development programs. Figure 16.1 provides an example of a self-assessment exercise used to assess one's leadership abilities.

INTERNSHIP PROGRAMS

One library system in Ft. Lauderdale, Florida, reported great success with graduate intern programs. They recruited college graduates from their support staff or from outside of it. They also supported their library school education and let them "learn while they earn." The system also uses a tuition reimbursement program to grow and develop talent in the organization. Also, they reimburse non-tuition–associated expenses such as additional fees, books, supplies, childcare, and transportation. In response to the number of expected retirements, the Broward Public Library Foundation created the BCL Library Leadership Institute. In this 12-month program, library staff who have demonstrated leadership potential, as well as enthusiasm, optimism, and vision for the library services of tomorrow, meet for 10 sessions spread out over the year. Each section includes a "Personal Reflections on Leadership" segment in which current leaders from another county present the leadership qualities that they believe were important in their careers. Other activities involve group exercises that explore topics such as modeling, team building, communication, vision, empowerment, and various other topics including a special session on "Encouraging the Heart."[9]

Library schools can also contribute to the development and nurturing of potential library leaders. Brinley Franklin, director of the University of Connecticut library, told the author in a recent interview that library schools

Figure 16.1
Sample Leadership Self-Assessment Exercise

SELF-ASSESSMENT EXERCISE

The following statements describe aspects of leadership. Respond to each statement depending on the way you would most likely act if you were the leader of a work group. Circle the letter that indicates how often you would behave in the described way: (A) always; (F) frequently; (O) occasionally; (S) seldom; (N) never.

1	I would most likely act as the spokesperson for the group	A F O S N
2	I would encourage overtime work	A F O S N
3	I would allow members complete freedom in their work	A F O S N
4	I would encourage the use of uniform procedures	A F O S N
5	I would permit the members to solve their own problems	A F O S N
6	I would stress being ahead of competing groups	A F O S N
7	I would speak as a representative of the group	A F O S N
8	I would needle members for greater effort	A F O S N
9	I would try out my ideas in the group	A F O S N
10	I would let the members do their work the way they think best	A F O S N
11	I would be working hard for a promotion	A F O S N
12	I would tolerate postponement and uncertainty	A F O S N
13	I would speak for the group if there were visitors present	A F O S N
14	I would keep the work moving at a rapid pace	A F O S N
15	I would turn the members loose on a job and let them go to it	A F O S N
16	I would settle conflicts when they occur in the group	A F O S N
17	I would get swamped by details	A F O S N
18	I would represent the group at outside meetings	A F O S N
19	I would be reluctant to allow the members any freedom of action	A F O S N
20	I would decide what should be done and how it should be done	A F O S N
21	I would push for increased production	A F O S N
22	I would let some members have authority that I could keep	A F O S N
23	Things would usually turn out as I predicted	A F O S N
24	I would allow the group a high degree of initiative	A F O S N
25	I would assign group members to particular tasks	A F O S N
26	I would be willing to make changes	A F O S N
27	I would ask the members to work harder	A F O S N
28	I would trust the group members to exercise good judgment	A F O S N
29	I would schedule the work to be done	A F O S N
30	I would refuse to explain my actions	A F O S N
31	I would persuade others that my ideas are to their advantage	A F O S N
32	I would permit the group to set its own pace	A F O S N
33	I would urge the group to beat its previous record	A F O S N
34	I would act without consulting the group	A F O S N
35	I would ask that the group follow standard rules and regulations	A F O S N

Source: Keith Reynolds, "I Am Their Leader, I Must Follow Them!," *Management Accounting* 77 (December 1999): 70–72.

can nurture potential leaders by having professors identify leadership qualities in their students. Once the potential leaders have been identified, they can be placed in the appropriate courses that will develop both their strengths as leaders and the career path best suited for them. The assumption is that the students are willingness to accept such placement and see how the courses will advance their careers and relate to their work interests.

LEADERSHIP TRAINING PROGRAMS

In addition to formal graduate programs in colleges, there are many different leadership training programs in the library profession. These programs include skill building, intensive feedback, conceptual approaches, and personal growth approaches. Skill-building approaches use simulation exercises to develop relevant leadership skills. Trainers generally model behaviors and video case studies may also be used. Intensive feedback approaches use 360-degree feedback, observational exercises, and verbal feedback from trainers, participants, and colleagues. Conceptual approaches develop leaders through the use of mental models using frameworks that are often built around contrasts. These leadership training programs use lectures, video case studies, and discussion groups. Personal growth training programs, such as the Snowbird Institute, use emotional and physical challenges to force reflective learning about one's own behavior, work views, and personal aspirations. They frequently use methods such as outdoor adventures that emphasize risk-taking, teamwork, and personal values exploration.[10]

Despite the proliferation of leadership programs, it has been difficult to assess how well these programs develop leaders. One of the key challenges in determining how well these programs develop leaders is that there is a lack of consensus on a definition of *leadership skills* in the library profession. Most evaluation methods for the programs rely on self-reports; very little empirical research exists on how well these programs develop leaders.[11] (Chapter 17 presents a complementary program that addresses some weaknesses associated with leadership programs.)

MENTORING

According to a recent study, potential leaders avoid management because of their own previous bad experiences.[12] This problem can be avoided if managers take the time to mentor newer members of their staff. Mentoring can be formal or informal. In most instances, the mentor and mentee create objectives and goals that they align with organizational goals. According to Gordon:

mentoring helps bring in a fresh viewpoint and way of thinking, and discussions with newer librarians helped managers to clarify their own thoughts and positions . . . Mentoring also makes managers aware that they serve as role models, and more thoughtful about their own actions. . . Managers can convey what they wish they had known to those they mentor, helping them to learn by example.[13]

Studies of mentoring in library organizations have found that it is a valuable tool for professionals to advance in their careers and to feel satisfied in their work life. Problems associated with mentoring include finding appropriate and good mentors, as well as adequate funding. Most libraries do not have financial support for mentoring and finding volunteers to work for free can be difficult. The upside potential is great; mentors provide needed inspiration, meaningful interaction, and reduce the feeling of burnout.[14] Also, mentoring has professional benefits for the mentor, mentee, and the organization. The mentee gains include emotional support, feedback, receiving tenure, social benefits, and gaining confidence. The mentor benefits through offering support, providing a means for staff growth, and the ability to learn new ideas and perspectives. The organization improves through the retention of experienced staff and the application of insights gained through the process.[15]

DEVELOPMENT

Encouraging professional development is another way to nurture potential library leaders. In this way, high potential library staff can develop skills needed to grow into leadership positions. Also, employees who are sent to training programs feel rewarded and recognized for their talents. Gordon found that the more energetic and talented a library's staff, and the younger the staff, the more that professional development opportunities are essential to them, to their job satisfaction, and to their continuing development.[16] These staff members should be encouraged to seek out opportunities on their own and attend conferences and workshops. Clearly, providing professional development opportunities is a key component of developing new library leaders. One head librarian went so far as to state, "Leaders who do not provide for professional development are failing both the profession and their colleagues."[17]

To ensure that the programs are developing library leaders, efforts should be undertaken to ensure they are effective: accomplish their goals and do not waste training dollars. It is important that their evaluation go beyond self-reports gathered from participants and documenting the extent of their satisfaction with those programs.

CHALLENGE

Another way to build skills in nascent library leaders is by involving them in projects that stretch their abilities. Library managers can encourage them to take on challenging projects and assume new responsibilities to help them develop the skills that will help them to move up in the organization. By encouraging new initiatives, managers can harness the energy from the newer staff and help energize the entire organization. When others in the library see that creativity and innovation is rewarded, they, too, may find new solutions to existing problems.[18]

The importance of gaining diverse experiences in libraries is also a way for potential leaders to grow and learn. In a study conducted by Peter Hernon and Nancy Rossiter, one library director stated that: "The best learning experiences are those that are long term and give opportunities for personal growth." Other library directors discussed mentoring, involvement in professional associations, leadership institutes, and participation in library consortia as means of developing potential leaders.[19]

SUPPORT

If library leaders are going to challenge new library managers, then the leaders must tolerate, if not encourage, a certain degree of failure. It might be appropriate to view failure not as a negative aspect but rather as a learning opportunity. Still, library leaders will have to work with emerging leaders to ensure that there are not too many of such experiences.

Gordon found an openness to change, encouragement of new ideas, and willingness to listen to all points of view is necessary to keep and engage the leaders of the future. Healthy and open organizations are able to satisfy staff, engage a new generation of librarians, and serve a new generation of patrons.[20] Support also generally involves resources; time and money should therefore be allocated to developing the leaders of the future.

WHAT TO NURTURE?

Dale Buss's research indicates that leaders must master and demonstrate caring, communication, and courage. Caring refers to the ability of leaders to elicit creative ideas from tier subordinates. Communication is the ability to get the message across in a fast-paced world where leaders need to make decisions quickly. They also should be able to express their own insights and convictions clearly and forcefully. As Buss states: "You can teach people the intrapersonal and interpersonal skills necessary to communicate, inspire, enroll, and motivate people." Courage means taking over leadership during a crisis. However, Buss also refers to "everyday courage," meaning taking small challenges and facing fears.[21] By nurturing, caring, communication, and courage, library leaders will be able to advance the leaders of the future.

CONCLUSION

As library directors and the profession prepares for the next generation of library leaders, they should work with schools of library and information science to ensure that master's programs are turning out graduates who can engage in analytical thinking and problem solving, and who have good oral and written communication skills, as well as intellectual curiosity. Perhaps the competences for research libraries that the Association of Southeastern Research Librarians (ASERL) developed might form the basis for hiring decisions.[22] Once hired, the new librarians, along with the other librarians, should receive extensive professional training to build on the ASERL competencies, especially for those with management and leadership potential. It is time for libraries to invest in staff training like many private sector organizations do.

In *Good to Great,* Collins states that great leaders take the necessary steps to ensure that the leaders that follow in their footsteps are well prepared to lead the organization.[23] Library leaders should ensure the success of the following generations of leaders by seeing that they are well prepared as they pursue their careers.

To counteract a negative image of library leadership, library directors should spend time connecting with the other levels in the library, perhaps engaging in more "managing by wandering aroun" or scheduling some time to spend with those on the front lines. This type of activity can go far in showing younger staff, paraprofessional staff, and people outside of leadership positions that library leaders do indeed care about the individuals. Also, leaders should cultivate potential new leaders by watching for attributes that have been found to be successful and develop these qualities. By doing so, library leaders will be able to have a pool of qualified candidates to run the organization, rather than facing a shortage resulting from turnover and retirements.

"The task of the leader is to get people from where they are to where they have not been."[24]

NOTES

1. Tom Peters, "Leadership and Change," *Finance Week* (June 21, 2004): 66.

2. Jim Collins, *Good to Great: Why Some Companies Make the Leap and Others Don't* (New York: Harper Collins, 2001).

3. Rachel Singer Gordon, "Nurturing New Leaders by Demonstrating Quality Leadership," *JLAMS* [*Journal of the Library Administration and Management Section of the New York Library Association*] 1, no. 2 (2004–2005): 23–38.

4. Peter Hernon, Ronald Powell, and Arthur Young, *The Next Library Leadership: Attributes of Academic and Public Library Directors* (Westport, CT: Libraries Unlimited, 2003).

5. Carole McConnell, "Staff and Leadership Shortages? Grow Your Own," *American Libraries* 35, no. 9 (October 2004): 34–36.

6. Gordon, "Nurturing New Leaders by Demonstrating Quality Leadership," 29.

7. Jack Welch and Suzy Welch, *Winning* (New York: HarperBusiness, 2005).

8. Mary Brandel "Skill Set Soul Searching," *Computerworld* 34 (2000): 87.

9. McConnell, "Staff and Leadership Shortages?"

10. Florence Mason and Louella Wetherbee, "Learning to Lead: An Analysis of Current Training Programs for Library Leadership," *Library Trends* 53 (Summer 2004): 187–217.

11. Ibid.

12. Gordon, "Nurturing New Leaders by Demonstrating Quality Leadership."

13. Ibid., 33–4.

14. Claire Nankivell and Michele Shoolbred, "Mentoring in Library and Information Services: A Literature Review and Report on Recent Research," *New Review of Academic Librarianship* 3 (1997): 102.

15. Hernon, Powell, and Young, *The Next Library Leadership.*

16. Gordon, "Nurturing New Leaders by Demonstrating Quality Leadership."

17. Charles Townley, "Nurturing Library Effectiveness: Leadership for Personnel Development," *Library Administration and Management* 16 (Winter 1989): 18.

18. Gordon, "Nurturing New Leaders by Demonstrating Quality Leadership."

19. Peter Hernon and Nancy Rossiter, "Emotional Intelligence: Which Traits Are Most Prized?" *College & Research Libraries* 67 (May 2006), 270–271.

20. Gordon, "Nurturing New Leaders by Demonstrating Quality Leadership."

21. Dale Buss, "When Managing Isn't Enough: Nine Ways to Develop the Leaders You Need," *Workforce* 80, no. 12 (December 2001): 44–47.

22. Hernon, Powell, and Young, *The Next Library Leadership*, 43–44.

23. Collins, *Good to Great.*

24. "Henry Kissinger." Available at http://www.nwlink.com/~donclark/leader/leadqot.html (accessed May 11, 2006).

17

MANAGERIAL LEADERSHIP AS AN AREA OF DOCTORAL STUDY

Peter Hernon, Candy Schwartz, and Caryn Anderson

"The doctoral program in managerial leadership can draw from many rich sources of research and experience in order to cultivate leadership within the students."[1]

Libraries and other information-related organizations are undergoing profound change. Institutional environments are increasingly complex, both structurally and conceptually. Boundaries are blurring among libraries, technology centers, and community/social destinations and between the development and delivery of information services and information products. For example, university libraries might have a unit for information and communications technologies that provides services to external clients or might have contracted services onsite (e.g., cafes or coffee bars). Cross-disciplinary fields of inquiry are growing. The nature of the services that information organizations are expected to deliver is evolving rapidly, and these organizations are more actively involved in the provision of significant primary and secondary literature to the scholarly community. Recent years have seen seismic shifts from print to electronic resources, from on-site to remote access, from service provided during opening hours to 24/7/365 access, and from repository to synthesizing and publishing functions. Also, in settings where the users of a given library have never visited the physical building, managing intellectual property rights and even coping with institutional issues of accountability, effectiveness, and efficiency have become more complicated.

These characteristics of modern information environments make them time-consuming to assess and manage, often intellectually challenging, and even politically explosive. To be resilient in this atmosphere of complexity and change, the information professions need leaders with unique combinations of intellectual and interpersonal assets that can best be described as effective management and inspiring, ethical leadership.

Against this background, the purpose of this chapter is to discuss the PhD in managerial leadership in the information professions (MLIP), which the Simmons College Graduate School of Library and Information Science developed and which the Institute of Museum and Library Services (IMLS) and Simmons College have funded for more than $1.53 million.

MANAGERIAL LEADERSHIP

Managerial leadership focuses on the knowledge, abilities, and skills of middle to senior-level managers in the information professions to help an organization establish and accomplish its purpose and direction (as reflected in mission and vision statements and strategic plans). Effective managerial leadership depends on individuals who continue to develop as both managers and leaders. Development refers to engaging in rigorous self-assessment, offsetting critical weaknesses, understanding and shaping organizational culture, and using research to enhance organizational efficacy.

The term *managerial leadership*, which has been used indiscriminately, recognizes that people in significant positions in the profession and in areas such as higher education need knowledge, skills, and abilities related to *both* management *and* leadership. A number of descriptions of managerial leadership really equate leadership with leadership theories and styles or focus on effective leadership. We interpret managerial leadership as requiring competency in both management and leadership, but the focus is more on leadership, thus distinguishing between a program in managerial leadership and, for instance, one in business administration where the focus is on training in the theory and practice of business management. Further, we place the study of managerial leadership in the context of the information professions.

Evolution from Doctor of Arts Degree

Responding to the Carnegie Foundation and its call for a doctor of arts (DA) degree, Simmons College began a DA program in library and information science in 1973. The program, which was designed to meet the ongoing needs of administrators of libraries, information centers, and information systems, maintained that management is an applied discipline that requires both academic preparation and substantial work experience. Graduates of the program, of whom there have been more than 70, work in various library settings in the United States and internationally.

The new PhD program was first brought to the faculty as a whole in 2001, through discussion of a white paper on the development of doctoral study in managerial leadership. The faculty passed a motion "accepting, in principle, the concept of a PhD degree (in managerial leadership)," but with the understanding that resources would need to be secured for this program to be successful. Receipt of funding, in 2005, from IMLS provided the impetus for moving the program from a concept into practice.

THE PROGRAM

The doctoral program in managerial leadership in the information professions is a cohesive program that concentrates on:

- A set of courses all centered on managerial leadership;
- A comprehensive understanding of diverse issues;
- A strong foundation in critical thinking, problem solving, practice-based research, and effective writing;
- The knowledge and skills necessary for those who would be change agents in an increasingly digital world; and
- A supportive and nurturing environment of individualized study that combines technological applications, research methods, and political realities with management and leadership theory and practice.

Another way to envision the program is to recognize that it has four components: (1) domain knowledge related to managerial leadership within library and information science, (2) expansion of the management and leadership literatures with relevant case studies and other types of innovative writings, (3) the enhancement of students' leadership abilities through self-improvement and nurturing from both full-time faculty members and key figures in the profession who lead complex organizations, and (4) production of research (both theoretical and applied) that adds to the professional literature.

Through flexible scheduling and a combination of classroom and Web-based learning, the program accommodates those individuals who are already employed in full-time managerial roles and who do not want to leave their positions to earn a degree. A portion of the program is self-directed, giving each student the opportunity to customize studies and research to address the unique environment and needs of an individual organization and the community it serves. Simultaneously, students gain a broad perspective by interacting with leaders throughout the professional community.

Program Goals

The goals of the program are to:

- Prepare individuals for careers as change agents and leaders in managing libraries and other information-related organizations in an environment of globalization and convergence of disciplines;

- Create a leading environment in which inquiry and critical questioning are valued and individual strengths are enhanced;
- Engender in students an ability to engage in analytical thinking and problem solving;
- Establish a culture that nurtures the advancement and dissemination of new knowledge related to managing libraries as complex organizations;
- Provide students with a conceptual understanding of organizations and behavior within them;
- Guide students in developing competencies in interpersonal and communication skills, leadership, and facilitation; and
- Foster an understanding of the role of technology in the management of change.

The goals will be accomplished through a program consisting of courses and modules that include case study development, presentations to different stakeholder groups, the composition of research and analytical papers of publishable quality, and the creation of practical planning documents related to activities such as strategic planning, project management, and capital campaign development. In addition to independent work, cohorts of students engage with each other, full-time and adjunct faculty, and professors of practice in collaborative projects. Activities are designed to enhance teamwork skills and to stimulate and nurture the intellectual exchange that is a fundamental characteristic of the doctoral experience.

Advisory Board

The board of advisors consists of current and past leaders of major professional organizations such as the American Library Association, the Association of College and Research Libraries, the Association of Research Libraries, the Association for Library and Information Science Education, the Special Libraries Association, the Council on Library and Information Resources, and the National Commission on Libraries and Information Science. Those individuals include:

- Camila A. Alire of the University of New Mexico;
- Ernest A. DiMattia, Jr. of The Ferguson Library;
- Susan S. DiMattia of DiMattia Associates;
- Robert E. Dugan of Suffolk University;
- Susan K. Martin of Marstons Mills Public Library;
- Elizabeth Martinez, consultant;
- James M. Matarazzo of Simmons College;
- Ann McLaughlin of Thomas Crane Public Library;
- Cheryl Metoyer of the University of Washington;
- James G. Neal of Columbia University;

- Danuta A. Nitecki of Yale University;
- Denise Stephens of the University of Kansas;
- James F. Williams, II of the University of Colorado, Boulder;
- Ann Wolpert of the Massachusetts Institute of Technology; and
- Jerome Yavarkovsky of Boston College.

Their role has been to advise the program directors in all phases of the program from the development of the conceptual model to matters related to the curriculum and the selection of the student body. They will remain as advisors throughout (and it is hoped beyond) the period of the federal grant and continue to provide feedback on the continued development and refinement of the program.

THE FACULTY

Members of the full-time faculty, nationally and internationally known practitioners (professors of practice), and adjunct faculty teach the courses and work with students on their research projects and completion of required independent modules. Each course is taught by several faculty members who work together to enrich the learning experience and to mentor student development—reinforcing the competencies specified in the leadership model, which is discussed later in the chapter. The professors of practice, including deans of libraries that are members of the Association of Research Libraries (ARL), are well-known and respected individuals recognized for their successful leadership. Such persons bring practical experience as leaders in their respective institutions and the profession, as well as a national and international reputation to the classroom, program, and the nurturing of students. The professors of practice work closely with students and with the professional community to strengthen the understanding and practice of managerial leadership through research, advocacy, and problem-based experiences. They emphasize the practical dilemmas encountered in modern information environments—integrating theory and practice to prepare students for leadership positions in the information professions.

STUDENT BODY

Information professionals who have already attained a middle to senior level in their career and are poised to make lasting contributions to the field constitute the candidate pool most likely to leverage the greatest value from program. These professionals are expected to complete the program within three years, while working full-time.

The program should attract and accept directors, assistant/deputy directors, and department heads from ARL and Association of College and Research

Libraries institutions, as well as large urban public libraries and other types of library and information settings.

This first cohort, which began the program in May 2006, represents the results of a competitive admissions process in which only 15 percent of the applicants were accepted. The five students bring a diversity of ages, ethnicities, and sectors of experience to the program. Two of them work in university libraries, one as the university librarian and the other as information services director for a research center. One student is branch services director for a bi-county public library system. One student heads up a multilibrary consortium, and another is director of a programmatic office in a large library association. Two of the students have been designated as *Movers & Shakers* by *Library Journal* (2002 and 2004). They are all active in their institutional and professional communities.

It is useful to start with a small group that can help to shape the details of implementing the program. As the program develops and matures, it will expand to include a greater number of students from a richer diversity of sectors and perspectives of librarianship and information management.

CURRICULUM

Managerial leadership, a dynamic and evolving direction for the information professions, offers opportunities for new collaborations and partnerships across disciplines. The curriculum model (Figure 17.1) outlines the intersecting relationships among management, leadership, and library and

Figure 17.1
Curriculum Model

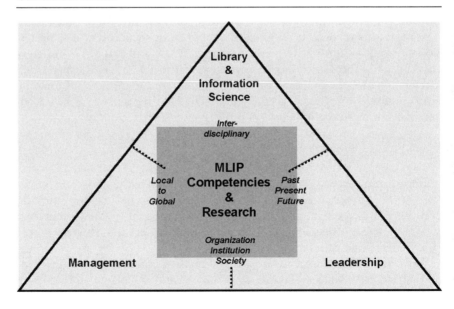

information science that the curriculum addresses. It also illustrates that the curriculum is crafted to recognize and integrate the disciplinary, temporal, spatial, and political contexts in which library and information enterprises operate. More specifically, this model will be used to ensure that courses:

- Contextualize topics in a chronological continuum (history, current frameworks, and potential changes);
- Demonstrate principles at local, regional, national, and global levels;
- Discuss impacts for organizations, institutions, and society; and
- Engage and consider the perspectives and effects of other disciplines (relevant theories and practical collaborators, constituencies, or stakeholders).

The curriculum explores such opportunities as students move through the program, while simultaneously expecting the students to make formative contributions to projects that will have value to their home institutions, the profession both nationally and globally, and their continued development (in accordance with the leadership model).

Program activities are provided via nontraditional methods of course delivery, including intensive instruction (both on-site and in remote locations), online instruction, and guided independent study. Student cohort meetings are held annually in early summer at Simmons College. All cohorts meet in the same week. Courses are offered in summer, fall, and spring and begin with three to five days of face-to-face intensive instruction either at Simmons College or an alternate location. Figure 17.2 depicts the required and elective components of the curriculum. The required courses and modules provide a foundation from which the independent study and elective courses build. Independent learning activities are scheduled at the discretion of the student, in consultation with faculty advisors.

OUTCOMES AND THEIR ASSESSMENT

Expectations related to student development throughout the program will be framed in terms of the leadership model depicted in Figure 17.3, which was adapted, with permission, from the National Center for Healthcare Leadership leadership competency model, version 2.0.[2] The diagram, definitions, and target competencies have been modified to reflect the distinctions of managerial leadership in the information professions. The leadership model groups competencies into three primary leadership domains:

1. *Transformation* refers to abilities in visioning, energizing, and stimulating a change process that coalesces communities, patrons, and professionals around new models of managerial leadership in the information professions. Transformation outcomes include understanding and demonstration of achievement orientation, analytical thinking/problem-solving, community orientation, financial skills, information discovery, innovative thinking, and strategic orientation.

Figure 17.2
The Curriculum

FOUNDATION (Required)	LIS 671, Managerial Leadership	This course reviews the major contributions to contemporary managerial leadership research, theory, and practice, including such areas as leadership theory, leadership styles, strategic planning, change management, ethics, and team building. It also places emphasis on a greater awareness of one's behavior, its impact on others, and the elements needed to influence people to accomplish desired goals in information organizations.
	LIS 672, Research for Managerial Leadership	Research for managerial leadership is positioned within the larger context of social science research. The course examines the research process from conceptualization of a researchable problem, through the reflective inquiry process, to completion (including review of the publication process). The need for research in library and information science is discussed, as well as trends and issues, types of research studies, problem identification, and the setup and reporting activities of a research study.
	LIS 675, Statistics for Evaluating Library and Information Services	The principles of evaluation research are applied to contemporary information management problems that have a leadership component. Building on *Research for Managerial Leadership*, this course covers the fundamentals of identifying and investigating problems relevant to information services delivery, including continuous quality improvement. Topics include obstacles and opportunities in evaluation research, systems models, measurement concepts (inputs, outputs, outcomes), and statistics (descriptive and inferential). The course also explores the ways in which evaluation and

Figure 17.2
The Curriculum (Continued)

		measurement are integrated with planning activities and the challenges associated with communicating results to decision makers.
	LIS 676, Financial Management of Library and Information Systems	An overview of budget management for libraries, information-related institutions, and projects is explored in this course. Understanding, planning, developing, justifying, and presenting budgets are discussed relative to money management tools and techniques. Alternate revenue sources, including the establishment and growth of foundations and endowments, as well as investments, audits, and risk management, are also explored.
	LIS 677, Human Resources Management	The fundamental aspects of managing and motivating staff are critical parts of effective leadership and management. This course examines labor relations, conflict resolution, and team leadership (including negotiation, mediation and facilitation). Communication, relationship building, and talent development are also explored in the context of supervising others.
	LIS 678, Managing and Leading in a Political Context	This course covers the skills necessary for interacting with the larger communities in which libraries and information centers operate (academic institutions, municipalities, corporations). It addresses specifically address advocacy and cooperation within complex, multi-stakeholder power structures as encountered when working with administrators, political leaders, and community groups (e.g., citizens, faculty, and students). The effect of political contexts on planning activities are also covered.

Figure 17.2
The Curriculum (Continued)

INVESTIGATION (Required)	LIS 680, Independent Inquiry	Students execute two managerial leadership research studies in collaboration with doctoral colleagues. This learning activity has a flexible time frame. Sample research areas may include program and institutional assessment (and/or accreditation), customer service, influencing organizational culture, leadership assessment and improvement, managing collections (digital and print; special collections), scholarly communication, and futurism (the future of information professions). Activity may begin on completion of *Evaluation of Information Services*, and must be completed as a prerequisite to *Issues in Managerial Leadership and Change*.
	LIS 681, Financial Management Independent Module	Students will explore a topic of their own choosing as an extension of *Financial Management of Library and Information Systems*. They investigate the issue independently and produce two papers of publishable quality: a case study and an analytical paper.
	LIS 682, Human Resource Management Independent Module	Students explore a topic of their own choosing as an extension of *Personnel Management*. They investigate the issue independently and produce two papers of publishable quality: a case study and an analytical paper.
	LIS 683, Political Context Independent Module	Students explore a topic of their own choosing as an extension of *Managing and Leading in a Political Context*. They investigate the issue independently and produce two papers of publishable quality: a case study and an analytical paper.

Figure 17.2
The Curriculum (Continued)

INVESTIGATION (Electives)	LIS 687, Issues in Information Policy	This course covers a wide range of issues associated with government, national and international, of importance to various stakeholder and interest groups. The course, which is intended for information managers, focuses mostly on national governments, and it specifically examines basic information policies and, to some extent, those of international organizations; the policy formulation and review process; the political economy of information; information management in the context of life cycle management; and especially intersections and differences between and among stakeholders and interest groups.
	LIS 688, Fundraising and Entrepreneurial Strategies	This course examines aspects of successful institutional and project-based fundraising, including the diverse skills necessary to engage existing donors, identify and approach prospective donors, write compelling grant proposals, execute and report on received grants, and monitor industry and society to identify creative fundraising opportunities.
	LIS 689, Information Technology Management for Leaders	This course is designed to enable directors of library and information enterprises to effectively hire and manage senior information technology personnel, remain appropriately current with relevant developments in technology, understand the risks and benefits of technology for their operation (including social informatics issues), assess the value of potential information technology projects, and, using an information technology project as a model, successfully manage

Figure 17.2
The Curriculum (Continued)

		and implement special projects of all kinds (including needs assessments, environmental scanning, budgeting, task projection and management, personnel management, assessment, etc.). The project management component focuses on helping students to view projects in a nonlinear and continuous manner to recognize that one project might be leveraged on another. The course also encourages students to "think outside the box."
	LIS 690, Marketing and Advocacy	Library leaders must be strong advocates for their organizations and be able to position their services appropriately to recognized and new target populations. This course discusses market research, planning, presentation, communication, implementation, and evaluation techniques. Advertising, public relations, publicity, promotion, and advocacy approaches to attracting and serving customers are also considered.
DEMONSTRA-TION	LIS 691, Issues in Managerial Leadership and Change	This capstone course involves sustained interaction with other doctoral students in examining issues critical to managerial leadership. It draws on all the theories and skills explored in previous coursework and independent investigation to develop case studies and issue briefs. Content will be flexible to serve the competencies, needs, and interests of the student cohort.
	Comprehensive Assessment	This assessment occurs on completion of the capstone course. The student revisits the paper prepared for that course, addressing any comments and making an oral presentation. The student also defends the first chapter of the dissertation. As well,

Figure 17.2
The Curriculum (Continued)

		the final annual review of student progress is conducted.
	LIS 699, Dissertation	The dissertation is a culminating experience intended to demonstrate student mastery of all areas of the MLIP leadership model, integrated with the disciplinary, temporal, spatial, and political contexts of the MLIP curriculum model. It serves as a comprehensive examination of the student's knowledge and skill development. It is also expected to make a significant contribution to the body of scholarship on managerial leadership in the information professions.

Figure 17.3
Leadership Model*

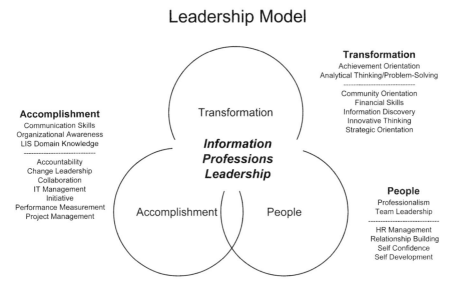

Leadership Model

Transformation
Achievement Orientation
Analytical Thinking/Problem-Solving

Community Orientation
Financial Skills
Information Discovery
Innovative Thinking
Strategic Orientation

Accomplishment
Communication Skills
Organizational Awareness
LIS Domain Knowledge

Accountability
Change Leadership
Collaboration
IT Management
Initiative
Performance Measurement
Project Management

People
Professionalism
Team Leadership

HR Management
Relationship Building
Self Confidence
Self Development

Transformation

Information Professions Leadership

Accomplishment   People

Note: Competencies listed above the line are primary and those below the line are secondary.

2. *Accomplishment* refers to abilities in translating vision and strategy into optimal organizational performance. Accomplishment outcomes include understanding and demonstration of communication skills, organizational awareness, library and information science domain knowledge, accountability, change leadership, collaboration, information technology management, initiative, performance measurement, and project management.

3. *People* refers to abilities in creating an organizational climate that values employees from all backgrounds and provides an energizing environment for them. It also includes the leader's responsibility to understand his or her impact on others and to improve his or her capabilities, as well as the capabilities of others. People outcomes include understanding and demonstration of human resources management, team leadership, professionalism, relationship building, self-confidence, and self-development.

Each course identified in Figure 17.2 deals with a particular set of the leadership outcomes. For example:

- LIS 671, Managerial Leadership, includes *transformation* (achievement orientation, analytical thinking/problem solving, community orientation, innovative thinking, and strategic orientation), *accomplishment* (communication skills, organizational awareness, domain knowledge, change leadership, collaboration, and initiative), and *people* (professionalism, team leadership, relationship building, self-confidence, and self-development).

- LIS 687, Issues in Information Policy, covers *transformation* (analytical thinking/ problem solving and strategic orientation), *accomplishment* (communication skills and domain knowledge), and *people* (professionalism).

- LIS 688, Fundraising and Entrepreneurial Strategies, addresses *transformation* (community orientation and strategic orientation) and *accomplishment* (communication skills, domain knowledge, and accountability).

Definitions of Leadership Competencies

Transformation

Under *transformation* (visioning, energizing, and stimulating a change process that coalesces communities, patrons, and professionals around new models of managerial leadership), the program emphasizes two primary competencies:

- *Achievement orientation*: A concern for surpassing a standard of excellence. The standard may be one's own past performance (striving for improvement), an objective measure (results orientation), outperforming others (competitiveness), challenging assumptions about goals or previous practices, or something that has been done previously (innovation).

- *Analytical thinking/problem solving*: The ability to understand a situation, issue or problem by breaking it into smaller pieces or tracing its implications in a step-by-step way.

It includes organizing the parts of a situation, issue, or problem systematically; making systematic comparisons of different features or aspects; setting priorities on a rational basis; and applying appropriate methods to explore fully and attack a problem.

Other *transformation* competencies include:

- *Community orientation*: The ability to align one's own and the organization's priorities with the needs and values of the community, including its cultural and ethnocentric values and to move managerial leadership in the information professions forward. It includes a service orientation to both external and internal "customers" and constituencies.

- *Financial skills*: The ability to understand and explain financial and accounting information, prepare and manage budgets, and make sound long-term investment decisions.

- *Information discovery*: An underlying curiosity and desire to know more about things, people, or issues, including the desire for knowledge and staying current with disciplinary, organizational, and professional trends and developments. It includes pressing for exact information, while also being able to judge when available information is sufficient to support a decision or action; resolving discrepancies by asking a series of questions; and scanning for potential opportunities or information that may be of future use; as well as staying current and seeking best practices for adoption.

- *Innovative thinking*: The ability to apply complex concepts, develop creative solutions, or adapt previous solutions in new ways.

- *Strategic orientation*: The ability to consider the business, demographic, ethnocultural, political, and regulatory implications of decisions and develop strategies that continually improve the long-term success and viability of the organization. It includes assessing risk and regularly taking educated risks where appropriate.

Accomplishment

Turning to the second domain, *accomplishment* (translating vision and strategy into optimal organizational performance), the following competencies emerge as a primary focus of the program:

- *Communication skills*: The ability to speak and write in a clear, logical, and grammatical manner in formal and informal situations; to prepare cogent business presentations; and to facilitate a group. This includes the ability to persuade, convince, influence, or impress others (individuals or groups) to get them to go along with or to support one's opinion or position.

- *Organizational awareness*: The ability to understand and learn the power relationships in one's own organization or in other organizations (e.g., stakeholders and suppliers). This includes the ability to identify who the real decision makers are; the individuals who can influence them; and to predict how new events or situations will affect individuals and groups within the organization.

- *Domain knowledge* (mastery of library and information science): A broad knowledge of the operational components of libraries and information centers and the current research and best practices associated with these components and related issues in library and information science. Components and issues include collection management and development, intellectual property rights, scholarly communication, and information access. Additional elements include the unique application of user needs analysis, ethics, marketing and advocacy, information technology, and outcomes assessment in information institutions.

Supporting competencies include:

- *Accountability*: The ability to hold people accountable to standards of performance or ensure compliance using the power of one's position or force of personality appropriately and effectively, with the long-term good of the organization in mind. This includes involving people in the development of the standards that impact their performance measurement.
- *Change leadership*: The ability to energize stakeholders and sustain their commitment to changes in approaches, processes, and strategies.
- *Collaboration*: The ability to work cooperatively with others, to be part of a team, to work together, as opposed to working separately or competitively. Collaboration applies when a person is a member of a group of people functioning as a team, but not the leader.
- *Information technology management*: The ability to see the potential in and to understand and use administrative information tools, including active sponsorship of system use and the continuous upgrading of information management capabilities.
- *Initiative*: The ability to make decisions and solve problems proactively—identifying a problem, obstacle, or opportunity and taking action in light of this identification to address current or future problems or opportunities. In this context, initiative also includes the ability to involve staff or other stakeholders in the decision-making and problem-solving processes to ensure greater cooperation and accountability among those implementing or affected by the decision/solution.
- *Performance measurement*: The ability to understand and use statistical and financial methods and metrics to set goals and measure organizational performance; commitment to and employment of evidence-based techniques. Includes measurement of customer expectations (satisfaction and service quality).
- *Project management*: The ability to plan and execute a project with significant scope and impact as well as manage a team. Examples include the construction of a major building or development of a new service.

People

The third domain area covers *people* (creating an organizational climate that values employees from all backgrounds and provides an energizing environment for them). Two competencies, professionalism and team leadership, stand out:

1. *Professionalism* includes the demonstration of (and commitment to) ethics, sound professional practices, social accountability, and community stewardship. The

desire to act in a way that is consistent with one's values and what one says is important.

2. *Team leadership* encompasses how a person sees himself or herself as a leader of others, from forming a team that possesses balanced capabilities to setting its mission, values and norms, as well as to holding the team members accountable individually and as a group for results, socialization, and professional development. Team leadership includes cross-cultural sensitivity and an ability to interact productively with different personality types; taking a personal interest in coaching and mentoring high-potential leaders; and the leader's responsibility to understand his or her impact on others and to improve his or her capabilities, as well as the capabilities of others.

Secondary competencies include:

- *Human resources management*: The ability to implement employment practices that comply with legal and regulatory requirements, and to represent contemporary approaches to human resources policies.

- *Relationship building*: The ability to establish, build, and sustain professional contacts for the purpose of building networks of people with similar goals and that support similar interests.

- *Self-confidence*: A belief in one's own capability to accomplish a task or select an effective approach to a task or problem. This includes confidence in one's ability as expressed in increasingly challenging circumstances and confidence in one's decisions or opinions. It also includes an ability to demonstrate emotional intelligence in regard to one's self and others.

- *Self-development*: The ability to have an accurate view of one's own strengths and development needs, including the impact that one has on others. A willingness to engage in regular self-assessment and to regulate needs through self-directed learning and trying new approaches.

Measurement of Course and Program Assessment

Demonstration of the mastery of competencies is drawn from structured self-assessment; an annual review of each student, involving all faculty members who taught that person; a portfolio of publishable case studies, issue briefs, scenario plans, and research and analytical papers; a comprehensive assessment; and a formal dissertation with oral defense. There will also be cohort peer review, which includes presentations to the cohort with feedback (during cohort meetings). Furthermore, there is an external review that involves both employers and members of the program advisory board.

After completion of the two research-based courses (LIS 672 and LIS 675) and before undertaking the dissertation, students complete two independent research studies that relate to planning and decision making but have a theoretical application. In many courses, they develop case studies (modeled on the problem-solving model developed by A.J. Anderson, professor emeritus of Simmons College) and present them to different stakeholders. They also engage in scenario planning, which identifies trends and explores the implications (political, economic, social and technological) of projecting them forward. Scenarios suggest possibilities and, it is hoped, enable managers to act rapidly if a situation develops.[3] Issue briefs are analyses of the literature on a significant topic that identify the issues and their key aspects, recent developments, selected key readings, and leaders on the topic. Depending on the audience, their length might be a maximum of one, two, or three pages.

The Particulars of Program Assessment

Assessment occurs at both the program and course levels, and it establishes clear, measurable expected outcomes of, and priorities for, student learning. It is also important to ensure that students have every opportunity to achieve the leadership competencies (specified in Figure 17.3); systematically gather, analyze, and interpret evidence to determine how well student learning matches program expectations; and use the data gathered to understand better and to improve student learning.

One of the key program outcomes relates to communications skills, both oral and written. Effective leaders must be able express themselves clearly and persuasively to different stakeholders and to do so within a limited amount of time. Figure 17.4 covers components for oral communication skills. During the first cohort meeting, the oral communication skills of each student will be assessed, and each student will be identified as performing at a *novice, proficient,* or *mastered* one of the five levels (see p. 249). Because course activities and program assessment focus on oral communication skills, students will have learning experiences and feedback that should enable them to communicate at the mastered level once they graduate.

Assessment of the secondary student competencies depicted in Figure 17.3 is conducted periodically throughout the program using the *Leadership Competencies Assessment Form* (Figure 17.5). Students will complete the form as part of the cohort orientation as they consider and respond to the leadership areas highlighted in the leadership model (Figure 17.3). The assessment form depicted in Figure 17.5 will also be addressed at each annual review (to review their progress and identify areas for further focus), on completion of the capstone course (to demonstrate the knowledge and experience gained), and at the comprehensive review.

Finally, a separate board for program assessment has been established to conduct an independent audit and address the extent to which students have learned. Learning, as defined by Peggy L. Maki, "encompasses not only knowledge leading to understanding but also abilities, habits of mind, ways of knowing, attitudes, values, and other dispositions that an institution and its programs and services assert they develop."[4] The knowledge gained

Figure 17.4
Oral Presentation Component of Communication Skills

Indicators	
Expresses purpose clearly	
Gives appearance of feeling at ease	
Gauges audience	Understands background of audience
	Monitors audience level of engagement
Presents arguments persuasively	
Stays within allotted time	
Structures presentation	Clear opening and closing
	Logical development flow
Exhibits good verbal delivery	Correct use of grammar and syntax
	Varied voice (avoids monotone)
Nonverbal behavior strengthens presentation	Appropriate body language
	Consistent eye contact
Instructional aids contribute to the quality of the presentation	
Uses domain knowledge and vocabulary appropriately	
Manages question-and-answer session well	

Student Self-Assessment Rating Scale:

1—Unfamiliar   This is not an element with which I am familiar.

2—Learning   I am learning the principles of this element.

3—Advancing   I am advancing my knowledge and practice of this element.

4—Competent   I am reasonably knowledgeable and effective in this element.

5—Mastered   I am experienced in applying my knowledge of this element

in practice.

Faculty/Employer Rating Scale:

1—Not Present   Element is not manifested in student's work.

2—Learning   Element is present but is poorly developed.

3—Advancing   Element is present and adequate but could be better.

from assessing the program as a whole is useful for improving "pedagogy, instructional design, curricular and co-curricular design, institutional programs and services that support, complement, and advance student learning, educational resources and tools, . . . [and] advising."[5]

Figure 17.5
Leadership Competencies Assessment Form

Please assess [yourself / the student / your colleague] by ranking [your / their] current competency in each leadership area according to the appropriate five-point scale given below. Use the "Assessment Description" area to record brief notes for future reference and discussion.

Leadership Areas*	Competency Ranking (1 – 5)	Assessment Description
Transformation		
Achievement orientation		
Analytical thinking/problem solving		
Community orientation		
Financial skills		
Information discovery		
Innovative thinking		
Strategic orientation		
Accomplishment		
Communication skills		
Organizational awareness		
LIS domain knowledge		
Accountability		
Change leadership		
Collaboration		
IT management		
Initiative		
Performance measurement		
Project management		

Figure 17.5
Leadership Competencies Assessment Form (continued)

People		
Professionalism		
Team leadership		
Human resources management		
Relationship building		
Self-confidence		
Self-development		

Student Self-Assessment Rating Scale:

1—Unfamiliar   This is not an element with which I am familiar.

2—Learning   I am learning the principles of this element.

3—Advancing   I am advancing my knowledge and practice of this element.

4—Competent   I am reasonably knowledgeable and effective in this element.

5—Mastered   I am experienced in applying my knowledge of this element

in practice.

Faculty/Employer Rating Scale:

1—Not Present   Element is not manifested in student's work.

2—Learning   Element is present but is poorly developed.

3—Advancing   Element is present and adequate but could be better.

CONCLUSION

The purpose of this new doctoral program—the first in the profession to focus exclusively on managerial leadership—is to contribute to the successful future of leadership in library and information settings by creating a flexible, innovative program that:

- Strengthens the intellectual and interpersonal assets of students as working managers;
- Actively involves leading practitioners in shaping the educational experience; and
- Generates rigorous research to improve the knowledge base and the practice of managerial leadership.

Students develop and demonstrate abilities related to the leadership model and its focus on transformation, accomplishment, and people. Critical to accomplishment is mastery of domain knowledge as reflected in the courses, the culminating assessment, and the dissertation.

Once the initial phase of the program has been completed—the first three years will rely on funding from the Institute of Museum and Library Services—Simmons College can expand the number of students in the program and develop collaborative partnerships with other universities as the program assumes more of a national and international presence. The need for this program is clearly attested by the willing participation of so many leaders in the profession. This commitment is expected to continue, with more leaders playing a role in the program. The challenge for library and information science education will be to move management and leadership into core courses at the master's level and to develop the pool of qualified and experienced full-time faculty members who can teach in such programs and contribute to the scholarly literature.

Simmons' new PhD in Managerial Leadership in the Information Professions will be an invaluable contribution to the profession of librarianship in that it will fill a long-standing educational lack and will provide a cadre of library leaders for the future.[6]

NOTES

1. Cheryl Metoyer of the University of Washington in an e-mail message to Caryn Anderson, February 8, 2006.

2. National Center for Healthcare Leadership, "NCHL Leadership Model, Version 2.0" (Chicago: National Center for Healthcare Leadership, 2004).

3. See Joan Giesecke, ed., *Scenario Planning for Libraries* (Chicago: American Library Association, 1998).

4. Peggy L. Maki, *Assessing for Learning: Building a Sustainable Commitment across the Institution* (Sterling, VA: Stylus Publishing, 2004), 3.

5. Ibid.

6. Michael Gorman, then president of the American Library Association in an e-mail message to Caryn Anderson, February 8, 2006.

18

LEADERSHIP IN ACADEMIC LIBRARIES IS NO FAD

Peter Hernon

"Leadership is a tricky business."[1]

Leadership does not exist in a vacuum; it needs a context. That context is the shared vision that institutional and organizational leaders develop to guide their planning, activities, and decision making. Leaders must understand both institutional and organizational cultures if they are going to be successful in creating positive change. Central to leadership, which is defined as influencing others to accomplish organizational goals, is the ability to motivate, inspire, and persuade others to achieve a vision, while maintaining the trust of the group. Effective managers are leaders, but team leadership is not limited to individuals with line authority. As a consequence, the term *managerial leadership* refers to individuals who are both managers and leaders. In a team setting, leaders may not have managerial responsibilities. As a result, managerial leadership does not include all leadership that occurs in institutions and organizations.

The purpose of this chapter is to build on some of the themes discussed in previous chapters and to reinforce the importance of leadership. As academic librarianship progresses in the twenty-first century, leadership will become more important as librarians interact directly with a more diverse set of stakeholders inside and outside the library and as they create a better understanding of how the library's mission helps the institution achieve its own mission. As more librarians develop their campus presence and play a partnership in information literacy with the teaching faculty (as many regional accrediting organizations expect),[2] there will be interesting opportunities for them to be a leader in showing faculty and administrators how to develop an appropriate assessment framework for measuring student learning outcomes. Involvement in information policy issues at the local, state, national, or international levels will lead to direct interaction with policymakers and coalition building with interested faculty and other stakeholders. In such circumstances, leadership is not necessarily confined to library directors and other members of the senior management team.

WORK SETTING

As shown in *The Next Library Leadership* and elsewhere,[3] there is a projected shortage of graduates of library and information studies (LIS) master's programs to fill every position resulting from retirements in the profession. A further complication is that not all libraries want to (or are in a position to) fill those positions. Libraries need to reexamine professional and paraprofessional positions on a regular basis, identify what types of expertise and credentials they need, and determine where accredited LIS programs can supply the right types of workers. The workforce of today and tomorrow consists of librarians with the master's degree in LIS, as well as others with degrees and expertise coming from other subject areas (e.g., engineering, computer science, publishing, law, donor relations, and human relations), with specific language or technological skills, or with teaching experience (for partnering with faculty teaching information literacy). At the same time, some of the work that librarians have traditionally performed has been assigned to paraprofessional staff.

As James G. Neal argues, the professional workforce in university libraries at present does not share a common background and "set of values, outlooks, styles, and expectations."[4] He foresees "new tensions among different types of library professionals,"[5] and staffing patterns that will complicate socialization into the profession, as well as "employee relations, training, management, and leadership."[6] Two questions arise: What percentage of the professional workforce in university libraries will have the master's degree in LIS? Will that percentage increase, decrease, or remain the same over time? The professional workforce might even exist in smaller numbers than it does at present.

Those in leadership positions may come from diverse backgrounds, but they should be able to motivate the workforce to accomplish a shared vision and organizational goals. To do this will require increased knowledge about a workforce containing individuals representing different generations, backgrounds, expertise, and experiences who will likely "challenge the standards and practices of library professionalism."[7] Libraries will probably need to invest more time and resources in staff orientation and professional staff development, and in opening new lines of communication. They will also need to develop effective mentoring programs and techniques to integrate the workforce into the library profession. If, as Neal foresees, libraries adopt flexible compensation strategies,[8] will some personnel issues that managers address be harder to resolve?

MANAGERIAL LEADERSHIP

The term *managerial leadership*, which is not new, appears in the leadership literature as a way to link leadership and management, or to view management from the perspective of leadership. Some writings, however, merely equate the term with leadership theories, styles, and behaviors.[9] Management is the process of administering and coordinating resources to ensure that an organization accomplishes its goals. Leading, along with planning, organizing, and controlling, are managerial functions. As A. J. Anderson explains, "the leading aspect of management is the process of influencing others to attain group, organizational, and societal goals. The central attribute is 'social influence.'"[10] The development of leadership skills necessitates that libraries invest in difficult areas such as better people skills for managers and the personal development of leaders, as well as the ability of managers-leaders to cope with complex human behaviors, emotions, occupational stress, and burnout. Leaders must know how to mentor, motivate, coach others, give effective presentations, listen, and share what they know. Such attributes are associated with both emotional intelligence and transformational leadership.

Managerial leadership calls for individuals to possess a set of attributes that makes them effective managers and successful leaders. In effect, "leadership and vision without the courage to seize opportunities or without the day-to-day managerial follow through to make it happen does not 'get it done'. . . . [T]rue leaders [cannot] neglect the housekeeping and their other managerial roles."[11] As is evident, more attention must shift to managerial leadership and perhaps over time the program discussed in Chapter 17 will have a significant impact on the profession.

Emergence of the Phrase

No definition of the phrase "managerial leadership" has gained general acceptance. In fact, it is often referred to but left undefined. The assumption, even among dissertation authors (and by extension their committees), is that everyone understands what it means; however, dissertations and other works often mention managerial leadership in their titles and perhaps introductions, never to explain, or repeat use of, that phrase.

As Figure 18.1 indicates, when discussing managerial leadership, some authors focus exclusively on management (see *a* in the figure) and ignore the leadership component (see *b*), whereas others either reverse the focus or view managerial leadership as coverage of either management *or* leadership; most frequently they concentrate on managerial development. Others examine the intersection between management and leadership (see *c*), thereby

Figure 18.1
Depiction of Managerial Leadership

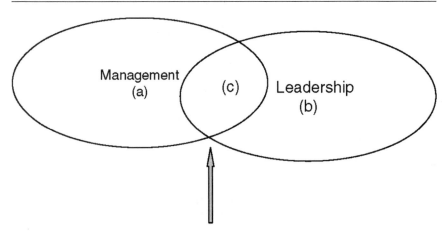

Managerial Leadership

examining the managerial leader—a position with leadership responsibility or someone seeking such responsibility. The assumption is that, like management, leadership is a formal position. For example, George S. Odiorne, in a book published in 1965, referred to management by objectives as a system or philosophy of managerial leadership. As he explains, managers need to identify and set objectives for themselves, their units, and their organizations.[12] Other than in the title, however, he does not deal with managerial leadership. Laurie Newman DiPadova related managerial leadership with organizational hierarchy; more specifically, she studied managerial roles, tasks, and responsibilities.[13] Lisa Deane McNary connected managerial leadership with the quality movement and the work of W. Edward Deming, and she developed a managerial leadership profile.[14]

In his 1951 dissertation at Cornell University, Chris Argyris studied the pattern of leadership and the interactions between the leader and the subordinates at an anonymous plant. In this instance managerial leadership is equated with the leader, presumably the boss.[15] In another dissertation, completed at the University of Michigan in 1957, James Kelso Dent equated managerial leadership with leadership style[16]; and, in a master's thesis, Wilbur M. Skidmore II investigated which leadership theory "is most relevant to effective management."[17]

More recently, Katherine M. Babiak defined managerial leadership "as the leadership process exercised by managers towards the members within the organization with the purpose of attaining the designated goals."[18] Manuel Guillén and Tomás F. González stressed that managerial leadership is a manager's commitment as a leadership to achieving total quality management systems.[19] Peter A. Topping referred to managerial leadership as "multidimensional" and seems to view the term in the context of "leadership challenges associated with managing others" and "interacting with the executives above and peers across the company." He believes that "to be effective a managerial leader needs to 'manage up' and to develop a network of relationships through the enterprise to get things accomplished."[20]

Turning now to the literature of library and information science, in 1987, Joanne R. Euster referred to the writings of D. E. Berlew, who viewed managerial leadership as one of the leadership stages that organizations might encounter. It ranks below an "excited organization," which experiences charismatic leadership. Berlew defines charisma in terms of:

- The development of a "common vision" for the organization related to values shared by the organization's members;
- The discovery or creation of value-related opportunities and activities within the framework of the mission and goals of the organization; and
- Making organization members feel stronger and more in control of their own destinies, both individually and collectively.[21]

The goal of an organization, Berlew maintains, is to advance to the stage of excitement. He considers managerial leadership as producing an organizational climate in which workers are highly productive and satisfied.[22]

From an examination of various literatures, managerial leadership might be viewed as the temperament, character, personality, behaviors, knowledge, skills, and abilities required to excel as a manager. The set of knowledge, skills, and abilities, however, might be linked with good management practices, leadership styles, and effective organizational results. In effect, managerial leadership is not a vision of leadership *versus* management or management *and* leadership. It is more the intersection or dynamic relationship *between* management and leadership (see *c* in Figure 18.1). The purpose of that intersection or relationship is to influence people to transform the organization through the achievement of its stated mission, vision, and goals.

For a PhD program, such as the one discussed in Chapter 17, the intersection or dynamic relationship focuses on leadership theories and styles, as well as the relevant research literature. Perhaps Figure 18.1 might be amended to include a third intersecting circle, one for research. The focus on research differentiates a graduate degree from a leadership program or institute.

Managerial leadership might address leadership efficacy or effectiveness, perhaps in dealing with subordinates and their job performance or satisfaction. Because leadership is not necessarily linked to a managerial position, managerial leadership does *not* encompass all leadership that might occur within a library. When managers encourage staff without line authority to be both leaders and followers, managerial leadership is not an appropriate term. The Simmons doctoral program (as discussed in Chapter 17, as a consequence, is aimed at individuals in managerial positions who are actual leaders or who want to develop their leadership potential. Managerial leadership might apply within the organization; however, it might also occur within the institution, in dealing with stakeholders, or while in participating in community engagement.

Research Agenda

To further illustrate what managerial leadership is, it might be helpful to identify some general research areas from which problem statements might be developed. Examples of research areas include:

- Analysis of gender and managerial leadership stereotypes: How do library managers compare with managers in other work environments?[23]
- Comparison between library directors and staff about the extent to which the director is a leader at the organizational level (comparison of the attributes related to emotional intelligence, for instance, that each claims the director possesses).
- Examination of how managerial leaders cope with dissent.[24]
- Faculty and upper administration perceptions of library managers as organizational and campus-wide leaders.
- Gender and other variables that might have an impact on library leadership effectiveness.
- Impact of managerial leadership in libraries on changing organizational culture.
- Importance of leadership in career advancement in library and information settings.
- Importance of librarians as campus leaders in achieving information literacy as a component of student learning outcomes for campus programs (undergraduate and graduate level).
- Importance of leadership and managerial traits and abilities in hiring library directors (including the perspectives of search committees and upper college and university administrators).
- Leadership challenges that arise in distributed digital environments in libraries.[25]
- Leadership role of senior managers in dealing with library stakeholders.
- Practice of resonant leadership among library directors.
- Prevalence of service leadership among academic libraries and, in the case of academic libraries, how well service covers the educational mission of academic institutions (e.g., how well it represents a learning environment).
- Professional communication networks that library directors (or a subset such as culturally diverse directors) use and the effect of those networks on leadership development.
- Role of library managers as opinion leaders in dealing with groups such as EDUCAUSE or government policymakers.

SOME MISPERCEPTIONS

An examination of the ACRLog, a blog of the Association of College and Research Libraries, revealed a discussion about "what makes a good academic library director." The core competencies that the authors highlighted related to their own work perspectives and contact with the library director. The authors identify those traits they believe directors should know to communicate better with them. For example, a librarian working as a Webmaster focused on "the technology aspects of library leadership" and identified the following abilities:

- An understanding of Web page development;
- Expertise with digital assets management;
- An ability to work with scholars and students to make the right information accessible;
- An ability to work well with information technologists (e.g., campus computing); and
- An ability to mentor others (help them keep up with the latest trends).

Other blog writers believe that "a critical attribute . . . is the ability to integrate the library into the curriculum, and that only happens when the director, working blog with library staff and other academic support professionals, is able to connect with faculty and encourage them to integrate library resources into their coursework."[26] In effect, the library director is a campus-wide "instructional leader."[27]

The director should be an educator who is familiar with student learning outcomes and the shift from teaching to learning. Thus the characterization of a director as an "instructional leader" may be too narrow. Such perceptions do not necessarily view the position of director from the perspective of the entire organization or the institution. Library directors must be informed about key issues confronting academic libraries and higher education and be able to develop and implement strategies to cope with those challenges. Directors probably do not need "expertise with digital assets management"; however, if the library has digital repositories, an associate or assistant director should possess that knowledge. Such knowledge may be important for an effective manager, perhaps one who is a member of the senior management team, but how does it apply to leadership?

PRESENT AND FUTURE CHALLENGES FOR MANAGERIAL LEADERSHIP

Instead of presenting a comprehensive list of challenges, this section identifies and briefly discusses some examples. With the realization that leadership is something that should be present throughout the organization and that individuals can be both leaders and followers depending on the situation and their knowledge and abilities, libraries need to engage in staff development that centers on empowerment, reasonable risk taking, and the meeting of organizational goals. Staff development programs might also focus on the role and importance of librarians interacting with stakeholders and being able to discuss with them the library's mission, vision, and goals in the context of a digital information age and recent trends in scholarly communication. As a result, staff development should introduce team leadership and the purpose of broad interaction with stakeholders; further an understanding of the library's mission, vision, and goals; and seek to improve the ability of librarians to engage in critical thinking and to practice good oral communication skills.[28] Another essential attribute is the ability to listen and to respond to what people are actually saying. Listening is directly related to good oral communication skills.

A closely related issue is the realization that many people still do not understand what makes someone a librarian and what that person actually does. This issue is not new; for example, more than a decade ago, a SPEC Kit of the Association of Research Libraries (ARL) explained,

With increasing frequency, professional position announcements make reference to educational and experiential requirements that are broader than, or in lieu of, the traditional M.L.S./library experience qualification. In the not-too-distant past, librarians were "forced" to assume professional roles beyond the immediate scope of librarianship (e.g., personnel officer, systems analyst, facilities administrator, fundraiser), but it now seems that library administrators are willing to seek and hire individuals with such specialized training and experience from within their respective professions or fields.[29]

The same SPEC Kit also noted that

a segment of the professional literature during the last decade or so, has vociferously argued in favor of moving beyond the standard M.L.S. pool of applicants and considering equally, if not giving preference to, candidates for librarian positions who possess other requisite educational qualifications and experience. Invariably, the main argument has revolved around the notion that to take full advantage of the opportunities presented by informational technologies, libraries need an infusion of diversified talent and a greater breadth of perspective than what the traditionally trained and oriented librarian brings.[30]

In informal discussions with library directors, some have noted that stakeholders have asked them to describe a librarian. The changing work force, the nature of the work that librarians do, the misperceptions that the Internet contains (or will contain) all (or most) information and knowledge, and a perceived decline in use of the physical library (Chapter 8 helps attack this misperception) create more confusion about libraries and librarians among stakeholders and the public. Dealing with such issues also addresses the outdated stereotype of a librarian as "quiet, mean or stern, single/unmarried, stuffy, and in glasses."[31]

Directly related to these challenges is that librarians tend to think organizationally, but function in an institutional setting. Library directors must think institutionally while carrying out their organizational responsibility. The challenge will be to get the library staff to move beyond their narrow role within an organization and to think both organizationally and institutionally.

SERVICE LEADERSHIP

In the digital information environment with ongoing changes in scholarly communication and an increased emphasis on information access, as opposed to physical ownership of materials and resources, the historical emphasis on judging libraries based on collection size has been replaced with a focus on the provision of more and better services. In this regard, some key questions become, "How do services exceed user expectations?" and "How is the definition of quality service changing?" For a library service quality encompasses the interactive relationship between the library and the people whom it serves. For more than a decade, librarians and LIS researchers have been interested in the research that Valarie Zeithaml, A. Parasuraman, Leonard L. Berry, and their disciples have conducted. Through this significant body of literature, academic librarians have become familiar with SERVQUAL and its library offspring, LibQUAL+™, which is available through the Association of Research Libraries (http://www.libqual.org/).

Traditionally, service quality has been associated with the gaps model of service and confirmation/disconfirmation theory.[32] In *Assessing Service Quality,* Peter Hernon and Ellen Altman link service quality and customer service.[33] Svafa Grönfeldt and Judith Stronther frame customer service as part of service leadership.[34] They argue that effective leadership will not guide service organizations unless the organizational culture centers on service excellence and an empowered staff delights the customers with the high quality of service provided. They downplay the importance of leadership styles and do not regard leadership as confined largely to the senior management team or the person serving as director, dean, chief information officer, or chief executive officer. Empowerment means that leadership is diffused throughout the organization so that everyone engages in self-leadership: people are able "to shape their own future and . . . cope with the changes that are part of it."[35] A "leadership mind-set" emerges when the entire organization practices collective leadership and works for sustained competitive advantage and continuous service improvement.[36] For Grönfeldt and Stronther, key traits of leadership become innovation, creativity, valuing customers, agility, teamwork, integrity diversity (attracting the best talent), responsibility (to the communities served as stated in the mission statement), inspiring trust, and accepting change. Such traits clarify the definition of service leadership as "the culture that empowers the organization to strategize its promises, design its processes, and engage its people in a proactive quest for competitive advantage."[37]

Service leadership is an intriguing concept that has application to the not-for-profit sector. For libraries, however, it neither replaces other leadership theories nor adequately reflects the mission of academic institutions and their libraries. Libraries can create a culture that empowers everyone in the organization to fulfill the promises implicit in service leadership. They can design service processes to change organizational culture, but, unlike for-profit organizations, there is not a systematic quest for competitive advantage. The challenge is to identify and include those parts of service leadership that are most useful to the organization and its broader institution.

Libraries are complex organizations whose organizational behavior cannot be explained entirely through either service leadership or customer service. This is not to say that both are not important. As libraries expand the types of individuals who enter their workforce, their cultures will include a more diverse set of beliefs, customs, knowledge, and practices. That culture will continue to change and will require different types of leadership and leadership styles. Emotional intelligence and transformational leadership will likely remain foundations from which new leadership theories and practices evolve. Leaders must stimulate, inspire, and motivate the people who work for (and with) them to change habits of mind, attitudes, behaviors, values, and skills so that they can accomplish organizational goals. They must also demonstrate strong communication skills and the other attributes covered in this book, and some will even be charismatic.

SUCCESSION MANAGEMENT

Succession management, which assumes a dynamic rather than a static operational environment, is more than succession planning. It involves an ongoing examination of the organization, its needs, expertise, and personnel. Its intent is to prepare for organizational change, deal with the retirement or otherwise departure of the professional staff, focus on staff retention, and ensure continuity in how the organization functions. If particular individuals leave, will job descriptions for new hires go unchanged, or will the organization reorganize and decide if it wants to move in a different direction? Succession management therefore is more than replacement planning. It involves a review of staff positions and sets strategic directions and priorities for the organization.

The typical approach to succession management is to develop a plan to guide the retention or replacement of middle or upper-level managers; however, the plan should also identify and nurture current and future leaders. Furthermore, the plan should discuss renewal—resonant leadership—so that leaders are not overwhelmed by occupational stress and burnout. They must renew themselves to cope with future challenges.

Succession management identifies those key positions where managerial leadership is essential. Potential candidates benefit from a wide variety of different work opportunities and experiences; these experiences, when possible, should be transformational. Senior managers often monitor staff, such as those involved on teams, and see how such individuals respond to leadership opportunities and challenges, while gaining more experience. Those with the greatest talent might be given line authority as they begin the transformation to managerial leadership. As Angela Bridgland notes, succession management requires opportunities for:

formal mentoring—mentors are teachers rather than figures in authority, and provide on-the-job advice about dealing with challenges presented by the work environment, including interpersonal problems and political issues. Mentors can reinforce the values of the organisation and can successfully model the critical competencies required for movement to higher levels.[38]

She explains that "organisations are increasingly making recruitment decisions based around two drivers: whether the position adds value and to what extent the job requires unique human capital." Furthermore, "where positions are deemed core and/or strategic, efforts must be made to ensure that a pool of knowledge and skills is created to ensure the ongoing success of these positions."[39] Clearly, succession management requires much thought and senior managers should continually revisit the plan, making changes as necessary.

BALDRIGE NATIONAL QUALITY PROGRAM

The purpose of the Baldrige National Quality Program, which the National Institute of Standards and Technology (NIST) administers in accordance with the Malcolm Baldrige National Quality Improvement Act of 1982, is to improve national competitiveness by developing partnerships in the private sector and all levels of government. The program has now been applied to public education and improved student performance. The American Society for Quality assists NIST, an agency of the Department of Commerce, in administering the Baldrige award program. One category for judging the award is leadership:

Leadership addresses how your senior leaders guide and sustain your organization, setting organizational vision, values, and performance expectations. Attention is given to how your senior leaders communicate with faculty and staff, develop future leaders, and create a learning environment that encourages ethical behavior and high performance. The Category also includes your organization's governance system, its legal and ethical responsibilities to the public, and how your organization supports its community.[40]

Senior leaders practice visionary leadership by demonstrating their "central role in setting values and directions, communicating, creating, and balancing value for all students and stakeholders, and creating an organizational bias for action."[41] They are future oriented and have a strong "commitment to improvement, innovation, and organizational sustainability. Increasingly, this requires creating an environment for empowerment, agility, and organizational learning."[42]

A core value and concept of leadership relate to learning-centered education, which places "the focus of education on learning and the real needs of students."[43] In the case of higher education, learning-centered education is similar to student learning outcomes and their assessment, which examines the impact of individual courses and programs of study on learning. Libraries should not be exempt from showing how they contribute both directly and indirectly to learning-centered education, as Richland College, one of seven institutions in the Dallas County Community College District, has done. In 2005, it became the first community college to receive the Baldrige award for organizational excellence. "The college previously received the 2005 Texas Award for Performance Excellence from the governor's office and the Quality Texas Foundation; was named a Best Practices Vanguard College by the League for Innovation in the Community College in 2000; was one of seven mentoring colleges for the American Association of Community Colleges' national Service Learning Project from 1998 to 2003; served as one of eight pilot institutions for the Southern Association of Colleges and Schools' new accreditation standards; and received the American Library Association's 2001 Library of the Future Award and the 2004 Excellence in Academic Libraries Award."[44] Instances such as these should be probed as libraries formulate a set of best practices based on the Baldrige criteria: leadership; strategic planning; customer and market focus; measurement, analysis and knowledge management; human resource focus; and process management.

PERSONALITY TRAITS

There is no single set of traits that an effective leader should possess. In today's corporate environment, a leader needs to build excellence in services and employees. Perhaps to reach excellence the person ought to a leader of good character; however, this point should not be overemphasized given all the accounts of people who were obviously leaders—perhaps for a long time—but lacked good character. In the nonprofit sector, including libraries, leaders should have good character and be ethical. They should also be reflective and forward-looking.

Leaders should have an accurate understanding of their personality and whether they are:

- Outgoing, talkative, sociable, assertive—*extraversion*;
- Trusting, good-natured, cooperative, soft hearted—*agreeableness*;
- Dependable, responsible, achievement oriented, persistent—*conscientiousness*;

- Relaxed, secure, and unworried—*emotional stability*; and
- Intellectual, imaginative, curious, broad minded—*openness to experience.*[45]

Depending on their personality traits, library directors tend to see members of the senior management team who offset their weaknesses.

Other influences on personality are the need for "achievement: desire to accomplish something difficult"; "affiliation: desire to spend time in social relationships and activities"; and "power: desire to influence, coach, teach or encourage others."[46] These factors should also be included in a 360-degree assessment and the maturation of effective leaders.

CONCLUSION

Given the importance of leadership development to organizational achievement, Stewart L. Tubbs and Eric Schulz developed a taxonomy of leadership that centers on one's core personality and values. Their taxonomy identifies a set of broad competencies related to "understanding the big picture," "attitudes are everything," "leadership, the driving force," "communication, the leader's voice," "innovation and creativity," "leading change," and "teamwork and followership." Each competency is divided into more specific competencies.[47] Combining this taxonomy with a characterization of leadership as emotional intelligence offers readers an excellent starting point to determine which competencies reflect managerial leadership and which ones can be developed over time. It is not likely that every leader possesses each competency; however, collectively, the senior management team should. Any replacement of senior managers should include an understanding of how new members complement the others in areas such as work experiences, managerial skills, and leadership competencies or attributes.

As Henry Mintzberg notes, leadership can be nurtured[48]; both the conditions that bring it out in people and many of the actual traits can be developed or refined, that, is at least to some extent. Where people might disagree is, "To what extent?" Potential leaders can be identified and given opportunities—formal and informal—to develop and demonstrate leadership styles and the mastery of specific attributes that transform a workforce to accomplish new tasks in innovative ways and to assume new roles and responsibilities as everyone works to accomplish a shared mission and specific goals. Effective leadership results from doing and reflecting on what is being learned.

The challenges confronting higher education and academic libraries will never lessen; some of them will remain unresolved and new ones will emerge. The twenty-first century librarian needs to be a leader and a follower, and the librarian who has managerial responsibilities and roles must also be an effective manager. The concept of managerial leadership will become more—not less—important as the century progresses. Librarians must view management from a leadership perspective. That perspective focuses on action and planning, both strategic and succession. It should embrace "managing quality" and avoid what Mintzberg refers to as "noisy words," ones that organizations adopt but superficially; actions should produce meaningful results. Change management, leadership, and empowerment are examples of "managerial noise."[49] Organizations must move beyond such noise and create a vision-driven organization in which the culture of leadership is inspirational, motivational, and transformational and displays emotional intelligence.

"A leader is a dealer in hope."[50]

NOTES

1. Henry Mintzberg, *Managers, not MBAs: A Hard Look at the Soft Practice of Managing and Management Development* (San Francisco: Berrett-Koehler Publishers, 2004), 213.

2. See Peter Hernon and Robert E. Dugan, *Outcomes Assessment in Higher Education* (Westport, CT: Libraries Unlimited, 2004); Peter Hernon, Robert E. Dugan, and Candy Schwartz, *Revisiting Outcomes Assessment in Higher Education* (Westport, CT: Libraries Unlimited, 2006).

3. For examples of those writings see chapter 1 of Peter Hernon, Ronald R. Powell, and Arthur P. Young, *The Next Library Leadership: Attributes of Academic and Public library Directors* (Westport, CT: Libraries Unlimited, 2003), 1–11.

4. James G. Neal, "Raised by Wolves," *Library Journal* 131, no. 3 (February 15, 2006): 42.

5. Ibid., 44.

6. Ibid., 42.

7. Ibid., 44.

8. Ibid.

9. See, for instance, Gary Yukl, "Managerial Leadership: A Review of Theory and Research," *Journal of Management* 15, no. 2 (1989): 251–89; Daniel R. Denison, Robert Hoojiberg, and Robert E. Quinn, "Paradox and Performance: Toward a Theory of Behavioral Complexity in Managerial Leadership," *Organization Science* 6, no. 5 (September-October 1995): 524–40. Available from JSTOR (accessed March 16, 2006).

10. See A. J. Anderson, unpublished course handout, LIS 404, "The Principles of Management" (Boston: Simmons College, 2000). R. Alex Mackenzie provides a more comprehensive view of managerial functions. He shows that leadership relates to decision making and better communication (influencing people to accomplish desired goals). See R. Alex Mackenzie, "The Management Process in 3-D," *Harvard Business Review* 47 (November-December 1969): 86–88.

11. E-mail message from Terrence Mech (King's College) to Peter Hernon, dated February 21, 2006.

12. George S. Odiorne, *Management by Objectives: A System of Managerial Leadership* (New York: Pitman Pub. Corp., 1965).

13. Laurie Newman DiPadova, *Managerial Leadership and Organizational Hierarchy: An Exploration of the Similarities and Differences in Managerial Roles at Hierarchical Levels* (Ph.D. diss., State University of New York at Albany, 1995).

14. Lisa Deane McNary, *The Deming Management Theory: A Managerial Leadership Profile for the New Economic Age* (Ph.D. diss., The University of New Mexico, 1993).

15. Chris Argyris, *A Study of a Pattern of Managerial Leadership* (Ph.D. diss., Cornell University, 1951).

16. James Kelso Dent, *Managerial Leadership Styles: Some Dimensions, Determinants and Behavioral Correlates* (Ph.D. diss., University of Michigan, 1957).

17. Wilbur M. Skidmore II, *A Functional Approach to Managerial Leadership* (master's thesis, The George Washington University, 1966), 2.

18. Katherine M. Babiak, *Managerial Leadership in Canadian NSOs: Values and Perceptions of Senior Staff Leaders and Their Staff Members* (master's thesis, University of Ottawa, 1994), 9.

19. Manuel Guillén and Tomás F. González, "The Ethical Dimension of Managerial Leadership: Two Illustrative Case Studies in TQM," *Journal of Business Ethics* 34 (2001): 173–89.

20. Peter A. Topping, *Managerial Leadership* (New York: McGraw-Hill, 2002), 145.

21. Joanne E. Euster, *The Academic Library Director: Management Activities and Effectiveness* (New York: Greenwood Press, 1987). See David E. Berlew, "Leadership and Organizational Excitement," in *Psychological Foundations of Organizational Behavior,* ed. Barry M. Shaw (Santa Monica, CA: Goodyear Pub. Co., 1977), 333.

22. Berlow, "Leadership and Organizational Excitement," 331.

23. See, for instance, Gary N. Powell, D. Anthony Butterfield?," and Jane D. Parent, "Gender and Managerial Stereotypes: Have the Times Changed?," *Journal of Management* 28, no. 2 (2002): 177–93.

24. Such a study might draw on Rosemary O'Leary, *The Ethics of Dissent: Managing Guerilla Government* (Washington, D.C.: CQ Press, 2006).

25. See Michael E. Brown and Dennis A. Gioia, "Making Things Click: Distributive Leadership in an Online Division of an Offline Organization," *The Leadership Quarterly* 13 (2002): 397–419. This article contains an excellent literature review.

26. Steven B., "What Makes a Good Academic Library Director," ACRLog (Association of College and Research Libraries). Available at http://acrlblog. org/2005/12/26/what-makes-a-good-academic-library-director/ (accessed March 20, 2006).

27. Scott Walter, "3 Responses to 'What Makes a Good Academic Library Director'," ACRLog (December 26, 2005). Available at http://acrlblog.org/2005/12/26/what-makes-a-good-academic-library-director/ (accessed March 20, 2006).

28. For an interesting and relevant discussion of university mission statements historically, see John C. Scott, "The Mission of the University: Medieval to Postmodern Transformations," *The Journal of Higher Education* 77 (January-February 2006): 1–39.

29. Association of Research Libraries, *Non-Librarian Professionals,* SPEC Kit 212 (Washington, D.C.: Association of Research Libraries, 1995). Available at http://www.arl.org/spec/212fly.html (accessed March 25, 2006).

30. Ibid.

31. See Stephen Walker and V. Lonnie Lawson, "The Librarian Stereotype and the Movies," *MC Journal: The Journal of Academic Media Librarianship* 1 (Spring 1993): 16–28. Available at http://wings.buffalo.edu/publications/mcjrnl/v1n1/image.html (accessed March 25, 2006). They note that these were the top characteristics that a survey group of 100 people on the Family Feud game used to describe a typical "librarian."

32. See Terry V. Vavra, *Improving Your Measurement of Customer Satisfaction: A Guide to Creating, Conducting, Analyzing, and Reporting Customer Satisfaction Measurement Programs* (Milwaukee, WI: American Society for Quality Press, 1997).

33. Peter Hernon and Ellen Altman, *Assessing Service Quality: Satisfying the Expectations of Library Customers* (Chicago: American Library Association, 1998).

34. Svafa Grönfeldt and Judith Stronther, *Service Leadership: The Quest for Competitive Advantage* (Thousand Oaks, CA: SAGE, 2006).

35. Ibid., 49.

36. Ibid., 6.

37. Ibid., 5.

38. Angela Bridgland, "To Fill, or How to Fill—That Is the Question: Succession Planning and Leadership Development in Academic Libraries," *Australian Academic & Research Libraries* 30, no.1 (March 1999). Available from Expanded Academic ASAP (accessed March 11, 2006).

39. Ibid.

40. *Baldrige National Quality Program: Education Criteria for Performance Excellence* (Gaithersburg, MD: National Institute of Standards and Technology, 2006), 39.

41. Ibid.

42. Ibid.

43. Ibid., 1.

44. Dallas County Community College District, Press Release: "Baldrige Award Goes to Richland College" (Dallas, TX: Dallas County Community College District, 2006). Available at http://www.dcccd.edu/About+DCCCD/News+and+Events/News/RLC/Baldrige+Award+Goes+to+Richland+College+11.22.05.htm (accessed March 16, 2006).

45. Steward L. Tubbs and Eric Schulz, "Exploring a Taxonomy of Global Leadership Competencies and Metacompetencies," *Journal of the American Academy of Business* 8, no. 1 (March 2006): 30.

46. Ibid.

47. Ibid.

48. Mintzberg, *Managers, not MBAs,* 215.

49. Henry Mintzberg, "Managing Quietly," *Leader to Leader* 12 (Spring 1999). Available at http://www.pfdf.org/leaderbooks/121/spring99/mintzberg.html (accessed March 15, 2006).

50. "Best Leadership Quotes: Napoleon Bonaparte." Famous-Quotes-and-Quotations.com (Boone, NC: Famous-Quotes-and-Quotations.com, n.d.). Available at http://www.famous-quotes-and-quotations.com/leadership-quotes.html (accessed March 16, 2006).

BIBLIOGRAPHY

ARTICLES

Alire, Camila A. "Diversity and Leadership: The Color of Leadership." *Journal of Library Administration*™ 32, no. 2/4 (2001): 95–109.

Alon, Illan, and James Higgins. "Global Leadership Success through Emotional and Cultural Intelligences." *Business Horizons* 48 (2005): 501–12.

Ardichvili, Alexander. "Leadership Styles of Russian Entrepreneurs and Managers." *Journal of Developmental Entrepreneurship* 6 (2001): 169–88.

Armitage, James W., Nancy Brooks, Matthew Carlen, and Scott Schulz. "Remodeling Leadership." *Performance Improvement* 45, no. 2 (February 2006): 40–48.

Atwater, Leanne, Shelly Dionne, John Camobreco, Bruce Avolio, and Alan Lau. "Individual Attributes and Leadership Style: Predicting the Use of Punishment and its Effects." *Journal of Organizational Behavior* 19 (1998): 559–76.

Avolio, Bruce J. "Leadership: Building Vital Forces into Highly Developed Teams." *Human Resource Management Journal* 11 (1995): 10–15.

Bass, Bernard. "Does the Transactional-Transformational Leadership Paradigm Transcend Organizational and National Boundaries?" *American Psychologist* 52 (1997): 130–39.

Bass, Bernard, and Bruce J Avolio. "The Transformational and Transectional Leadership of Men and Women." *Applied Psychology: An International Review* 45, no.1 (1996): 5–34.

Bender, Laura. "Team Organization-Learning Organization: The University of Arizona Four Years into It." *Information Outlook* 1 (1997): 19–22.

Blake, Robert, and Jane Mouton. "Management by Grid." *Group and Organization Studies* 6 (1981): 439–55.

Blanchard, Kenneth. "Assessing Your Leadership Skills." *Executive Excellence* 7, no. 5 (May 1990): 21–22.

Bloss, Alex, and Don Lanier. "The Library Department Head in the Context of Matrix Management and Reengineering." *College & Research Libraries* 58 (1997): 499–508.

Boal, Kimberly B. "Strategic Leadership Research: Moving on." *Leadership Quarterly* 11 (2001): 515–50.

Bornstein, Rita. "The Nature and Nurture of Presidents." *The Chronicle of Higher Education* (November 4, 2005): B10-B11.

Boujnah, Marc. "L'Inegalite des Femmes." *Air France Areo Magazine* 6 (2002): 43.

Bowers, Matthew, Linda DeBeau-Melting, John DeVries, and Merry Schellinger. "Organizational Restructuring in Academic Libraries: A Case Study." *Journal of Library Administration* 22 (1996): 33–44.

Brandel, Mary. "Skill Set Soul Searching." *Computerworld* 34 (2000): 87.

Brown, F. William, and Dan Moshavi, "Transformational Leadership and Emotional Intelligence: A Potential Pathway for an Increased Understanding of Interpersonal Influence." *Journal of Organizational Behavior* 26 (2005): 867–71.

Brown, Michael E., and Dennis A. Gioia. "Making Things Click: Distributive Leadership in an Online Division of an Offline Organization." *The Leadership Quarterly* 13 (2002): 397–419.

Buckingham, Marcus. "What Great Managers Do." *Harvard Business Review* 20 (2005): 20–26.

Buss, Dale. "When Managing Isn't Enough: Nine Ways to Develop the Leaders You Need." *Workforce* 80, no. 12 (December 2001): 44–47.

Calhoun, Karen, Zsuzsa Koltay, and Edward Weissman. "Library Gateway: Project Design, Teams and Cycle Time." *Library Resources and Technical Services* 43 (1999): 114–22.

Campbell, Jerry D. "The Academic Library as a Virtual Destination." *Educause Review* 41 (January/February 2006): 16–30.

"The Chronicle Survey of Presidents of 4-Year Colleges." *The Chronicle of Higher Education* (November 4, 2005): A37-A39.

Clutterbuck, David, and Sheila Hirst. "Leadership Communication: A Status Report." *Journal of Communication Management* 6 (2002): 351–54.

Collins, Jim. "Level 5 Leadership." *Harvard Business Review* 83 (2005): 136–46.

Cornell, S. "Growing Leaders." *Public Library Journal* 17, no. 4 (Winter 2002): 115–16, 118.

deJager, G.J.J., and Adeline S.A. duToit. "Self Directed Work Teams in Information Services: An Exploratory Study." *South African Journal of Library & Information Science* 65 (December 1997): 194–98.

Demirhan, Amed. "Developing Leadership through Mentoring." *Florida Libraries* 48, no. 2 (Fall 2005): 15–16.

Dewey, Barbara I. "Leadership and University Libraries: Building to Scale at the Interface of Cultures." *Journal of Library Administration* 42, no. 1 (2005): 41–50.

Diaz, Joseph R., and Chestalene Pintozzi. "Helping Teams Work: Lessons Learned from the University of Arizona Library Reorganization." *Library Administration & Management* 13 (Winter 1999): 27–36.

Dorfman, Peter, and Jon Howell. "Leadership in Western and Asian Countries: Commonalities and Differences in Effective Leadership Processes across Cultures." *Leadership Quarterly* 8 (1997): 234–64.

Eagly, Alice, and Mary C. Johannnesen-Schmidt. "Leadership Styles of Women and Men." *Journal of Social Issues* 57, no, 4 (2001): 781–97.

Eales-White, Rupert. The COGAL Concept of Leadership." *Industrial and Commercial Training* 35 (2003): 203–207.

Echt, Rita. "The Realities of Teams in Technical Services at Michigan State University Libraries." *Library Acquisitions: Practice and Theory* 21 (Summer 1997): 179–87.

Eddy, Pamela L. "Nested Leadership: The Integration of Organizational Change in a Multicollege System." *Community College Journal of Research and Practice* 30, no. 1 (January 2006): 41–51.

Edgerly, Mary Spalding, and D. Michele Beaulieu. "Bringing Effective Skills & Technology Together: Leadership Opportunities for Rural Librarians." *Rural Libraries* 23, no. 2 (2003): 7–19.

Euster, Joanne R. "Teaming Up." *Wilson Library Bulletin,* 69 (January 1995): 57–59.

Flaga, Catherine T. "The Process of Transition for Community College Transfer Students." *Community College Journal of Research and Practice* 30, no. 1 (January 2006): 3–19.

Flynn, Gillian. "Xers vs. Boomers: Teamwork or Trouble." *Personnel Journal* 75 (November 1996): 86–90.

"Gen X Bites Back." *American Libraries* 35 (September 2004): 43–45.

"Generation X Professionals: Assumptions and Realities." *Worklife Report* 14 (Winter 2002): 10.

Geoffee, Robert, and Gareth Jones, "Why Should Anyone Be Led by You?" *Harvard Business Review* 78 (2000): 62–70.

George, Jennifer. "Emotions and Leadership: The Role of Emotional Intelligence." *Human Relations* 53 (2000): 1027–56.

———. "Leader Positive Mood and Group Performance: The Case of Customer Service." *Journal of Applied Psychology* 25 (1995): 778–94.

George, Jennifer, and Ken Bettenhausen. "Understanding Pro-Social Behavior, Sales Performance, and Turnover: A Group-Level Analysis in a Service Context." *Journal of Applied Psychology* 75 (1990): 75–109.

Golden, Janine. "Leadership Development and Staff Recruitment . . . Florida Style." *Florida Libraries* 48, no. 2 (Fall 2005): 17–20.

Goleman, Daniel. "Leadership That Gets Results." *Harvard Business Review* 78 (March-April 2000): 78–90.

———. "What Makes a Leader?" *Harvard Business Review* 82 (January 2004): 82–91; *Harvard Business Review* 5 (November-December 1998): 93–102.

Goleman, Daniel, Richard Boyatzis, and Annie McKee. "Primal Leadership: The Hidden Driver of Great Performance." *Harvard Business Review* 79 (2001): 42–51.

Gordon, Rachel Singer. "NEXTGEN: What We Really Want." *Library Journal* 129 (October 15, 2004): 46.

———. "Nurturing New Leaders by Demonstrating Quality Leadership." *JLAMS* [*Journal of the Library Administration and Management Section of the New York Library Association*] 1, no. 2 (2004–2005): 23–38.

———. "Time to Make Some Change." *Library Journal* 129 (August 2004): 51.

Guillén, Manuel, and Tomás F. González. "The Ethical Dimension of Managerial Leadership: Two Illustrative Case Studies in TQM." *Journal of Business Ethics* 34 (2001): 173–89.

Harari, Oren. "Proven Leadership Principles." *Executive Excellence* 19 (2002): 3.

Hernon, Peter, and Nancy Rossiter. "Emotional Intelligence: Which Traits Are Most Prized?" *College & Research Libraries* 67 (May 2006): 260–75.

Hernon, Peter, Ronald Powell, and Arthur Young. "Academic Library Directors: What Do They Do?" *College & Research Libraries* 65 (November 2004): 538–63.

———. "University Library Directors in the Association of Research Libraries: The Next Generation, Part One." *College & Research Libraries* 62 (March 2001): 116–45.

———. "University Library Directors in the Association of Research Libraries: The Next Generation, Part Two." *College & Research Libraries* 63 (January 2002): 73–90.

Hosking, Dian Marie. "Organizing Leadership and Skillful Process." *Journal of Management Studies* 25, no. 2 (March 1988): 147–67.

House, Robert. "A Path-Goal Theory of Leadership Effectiveness." *Administrative Science Quarterly* 16 (1971): 321–39.

Isen, Alice, Kimberly Daubman, and Gary Nowicki. "Positive Affect Facilitates Creative Problem Solving." *Journal of Personality and Social Psychology* 52 (1987): 1122–31.

Jaramillo, George R. "Utilization of Teams in an Academic Library Environment." *Colorado Libraries* 22 (1996): 17–23.

Katzenbach, Jon R., and Douglas K. Smith. "The Discipline of Teams." *Harvard Business Review* 71, no. 2 (March-April 1993): 111–20.

Kear, Robin. "Learning to Be a Library Leader: Leadership Development Opportunities in Florida and Beyond." *Florida Libraries* 48, no. 2 (Fall 2005): 22–23.

Kellerman, Barbara. "How Bad Leadership Happens." *Leader to Leader* 35 (Winter 2005): 41–46.

Kotter, John P. "What Leaders Really Do (Managers Promote Stability While Leaders Press for Change)." *Harvard Business Review* 79, no.11 (December 2001): 85–96 (A reprint of a 1990 article).

Kuhnert, Karl W., and Phillip Lewis. "Transactional and Transformational Leadership: A Constructive/Developmental Analysis." *Academy of Management Review* 12 (1994): 648–57.

"Leadership: What Makes Us Tick?" *Library Media Connection* 24, no. 6 (March 2006): 15–19.

Lord, Robert, Christy DeVader, and George Alliger. "A Meta-Analysis of the Relation between Personality Traits and Leadership Perceptions: An Application of Validity Generalization Procedures." *Journal of Applied Psychology* 71 (1986): 402–10.

Losada, Marcial, and Emily Heaphy, "The Role of Positivity and Connectivity in the Performance of Business Teams." *American Behavioral Scientist* 47 (2004): 740–65.

Lubans, John. "'I Ain't No Cowboy, I Just Found This Hat:' Confessions of an Administrator in an Organization of Self-managing Teams." *Library Administration & Management* 10 (1996): 28–40.

Lutz, Charles. "Leading by Example." *Security Management* 49 (2005): 44–47.

Mackenzie, R. Alex. "The Management Process in 3-D." *Harvard Business Review* 47 (November-December 1969): 86–88.

Mann, R. D. "A Review of the Relationship between Personality and Performance in Small Groups." *Psychological Bulletin* 56 (1959): 241–70.

Manning, Tracy. "Leadership across Cultures: Attachment Style Influences." *Journal of Leadership and Organizational Studies* 9 (2003): 20–32.

Martin, Elaine R. "Team Effectiveness in Academic Medical Libraries: A Multiple Case Study," *Journal of the Medical Library Association* 94, no. 3 (July 2006): 271–278.

Mason, Florence M., and Louella V. Wetherbee. "Learning to Lead: An Analysis of Current Training Programs for Library Leadership." *Library Trends* 53, no. 1 (Summer 2004): 187–217.

Matthews, Catherine J. "Becoming a Chief Librarian: An Analysis of Transition Stages in Academic Library Leadership." *Library Trends* 50, no. 4 (Spring 2002): 578–602.

Mavrinac, Mary Ann. "Transformational Leadership: Peer Mentoring as a Values-based Learning Process." *portal: Libraries and the Academy* 5, no. 3 (2005): 391–404.

Mayer, John, Peter Salovey, David Caruso, and Gill Sitarenios. "Measuring and Modeling Emotional Intelligence with MSCEIT V 2.0." *Emotion* 3 (2003): 97–105.

McAdam Tim, and Nancy M. Stanley, "Implementing Teams for Technical Services Functions." *The Serials Librarian* 28 (1996): 361–365.

McClain, Charles J. "Leadership with Integrity: A Personal Perspective." *Innovative Higher Education (Historical Archive)* 17, no. 1 (September 1992): 9–17.

McConnell, Carole. "Staff and Leadership Shortages? Grow Your Own." *American Libraries* 35, no. 9 (October 2004): 34–36.

McDowell-Larson, Sharon, Leigh Kearney, and David Campbell, "Fitness and Leadership: Is There a Relationship?" *Journal of Managerial Psychology* 17 (2002): 316–25.

McGregor, Douglas. "Human Side of Enterprise." *Management Review* 46, no. 11 (1957): 22–28.

McManus, Kevin. "The Leadership Gap." *Industrial Engineer* 37 (2005): 20.

Mickan, Sharon, and Sylvia Rodger. "Characteristics of Effective Teams: A Literature Review." *Australian Health Review* 23, no. 3 (July 2000), 201–208.

Mosby, Anne Page, and Judith D. Brook. "Devils and Goddesses in the Library: Reflections on Leadership, Team Building, Staff Development, and Success." *Georgia Library Quarterly* 42, no. 4 (Winter 2006): 5–10.

Mosley, Pixey Anne. "Mentoring Gen X Managers: Tomorrow's Library Leadership Is Already Here." *Library Administration & Management* 19, no. 4 (Fall 2005): 185–190, 191–192.

Mumford, Michael, Michelle Marks, Mary Shane Connelly, Stephen Zaccaro, and Roni Reiter-Palmon. "Development of Leadership Skills: Experience and Timing." *Leadership Quarterly* 11 (2000): 87–114.

Nankivell, Claire, and Michele Shoolbred. "Mentoring in Library and Information Services: A Literature Review and Report on Recent Research." *New Review of Academic Librarianship* 3 (1997): 91–144.

Neal, James G. "Raised by Wolves." *Library Journal* 131, no. 3 (February 15, 2006): 42–44.

Peters, Tom. "Leadership and Change." *Finance Week* (June 21, 2004): 66.

Phelan, Daniel F., and Richard M. Malinski (Eds.). "Midlife Career Decisions of Librarians." *Library Trends* 50, no. 4 (Spring 2002): 575–758.

Pors, Niels Ole, and Carl Gustav Johannsen. "Library Directors under Cross-pressure between New Public Management and Value-based Management." *Library Management* 24, nos. 1/2 (2003): 51–60.

Powell, Gary N., D. Anthony Butterfield, and Jane D. Parent. "Gender and Managerial Stereotypes: Have the Times Changed?" *Journal of Management* 28, no. 2 (2002): 177–93.

Price, James. "Handbook of Organizational Measurement." *International Journal of Manpower* 18 (1997): 303–558.

Reynolds, Keith. "I Am Their Leader, I Must Follow Them!" *Management Accounting* 77 (December 1999): 70–72.

Riggs, Donald E. "The Crisis and Opportunities in Library Leadership." *Journal of Library Administration*™ 32, nos. 3/4 (2001): 5–17.

Roseman, Janet L. "On Leadership." *Dance/USA Journal* 14, no. 4 (Spring 1997): 15–19, 25.

Rotter, J.B. "Interpersonal Trust: Trustworthiness and Gullibility." *American Psychologists* 35 (January 1980): 1–5.

Russell, Carrie. "Using Performance Measurement to Evaluate Teams and Organizational Effectiveness at the University of Arizona." *Library Administration & Management* 12 (Summer 1998): 159–65.

Russell, Keith, and Denise Stephens (Eds.). "Organizational Development and Leadership." *Library Trends* 53, no. 1 (Summer 2004): 1–264.

Sala, Fabio. "Executive Blind Spots: Discrepancies between Self- and Other-Ratings." *Consulting Psychology Journal: Practice & Research* 55 (Fall 2003): 222–29.

Salovey, Peter, and John Mayer. "Emotional Intelligence." *Imagination, Cognition and Personality* 9 (1990): 185–211.

Sapp, Gregg. "James Neal on the Challenges of Leadership." *Library Administration and Management* 19, no. 2 (Spring 2005): 64–67.

Schaub, Diana. "On the Character of Generation X." *Public Interest* 137 (Fall 1999): 3–24.

Scott, John C. "The Mission of the University: Medieval to Postmodern Transformations." *The Journal of Higher Education* 77 (January-February 2006): 1–39.

Seligman, Martin E., and Michaly Csikszentmihalyi. "Positive Psychology: An Introduction." *American Psychologist* 55 (2000): 5–14.

Shaughnessy, Thomas W. "Lessons from Restructuring the Library." *The Journal of Academic Librarianship* 22 (July 1996): 251–57.

Sheehy, Carolyn A. "Synergy: The Illinois Library Leadership Initiative and the Development of Future Academic Library Leaders." *College & Undergraduate Libraries*™ 11, no. 1 (2004): 61–75.

Somerville, Mary M., Barbara Schader, and Malia E. Huston. "Rethinking What We Do and How We Do It: Systems Thinking Strategies for Library Leadership." *Australian Academic & Research Libraries* 36, no. 4 (December 2005): 214–27.

Spreitzer, Gretchen, Kimberly Hopkins Perttula, and Katherine Xin. "Traditionality Matters: An Examination of the Effectiveness of Transformational Leadership in the United States and Taiwan." *Journal of Organizational Behavior* 26 (2005): 205–27.

Stanley, Mary J. "Taking Time for the Organization." *College & Research Libraries News* 62 (October 2001): 900–902, 908.

Stodgill, Ralph M., "Personal Factors Associated with Leadership: A Survey of the Literature." *Journal of Psychology* 25 (1948): 35–71.

Sullivan, Leila Gonzālez. "Four Generations of Community College Leadership." *Community College Journal of Research & Practice* 25 (September 2001): 559–71.

Suutari, Vesa. "Global Leadership Development: An Emerging Research Agenda." *Career Development International* 7 (2002): 218–33.

Townley, Charles. "Nurturing Library Effectiveness: Leadership for Personnel Development." *Library Administration and Management* 16 (Winter 1989): 16–20.

Tubbs, Steward L., and Eric Schulz. "Exploring a Taxonomy of Global Leadership Competencies and Metacompetencies." *Journal of the American Academy of Business* 8, no. 1 (March 2006): 29–34.

Van Velsor, Ellen. "Assess, Challenge, and Support." *Executive Excellence* 17, no. 6 (June 2000): 19.

von Dran, Glsela. "Human Resources and Leadership Strategies for Libraries in Transition." *Library Administration & Management* 19, no. 4 (Fall 2005): 177–84.

Warner, Linda Sue, and Keith Grint. "American Indian Ways of Leading and Knowing." *Leadership* 2, no. 2 (May 2006): 225–44.

Weiner, Sharon Gray. "Leadership of Academic Libraries: A Literature Review." *Education Libraries* 26, no. 2 (Winter 2003): 5–18.

Whetstone, J. Thomas. "Personalism and Moral Leadership: The Servant Leader with a Transforming Vision." *Business Ethics: A European Review* 11, no. 4 (October 2002): 385–92.

Wiethoff, Carolyn. "Management Basics: Managing Generation X." *Indiana Libraries* 23 (2004): 53–55.

Williams, James F. II, and Mark D. Winston. "Leadership Competencies and the Importance of Research Methods and Statistical Analysis in Decision Making and Research and Publication: A Study of Citation Patterns." *Library & Information Science Research* 25 (2003): 387–402.

Wilson, Jane L. "360 Appraisals." *Training & Development* 51 (June 1997): 44–45.

Winston, Mark D. (Ed.). "Leadership in the Library and Information Science Professions: Theory and Practice." *Journal of Library Administration*™ 32, no. 3/4 (2001): 1–186.

Yamasaki, Erika. "Understanding Managerial Leadership as More Than an Oxymoron." *New Directions for Community Colleges* 27 (Spring 1999): 67–73.

Yankelovich, Daniel, and Isabella Furth. "The Role of Colleges in an Era of Mistrust." *The Chronicle of Higher Education* (September 16, 2005): B8-B11.

Young, Arthur P., Peter Hernon, and Ronald R. Powell, "Attributes of Academic Library Leadership: An Exploratory Study of Some Gen-Xers." *The Journal of Academic Librarianship* 32, no. 5 (September 2006): 482–502.

Young, Arthur P., Ronald R. Powell, and Peter Hernon. "What Will Gen Next Need to Lead?" *American Libraries* 35 (May 2004): 31–35.

Yukl, Gary. "Managerial Leadership: A Review of Theory and Research." *Journal of Management* 15, no. 2 (1989): 251–89.

Zaccaro, Stephen, Michael Mumford, Mary Shane Connelly, Michelle Marks, and Janelle Gilbert. "Assessment of Leader Problem-Solving Capabilities." *Leadership Quarterly* 11 (2000): 37–64.

BOOKS

Applebaum, Eileen, and Rosemary Batt. *The New American Workplace: Transforming Work Systems in the United States.* Ithaca, NY: ILR Press, 1994.

Barnard, Chester I. *The Functions of the Executive.* Cambridge, MA: Harvard University Press, 1938.

Barnett, Rosalind, and Caryle Rivers. *Same Difference: How Gender Myths Are Hurting Our Relationships, Our Children, and Our Jobs.* New York: Basic Books, 2004.

Bar-On, Reuvin. *The Emotional Quotient Inventory: A Measure of Emotional Intelligence.* Toronto, ON: Multi Health Systems, 1996.

Bass, Bernard M. *Bass and Stodgill's Handbook of Leadership.* 3d ed. New York: Free Press, 1990.

———. *Leadership and Performance beyond Expectations.* New York: Free Press 1985.

Bass, Bernard M., and Bruce Avolio. *Improvising Organizational Effectiveness through Transformational Leadership.* Thousand Oaks, CA: Sage, 1994.

———. *Transformational Leadership Development: Manual for the Multifactor Leadership Questionnaire.* Palo Alto, CA: Consulting Psychologists Press, 1990.

Bass, Bernard M., and Ronald E. Riggio. *Transformational Leadership.* 2d ed. Mahwah, NJ: Lawrence Erlbaum Associates, Publishers, 2006.

Belenky, Mary Field. *Women's Ways of Knowing: The Development of Self, Voice, and Mind.* New York: Basic Books, 1986.

Bennis, Warren G. *On Becoming a Leader.* Reading, MA: Addison-Wesley, 1989.

———. *Why Leaders Can't Lead: The Unconscious Conspiracy Continues.* San Francisco: Jossey-Bass Publishers 1989.

Bennis, Warren G., and Burt Nanus. *Leaders: The Strategies for Taking Charge.* New York: Harper & Row, 1985.

Bingham, William V. *Leadership: The Psychological Foundations of Management.* New York: Shaw, 1927.

Boyatzis, Richard, and Annie McKee. *Resonant Leadership: Renewing Yourself and Connecting with Others through Mindfulness, Hope, and Compassion.* Boston: Harvard Business School Press, 2005.

Bracken, D. W., M. A. Dalton, R. A. Jako, C. D. McCauley, and V. A. Pollman. *Should 360-degree Feedback Be Used Only for Developmental Purposes?* Greensboro, NC: Center for Creative Leadership, 1997; Norwood, MA: Books24X7.com [electronic resource].

Breivik, Patricia Senn, and E. Gordon Gee, *Higher Education in the Internet Age: Libraries Creating a Strategic Edge.* Westport, CT: Praeger, 2006.

Brown, David G. *University Presidents as Moral Leaders.* Westport, CT: Greenwood Press, 2005.

Buckingham, Marcus, and Donald O. Clifton. *Now, Discover Your Strengths.* New York: Free Press, 2001.

Burns, James MacGregor. *Leadership.* New York: Harper & Row, 1978.

Childers, Thomas A., and Nancy A. Van House. *"What's Good:" Describing Your Public Library's Effectiveness*. Chicago: American Library Association, 1993.

Cohen, Michael D., and James G. March. *Leadership and Ambiguity: The American College President*. New York: McGraw-Hill, 1974.

Collins Jim. *Good to Great: Why Some Companies Make the Leap and Others Don't*. New York: Harper Collins, 2001.

Covey, Steven. *The 8th Habit*. New York: Free Press, 2004.

———. *The Seven Habits of Highly Effective People*. New York: Simon & Schuster, 1989.

Crawford, Chris B., Curtis L. Brungardt, and Micol Maughan. *Understanding Leadership: Theories & Concepts*, 3d ed. New York: Wiley, 2004.

Derr, C. Brooklyn, Sylvie Roussillon, and Frank Bournois. *Cross-Cultural Approaches to Leadership Development*. Westport, CT: Quorum Books, 2002.

Early, P. Christopher, and Soon Ang. *Cultural Intelligence: Individual Interactions across Cultures*. Stanford, CA: Stanford Business Books, 2003.

Euster, Joanne E. *The Academic Library Director: Management Activities and Effectiveness*. New York: Greenwood Press, 1987.

Fielder, Fred E. *A Theory of Leadership Effectiveness*. New York: McGraw-Hill, 1967.

Fielder, Fred E., and Martin Chemers. *Improving Leadership Effectiveness*. New York: John Wiley, 1984.

Fine, Doris R. *When Leadership Fails: Desegregation and Demoralization in the San Francisco Schools*. New Brunswick, NJ: Transaction Books, 1986.

Freidel, Frank. *Franklin D. Roosevelt: A Rendezvous with Destiny*. Boston: Little, Brown & Co., 1990.

Gardner, John W. *On Leadership*. New York: The Free Press, 1990.

Giesecke, Joan (Ed.). *Scenario Planning for Libraries*. Chicago: American Library Association, 1998.

Gilligan, Carol. *In a Different Voice: Psychological Theory and Women's Development*. Cambridge, MA: Harvard University Press, 1993.

Goethals, George R., Georgia J. Sorenson, and James MacGregor Burns (Eds.). *Encyclopedia of Leadership*, 4 vols. Thousand Oaks, CA: Sage, 2004.

Goleman, Daniel. *Emotional Intelligence*. New York: Bantam Books, 1995.

Goleman, Daniel, Richard Boyatzis, and Annie McKee, *Primal Leadership: Realizing the Power of Emotional Intelligence*. Boston: Harvard Business School Press, 2002.

Goodwin, Doris Kearns. *Team of Rivals: The Political Genius of Abraham Lincoln*. New York: Simon & Schuster, 2005.

Gordon, Rachael Singer. *The Nextgen Librarian's Survival Guide*. Medford, NJ: Information Today, Inc., 2006.

Gortner, Harold. *Administration in the Public Sector*. 2d ed. New York: Wiley & Sons, 1981.

Grassian, Esther S., and Joan R. Kaplowitz. *Learning to Lead and Manage Information Literacy Instruction*. New York: Neal-Schuman, 2005.

Griffin, Ricky. *Fundamentals of Management, Core Concepts and Applications*, 4th ed. Boston: Houghton Mifflin, 2004.

Grönfeldt, Svafa, and Judith Stronther. *Service Leadership: The Quest for Competitive Advantage*. Thousand Oaks, CA: SAGE, 2006.

Hackman, J. Richard. *Leading Teams: Setting the Stage for Great Performances*. Boston: Harvard Business School Press, 2002.

Hackman, Michael Z., and Craig E. Johnson. *Leadership: A Communication Perspective*. Prospect Heights, IL: Waveland Press, Inc., 1991.

Heifetz, Ronald A. *Leadership without Easy Answers*. Cambridge, MA: Belknap Press of Harvard University Press, 1994.

Henri, James, and Marlene Asselin. *Leadership Issues in the Information Literate School Community*. Westport, CT: Libraries Unlimited, 2005.

Hernon, Peter, and Ellen Altman, *Assessing Service Quality: Satisfying the Expectations of Library Customers*. Chicago: American Library Association, 1998.

Hernon, Peter, and Philip Calvert. *Improving the Quality of Library Services for Students with Disabilities*. Westport, CT: Libraries Unlimited, 2006.

Hernon, Peter, and Robert E. Dugan. *Outcomes Assessment in Higher Education*. Westport, CT: Libraries Unlimited, 2004.

Hernon, Peter, Robert E. Dugan, and Candy Schwartz. *Revisiting Outcomes Assessment in Higher Education*. Westport, CT: Libraries Unlimited, 2006.

Hernon, Peter, Ronald R. Powell, and Arthur P. Young. *The Next Library Leadership: Attributes of Academic and Public Library Directors*. Westport, CT: Libraries Unlimited, 2003.

Hersey, Paul, and Kenneth Blanchard. *Management of Organizational Behavior: Using Human Resources*. Englewood Cliffs, NJ: Prentice Hall, 1969.

Hersey, Paul, and Kenneth Blanchard, and Dewey Johnson, *Management of Organizational Behavior: Utilizing Human Resources*. 7th ed. Englewood Cliffs, NJ: Prentice Hall, 1996.

Hofstede, Gert. *Culture's Consequences: International Differences in Work Related Values*. Beverly Hills, CA: Sage, 1980.

House, Robert, Paul Hanges, Mansour Javidan, and Peter Dorfman. *Culture, Leadership and Organizations: The GLOBE Study of 62 Societies*. Thousand Oaks, CA: Sage, 2004.

Howe, Neil, and William Strauss. *Millennials Rising: The Next Great Generation*. New York: Random House, 2000.

Jacobson, David. *Inspiration to Perspiration: The Four Essential Steps to Achieving Your Goals*. San Diego, CA: Goal Success, 2003.

Johnson, Spencer. *Who Moved My Cheese? An Amazing Way to Deal with Change in Your Work and in Your Life*. New York: Putnam, 1998.

———. *Who Moved My Cheese? Little Nibbles of Cheese*. Kansas City, MO: Stark Books, 2001.

Jones, John E., and William Bearley. *360 Feedback: Strategies, Tactics, and Techniques for Developing Leaders*. Amherst, MA: HRD Press; Minneapolis, MN: Lakewood Publications, 1996; Norwood, MA: Books24x7.com [electronic resource].

Kanter, Rosabeth Moss. *The Change Masters: Innovation and Entrepreneurship in the American Corporation*. New York: Touchstone/Simon and Schuster 1983.

Kaplan Robert E., and Charles J. Palus. *Enhancing 360-degree Feedback for Senior Executives: How to Maximize the Benefits and Minimize the Risks*. Greensboro, NC: Center for Creative Leadership, 1994; Norwood, MA: Books24X7.com [electronic resource].

Kellerman, Barbara. *Bad Leadership: What It Is, How It Happens, Why It Happens*. Boston, MA: Harvard Business School, 2004.

Krahenbuhl, Gary S. *Building the Academic Deanship: Strategies for Success.* Westport, CT: Greenwood Press, 2004.

Lancaster, Lynne C., and David Stillman. *When Generations Collide.* New York: HarperCollins Publishers, 2002.

Larson, Carl E., and Frank M. J. LaFasto. *Teamwork: What Must Go Right/What Can Go Wrong.* Newbury Park, CA: Sage Publications, 1989.

Maki, Peggy L. *Assessing for Learning: Building a Sustainable Commitment across the Institution.* Sterling, VA: Stylus Publishing, 2004.

McDonald Joseph A., and Lynda Basney Micikas. *Academic Libraries: The Dimensions of Their Effectiveness.* Westport, CT: Greenwood Press, 1994.

McGregor, Douglas. *The Human Side of Enterprise.* New York: McGraw-Hill 1960.

Mintzberg, Henry. *Managers, not MBAs: A Hard Look at the Soft Practice of Managing and Management Development.* San Francisco: Berrett-Koehler Publishers, 2004.

Moran, Barbara, and Robert Stuart. *Library and Information Center Management.* Englewood, CO: Libraries Unlimited, 2002.

Nadler, David A., Janet L. Spencer, & Associates. *Executive Teams.* San Francisco: Jossey-Bass, 1998.

Nanus, Burt. *Visionary Leadership: Creating a Compelling Sense of Direction for Your Organization.* San Francisco: Jossey-Bass Publishers, 1992.

Neck, Christopher. *Fit to Lead.* New York: St. Martin's Press, 2004.

Neufelt, Victoria (Ed.). *Websters' New World Dictionary of American English.* 3d ed. New York: Webster's New World. 1988.

Northouse, Peter G. *Leadership: Theory and Practice.* 3d ed. Thousand Oaks, CA: Sage, 2004.

Odiorne, George S. *Management by Objectives: A System of Managerial Leadership.* New York: Pitman Pub. Corp., 1965.

O'Leary, Rosemary. *The Ethics of Dissent: Managing Guerilla Government.* Washington, D.C.: CQ Press, 2006.

Peale, Norman Vincent, and Kenneth Blanchard. *Power of Ethical Management.* New York: Ballantine Books, 1989.

Peters, Tom. *Liberation Management.* New York: Knopf, 1992.

Pfeffer, Jeffrey. *Power in Organizations.* Marshfield, MA: Pitman Publishing, 1981.

Regenstein, Carrie E., and Barbara I. Dewey, *Leadership: Higher Education, and the Information Age: A New Era for Information Technology and Libraries.* New York: Neal-Schuman, 2003.

Rosen, Bernard Carl. *Masks and Mirrors: Generation X and the Chameleon Personality.* Westport, CT: Praeger, 2001.

Rosen, Robert, Patricia Digh, Marshall Singer, and Carl Phillips. *Global Literacies: Lessons on Business Leadership and National Cultures.* New York: Simon and Schuster, 2000.

Rost, Joseph. *Leadership for the Twenty-first Century.* New York: Praeger, 1991.

Selznick, Philip. *Leadership in Administration: A Sociological Interpretation.* Evanston, IL: Row, Peterson, 1957.

Senge, Peter. *The Fifth Discipline: The Art and Practice of the Learning Organization.* New York: Doubleday, 1990.

Shelton, Charlotte, and Laura Shelton. *The NeXt Revolution: What Gen X Women Want at Work and How Their Boomer Bosses Can Help Them Get It.* Mountain View, CA: Davies-Black Publishing, 2005.

Stogdill, Ralph M., and Bernard M. Bass. *Handbook of Leadership: A Survey of Theory and Research.* New York: The Free Press, 1974.

Tannen, Deborah. *You Just Don't Understand: Women and Men in Conversation.* New York: Morrow, 1990.

Taylor, Robert S. *The Making of a Library: The Academic Library in Transition.* New York: John Wiley, 1972.

Tead, Ordway. *The Art of Leadership.* New York: McGraw-Hill, 1935.

Topping, Peter A. *Managerial Leadership.* New York: McGraw-Hill, 2002.

Tornow, Walter W., and Manuel London. *Maximizing the Value of 360-degree Feedback: A Process for Successful Individual and Organizational Development.* San Francisco: Jossey Bass, 1998; Norwood, MA: Books24X7.com [electronic resource].

Trice, Harrison, and Janice Beyer. *The Cultures of Work Organizations.* Englewood Cliffs, NJ: Prentice Hall, 1993.

Ulrich, Dave, and Norm Smallwood. *Why the Bottom Line Isn't! How to Build Value through People and Organization.* New York: John Wiley & Sons, 2003.

Van Velsor, Ellen, Jean Brittain Leslie, and John W. Fleenor. *Choosing 360: A Guide to Evaluating Multi-rater Feedback Instruments for Management Development.* Greensboro, NC: Center for Creative Leadership, 1997; Norwood, MA: Books24X7.com [electronic resource].

Vavra, Terry V. *Improving Your Measurement of Customer Satisfaction: A Guide to Creating, Conducting, Analyzing, and Reporting Customer Satisfaction Measurement Programs.* Milwaukee, WI: American Society for Quality Press, 1997.

Ward, Peter. *360-Degree Feedback.* London: Institute of Personnel and Development, 1997; Norwood, MA: Books24x7.com [electronic resource].

Welch, Jack, and Suzy Welch. *Winning.* New York: HarperBusiness, 2005.

Wheatly, Margaret. *Leadership and the New Science.* San Francisco: Berrett-Koehler Publishers, 1994.

Wren, J. Thomas. *Leader's Companion: Insight in Leadership through the Ages.* New York: Free Press, 1995.

Yukl, Gary. *Leadership in Organizations.* Englewood Cliffs, NJ: Prentice Hall, 2002.

BOOK CHAPTERS

Bass, Bernard M. "Transformational Leadership: A Response to Critiques." In *Leadership Theory and Research: Perspectives and Directions,* ed. Martin M. Chemers & Roya Ayman. New York: Free Press 1996.

Berlew, David E. "Leadership and Organizational Excitement." In *Psychological Foundations of Organizational Behavior,* ed. Barry M. Shaw. Santa Monica, CA: Goodyear Pub. Co.

Gowing, Marilyn K. "Measurement of Individual Emotional Comptence." In *The Emotional Intelligent Workplace: How to Select for, Measure, and Improve Emotional Intelligence in Individuals, Groups, and Organizations,* ed. Cary Cherniss and Daniel Goleman. San Francisco: Jossey-Bass, 2001.

Hackman, J. Richard, and Richard E. Walton. "Leading Groups in Organizations." In *Designing Effective Work Groups,* ed. Paul S. Goodman and Associates. San Francisco: Jossey-Bass, 1986.

House, Robert. "Theory of Charismatic Leadership." In *Leadership: The Cutting Edge,* A symposium held at Southern Illinois University, Carbondale, October 27–28, 1976, ed. James G. Hunt and Lars L. Larson. Carbondale: Southern Illinois University Press, 1977.

Kotter, John P. "What Leaders Really Do." In *Harvard Business Review on Leadership.* Boston: Harvard Business School Publishing, 1998.

Lonner, Walter. "The Search for Psychological Universals." In *Handbook of Cross-cultural Psychology,* ed. Harry Triandis and W.W. Lambert. Boston: Allyn-Bacon, 1980.

Luthans, Fred, and Bruce Avolio. "Authentic Leadership: A Positive Development Approach." In *Positive Organizational Scholarship: Foundations of a New Discipline,* ed. Kim S. Cameron, Jane E. Dutton, and Robert E. Quinn. San Francisco: Barrett-Koehler, 2003.

Mayer, Jack, and Peter Salovey. "What Is Emotional Intelligence: Implications for Educators." In *Emotional Development, Emotional Literacy, and Emotional Intelligence,* ed. Peter Salovey and David Sluyter. New York: Basic Books, 1997.

Nitecki, Danuta A., and William Rando. "Evolving an Assessment of the Impact on Pedagogy, Learning, and Library Support of Teaching with Digital Images." In *Outcomes Assessment in Higher Education,* ed. Peter Hernon and Robert E. Dugan. Westport, CT: Libraries Unlimited, 2004.

St. Clair, Gloriana, and Erika Linke. "The Library of the Future." In *The Innovative University,* ed. Daniel P. Resnick and Dana S. Scott. Pittsburgh, PA: Carnegie Mellon University Press, 2004.

Weiss, Howard, and Russell Cropanzano. "Affective Events Theory." In *Research in Organizational Behavior,* ed. Barry Staw and Larry Cummings. Greenwich, CT: JAI Press, 1996.

Zaleznik, Abraham. "Managers and Leaders: Are They Different?" In *Harvard Business Review on Leadership.* Boston: Harvard Business School Publishing, 1998.

GOVERNMENT PUBLICATIONS

Baldrige National Quality Program: Education Criteria for Performance Excellence. Gaithersburg, MD: National Institute of Standards and Technology, 2006.

DISSERTATIONS AND THESES

Argyris, Chris. "A Study of a Pattern of Managerial Leadership" (Ph.D. diss., Cornell University, 1951).

Babiak, Katherine M. "Managerial Leadership in Canadian NSOs: Values and Perceptions of Senior Staff Leaders and Their Staff Members" (master's thesis, University of Ottawa, 1994).

Burbach, Mark. "Testing the Relationship between Emotional Intelligence and Full-Range Leadership as Moderated by Cognitive Style and Self-Concept." (Ph.D. diss., University of Nebraska, Lincoln, 2004).

Creswell, John W. "Department Chair Faculty Development Activities and Leadership Practices: University Libraries Faculty Perceptions" (Ph.D. diss., University of Nebraska-Lincoln, 2002).

Dent, James Kelso. "Managerial Leadership Styles: Some Dimensions, Determinants and Behavioral Correlates" (Ph.D. diss., University of Michigan, 1957).

DiPadova, Laurie Newman. "Managerial Leadership and Organizational Hierarchy: An Exploration of the Similarities and Differences in Managerial Roles at Hierarchical Levels" (Ph.D. diss., State University of New York at Albany, 1995).

McNary, Lisa Deane. "The Deming Management Theory: A Managerial Leadership Profile for the New Economic Age" (Ph.D. diss., The University of New Mexico, 1993).

Skidmore, Wilbur M. II. "A Functional Approach to Managerial Leadership" (master's thesis, The George Washington University, 1966).

WEB RESOURCES

American Association of Community Colleges. "Community College Leaders; Today and Tomorrow." Washington, D.C.: American Association of Community Colleges, n.d. Available at http://www.ccleadership.org/leading_forward/characteristics.htm (accessed November 5, 2005).

Association of Research Libraries, *Non-Librarian Professionals,* SPEC Kit 212. Washington, D.C.: Association of Research Libraries, 1995. Available at http://www.arl.org/spec/212fly.html (accessed March 25, 2006).

Association of Southeastern Research Libraries. "Shaping the Future: ASERL's Competencies for Research Libraries." Atlanta, GA: Association of Southeastern Research Libraries, 2000. Available at http://www.aserl.org/statements/competencies/competencies.htm (accessed September 9, 2005).

———. "Survey Report: ASERL Competencies for Research Librarians: Usage at ASERL Member Libraries." Atlanta, GA: Association of Southeastern Research Libraries, 2003. Available at http://www.aserl.org/aserlcompetencies.pdf (accessed September 9, 2005).

Baker, Shirley K. "Leading from Below: Or, Risking Getting Fired." St. Louis: Washington University, n.d. Available at http://www.wustl.edu/baker/leading.html (accessed November 18, 2005).

"Best Leadership Quotes: Napoleon Bonaparte." Famous-Quotes-and-Quotations.com. Boone, NC: Famous-Quotes-and-Quotations.com, n.d. Available at http://www.famous-quotes-and-quotations.com/leadership-quotes.html (accessed March 16, 2006).

"Big Dog's Leadership Quotes." Available at http://www.nwlink.com/~donclark/leader/leadqot.html (accessed May 1, 2006).

Brewer, Joseph M., Sheril J. Hook, Janice Simmons-Welburn, and Karen Williams. "Libraries Dealing with the Future Now," *ARL Bimonthly Report* 234 (Association of Research Libraries, June 2004). Available at http://www.arl.org/newsltr/234/dealing.html (accessed February 9, 2006).

Bridgland, Angela. "To Fill, or How to Fill—That Is the Question. Succession Planning and Leadership Development in Academic Libraries," *Australian Academic Research Libraries* 30 (March 1999). Available through Expanded Academic ASAP (accessed September 8, 2005).

Campbell, Jerry. D. "Changing a Cultural Icon: The Academic Library as a Virtual Destination," *Educause Review* 41 (January-February 2006): 16–31. Available at http://www.educause.edu/apps/er/erm06/erm0610.asp?bhcp = 1 (accessed May 25, 2006).

Carlson, Scott. "The Deserted Library," *The Chronicle of Higher Education* 48 (November 16, 2001). Available at http://chronicle.com/weekly/v48/i12/ 12a03501.htm (accessed February 28, 2006).

The Carnegie Classification of Institutions of Higher Education. Menlo Park, CA: Carnegie Foundation for the Advancement of Teaching, 2005. Available at http://www. carnegiefoundation.org/classifications/ (accessed February 8, 2006).

"Clemson University's Mission Statement." Clemson, SC: Clemson University, 2001. Available at http://www.clemson.edu/welcome/quickly/mission/index.htm (accessed September 7, 2005).

Clemson University. "Vision Statement." Clemson, SC: Clemson University, 2006. Available at http://www.clemson.edu/welcome/quickly/mission/index.htm (accessed February 16, 2006); http://www.clemson.edu/welcome/quickly/ mission/goals.htm (accessed February 16, 2006).

Dallas County Community College District. Press Release: "Baldrige Award Goes to Richland College" (Dallas, TX: Dallas County Community College District, 2006). Available at http://www.dcccd.edu/About+DCCCD/ News+and+Events/News/RLC/Baldrige+Award+Goes+to+Richland+Colleg e+11.22.05.htm (accessed March 16, 2006).

Denison, Daniel, R. Robert Hoojiberg, and Robert E. Quinn. "Paradox and Performance: Toward a Theory of Behavioral Complexity in Managerial Leadership," *Organization Science* 6, no. 5 (September-October 1995): 524–40. Available from JSTOR (accessed March 16, 2006).

"Draft Leadership Characteristics: President, University of Arizona." Tucson, AZ: University of Arizona, 2005. Available at http://www.abor.asu.edu/special_ editions/UA%20Search/Leadership%20Characteristics.pdf (accessed November 7, 2005).

Eisenhower Dwight D. "4th State of The Union Address" (1956). Available at http://www.theamericanpresidency.us/1956.htm (accessed March 1, 2006).

"Harvey S. Firestone Quotes." Thinkexist.com. Available at http://en.thinkexist. com/quotes/harvey_s._firestone (accessed April 18, 2006).

Heathfield, Susan M. "Your Guide to Human Resources: Generation X." Available at http://humanresources.about.com/od/glossaryg/g/gen_x.htm (accessed May 17, 2006).

"Henry Kissinger." Available at http://www.nwlink.com/~donclark/leader/ leadqot.html (accessed May 11, 2006).

Hisle, W. Lee. "Top Issues Facing Academic Libraries: A Report on the Focus on the Future Task Force," *College & Research Libraries* 63, no. 10 (November 2002). Available at http://www.ala.org/ala/acrl/acrlpubs/ crlnews/backissues2002/novmonth/topissuesfacing.htm (accessed February 15, 2006).

Ihrkey, Doug, and Larry Gates. "Leadership: What Does It Mean and How Do You Get It?" *Cacubo Annual Conference,* Milwaukee, WI, 2005. Available at http://www.cacubo.org/powerpoint/Milwaukee%20presentations/ Leaders hip%20Gates%20Ihrkey10%2017%202005.ppt (accessed April 27, 2006).

Johnson, Michael J., Donald E. Hanna, and Don Okcott, Jr., *Bridging the Gap: Leadership, Technology, and Organizational Change for University Deans and Chairpersons.* Aldgate, South Australia: Webcite, n.d. Available at http://www.webcite.com.au/prod14.htm (accessed November 14, 2005).

"Library Strategic Planning: Yale University Library Mission-Vision-Values." New Haven, CT: Yale University Libraries, 2003. Available at http://www.library.yale.edu/strategicplanning/mission.html (accessed September 7, 2005).

Mintzberg, Henry. "Managing Quietly," *Leader to Leader* 12 (Spring 1999). Available at http://www.pfdf.org/leaderbooks/121/spring99/mintzberg.html (accessed March 15, 2006).

"The Neuropsychology of Leadership." Available at http://www.sybervision.com/Leaders/ (accessed November 7, 2005).

New York University, Office of the Provost, "About the Office." New York: New York University, n.d. Available at http://www.nyu.edu/provost/about-statement.html (accessed November 14, 2005).

Null, Matthew. "Candidates List Desired Traits of College Presidents," *The Telescope* (October 31, 2005). Available at http://www.the-telescope.com/media/paper749/news/2004/10/11/News/Candidates.List.Desired.Traits.Of.College.President-746666.shtml (accessed November 7, 2005).

"101 Facts on the Status of Working Women." Washington, D.C.: Business and Professional Women/USA, 2005. Available at http://www.bpwusa.org/files/public/101FactsonWorkingwomen2005.pdf.pdf (accessed May 2, 2006).

Pors, Niels Ole. "Dimensions of Leadership and Service Quality: The Human Aspect in Performance Measurement," *Proceedings of the 4th Northumbria International Conference on Performance Measurement in Libraries and Information Services, Meaningful Measures for Emerging Realities* (Pittsburgh, PA, 2001; distributed by the Association of Research Libraries, Washington, D.C.), 245–251. See http://www.arl.org/stats/north/index.html (accessed April 24, 2006).

"Ray Kroc, Founder of McDonald's." Available at http://www.nwlink.com/~donclark/leader/leadqot.html (accessed May 11, 2006).

Rodriguez, Raul O., Mark T. Green, and Malcolm J. Ree. "Leading Generation X: Do the Old Rules Apply," *Journal of Leadership & Organizational Studies* 9 (Spring 2003). Available through Expanded Academic ASAP (accessed July 28, 2004).

"Role and Mission of UNK: Mission Statement." Kearney, NE: University of Nebraska at Kearney, 2005. Available at http://www.unk.edu/about/index.php?id = 124 (accessed September 7, 2005).

Smith, Brien. "Managing Generation X," *USA Today (Magazine)* 129 (November 2000). Available through Expanded Academic ASAP (accessed July 28, 2004).

Stanford University. "The Cares of the University." Palo Alto, CA: Stanford University, n.d. Available at http://www.stanford.edu/home/stanford/cares/noframes/crystal.html (accessed November 7, 2005).

Steven B. "What Makes a Good Academic Library Director," ACRLog (Association of College and Research Libraries). Available at http://acrlblog.org/2005/12/26/what-makes-a-good-academic-library-director/(accessed March 20, 2006).

Stoffle, Carla, Barbara Allen, David Morden, and Krisellen Maloney. "Continuing to Build the Future Academic Libraries and Their Challenges," *portal: Libraries*

and the Academy 3, no. 3 (July 2003), 365. [363–380] Available at http://
0-muse.jhu.edu.library.simmons.edu/journals/portal_libraries_and_the_academy/
v003/3.3stoffle.html (accessed February 15, 2006).

Troll, Denise. "How and Why Are Libraries Changing," CLIS *[Council on Library and Information Resources]* Issues, No. 21 (May/June 2001). Available at http://
www.clir.org/pubs/issues/issues21.html (accessed February 13, 2006).

University of Arizona, Office of the President. "Frey Leadership Institute Talk, Atlanta, GA." Tucson, AZ: University of Arizona, 2003. Available at http://
president.arizona.edu/communications/public-addresses/public-address02/
(accessed November 14, 2005).

University of North Carolina, School of Information and Library Science. "News Release: Provosts from the Triangle Discuss Issues Confronting Higher Education." Chapel Hill: University of North Carolina, 2005. Available at http://
sils.unc.edu/news/releases/2005/09_trlnpprovosts.htm (accessed February 9, 2006).

Walker, Stephen, and V. Lonnie Lawson. "The Librarian Stereotype and the Movies," *MC Journal: The Journal of Academic Media Librarianship* 1 (Spring 1993): 16–28. Available at http://wings.buffalo.edu/publications/mcjrnl/v1n1/
image.html (accessed March 25, 2006).

Walter, Scott. "3 Responses to 'What Makes a Good Academic Library Director'," ACRLog (December 26, 2005). Available at http://acrlblog.org/2005/12/26/
what-makes-a-good-academic-library-director/ (accessed March 20, 2006).

Wepner, Shelley B., Antonia D'Onofrio, Bernice Willis, and Stephen C. Wilhite. "Getting at the Moral Leadership of Education Deans," *The Qualitative Report*, 7, no. 2 (June 2002). Available at http://www.nova.edu/ssss/QR/QR7-2/
wepner.html (accessed November 12, 2005).

"Where the Jobs Are," *Library Journal*. Available at http://www.libraryjournal.
com/article/CA434433 (accessed July 29, 2004).

Wilder, Stanley. "The Changing Profile of Research Library Professional Staff," *ARL Bimonthly Report* 208/209. Available at http://www.arl.org/newsltr/208_
209/chgprofile/html (accessed September 8, 2005).

UNPUBLISHED SOURCES

Martin, Elaine R. "Team Effectiveness in Academic Medical Libraries: A Multiple Case Study." Paper for the doctor of arts degree. Boston: Simmons College, 2004.

National Center for Healthcare Leadership. "NCHL Leadership Model, Version 2.0." Chicago: National Center for Healthcare Leadership, 2004.

Simmons College. "Graduate School of Library and Information Science, Ph.D. Managerial Leadership in the Information Profession—Program Description." Boston: Simmons College, 2006.

Yancey, Margaret. "Work Teams: Three Models of Effectiveness." Denton, TX: University of North Texas Center for the Study of Work Teams, 1998. No longer available at http://www.workteams.unt.edu/reports/Yancey.html (accessed September 1, 2002).

INDEX

ABOUT THE EDITORS
AND CONTRIBUTORS

MIGNON ADAMS is the director of Library and Information Services at the University of the Sciences (Philadelphia, Pennsylvania 19104–4495, m.adams@usip.edu), a position she has held for 20 years. She previously held positions at the State University of New York at Oswego. For the past decade she has facilitated the annual seminar held for new college library directors, a role that has continually renewed her enthusiasm and interest in college librarianship. Professionally, she has chaired a number of committees in the College Library Section of ACRL, including the College Library Section, and has held leadership roles in her chapter of the Medical Library Association and the library section of the American Association of Colleges of Pharmacy. She is the author of numerous articles in library publications and a book on library credit courses.

CAMILA A. ALIRE is dean emeritus, University Libraries, University of New Mexico and Colorado State University (her e-mail address is calire@att. net) and currently serves as president of the Association of College and Research Libraries (ACRL). She presently sits on the board of directors of the Association of Research Libraries (ARL) and served on the ALA Executive Board. She served as REFORMA national president and on its executive board. She has written on the topic of leadership as well as conducted workshops on leadership development. She received her doctorate in Higher Education Administration from the University of Northern Colorado. She holds an MLS from the University of Denver and a bachelor of arts degree from Adams State College.

CARYN ANDERSON is program coordinator of the Ph.D. program in managerial leadership in the information professions at Simmons College, Graduate School of Library and Information Science (300 The Fenway, Boston, MA 02115–5898, caryn.anderson@simmons.edu). She also serves as consultant to research projects in digital libraries and public policy. Ms. Anderson received her bachelor of science degree from the College of Communication at Boston University in 1987 and spent much of her early career in nonprofit management and policy analysis in the arts and human services. She went on to achieve her master of science degree from Simmons College, Graduate School of Library and Information Science, in 2005. She is active in the American Society for Information Science and Technology, where she has co-founded the International Calendar of Information Science Conferences, received multiple awards, and held a variety of local and national level leadership positions.

STEVEN J. BELL is director of the Paul J. Gutman Library at Philadelphia University. He writes and speaks frequently on topics such as information retrieval, library and learning technologies, and academic librarianship. An adjunct professor at the Drexel University College of Information Science and Technology, he teaches courses in online searching, academic librarianship, and business information resources. He maintains a Web site and Weblog, "Steven Bell's Keeping Up Web Site" and "The Kept-Up Academic Librarian," which promote current awareness skills and resources. He is also a member of the ACRLog blogging team. He is a co-founder of the Blended Librarian's Online Learning Community on the Learning Times Network and has participated in numerous virtual presentations. (For additional information about him or to find links to the various Web sites he publishes and maintains, see http://staff.philau.edu/bells).

JOAN R. GIESECKE is the dean of Libraries, University of Nebraska-Lincoln (UNL) Libraries (318 Love Library, Lincoln, NE 68588–4100, jgiesecke1@unl.edu). She joined UNL in 1987 and became dean in 1996. Before this, she was the associate dean for collections and services. She has held positions at George Mason University in Fairfax, Virginia, Prince George's County Memorial Library System, and the American Health Care Association. She received a doctorate in public administration from George Mason University, a MLS from the University of Maryland, a master's degree in management from Central Michigan University, and a B.A. in economics from SUNY at Buffalo. Giesecke's research interests include organizational decision making and management skills. She has developed a training program for managers and has presented a variety of papers on management and supervisory skills. She is a former editor of the journal *Library Administration and Management* and has published numerous articles on management issues. Her books include *Practical Help for New*

Supervisors, Scenario Planning for Libraries, and *Practical Strategies for Library Managers.* She serves as president of the Homestead Girl Scout Council.

LARRY L. HARDESTY is Interim University Librarian, Winona State University (Winona, MN 55987-5837, lhardesty@winona.edu). Previous to assuming that position he served for nine years as college librarian at Austin College in Sherman, Texas, and for 12 years as director of library services at Eckerd College in St. Petersburg, Florida. He is currently a councilor at large of the Council of the American Library Association. In 1999–2000, he served as president of the Association of College and Research Libraries (ACRL). In 2001, he received the ACRL Academic/Research Librarian of the Year Award. He holds a Ph.D. in Library and Information Science from Indiana University-Bloomington, and a master in library science from the University of Wisconsin-Madison.

PETER HERNON is a professor at Simmons College, Graduate School of Library and Information Science (300 The Fenway, Boston, MA 02115–5898, peter.hernon@simmons.edu), where he teaches course on government information policy and resources, evaluation of information services, research methods, and academic librarianship. He received his Ph.D. from Indiana University and has taught at Simmons College, the University of Arizona, and Victoria University of Wellington (New Zealand). He is the co-editor of *Library & Information Science Research,* founding editor of *Government Information Quarterly,* and past editor of *The Journal of Academic Librarianship.* He is the author of approximately 260 publications, 44 of which are books. Among these are *Improving the Quality of Library Services for Students with Disabilities* (Libraries Unlimited, 2006), *Comparative Perspectives on E-government* (Scarecrow Press, 2006), *Revisiting Outcomes Assessment in Higher Education* (Libraries Unlimited, 2006), *Outcomes Assessment in Higher Education* (Libraries Unlimited, 2004), and *Assessing Service Quality* (American Library Association, 1998), which received the Highsmith award for outstanding contribution to the literature of library and information science in 1999.

THOMAS G. KIRK, JR. is library director and coordinator of information services at Earlham College (Richmond, Indiana 47374–4095, kirkto@earlham. edu). Previous to assuming this position, he was library director at Berea College (Berea, KY), and before that he was science librarian at Earlham with an interim year as acting director of library and media resources at the University of Wisconsin, Parkside. He served as president of the Association of College and Research Libraries (ACRL) and chaired an initiative of the ACRL Institute for Information Literacy to write "Characteristics of Best Practices in Information Literacy Programming." He is also involved in the development of library consortia and has served on the board of directors of SOLINET, the Southeast Library Network, and the OCLC Members Council representing SOLINET and INCOLSA (Indiana Cooperative Library Services Authority). Mr. Kirk chaired the Private Academic Library Network of Indiana (PALNI). His current project is helping plan and carryout a series of workshop for Council of Independent Colleges (CIC) on Transformation of the College Library.

ELAINE MARTIN is the director of Library Services, Lamar Soutter Library, University of Massachusetts Medical School (Worcester, MA 01655, elaine.martin@umassmed.edu). Since 2001, she has also directed the National Network of Libraries of Medicine, New England Region housed at the medical school. She received her doctor of arts degree from the Graduate School of Library and Information Sciences, Simmons College, Boston in January 2005. A medical librarian for more than 20 years, she is an active member of the Medical Library Association (MLA) and the Association of Academic Health Sciences Libraries (AAHSL).

TERRENCE MECH has been Director of the Library at King's College (133 North River Street, Wilkes-Barre, PA 18711–0801, tfmech@kings.edu) since 1982. He serves on the vice president for academic affairs' academic team and currently co-chairs the college's Institutional Planning and Resources Committee. He served as the college's vice president for information and instructional technologies for seven years (1994–2001). Dr. Mech was a member of the Middle States Commission on Higher Education Advisory Panel on Information Literacy that prepared *Developing Research & Communication Skills: Guidelines for Information Literacy in the Curriculum* (2003). He holds graduate degrees from Pennsylvania State University (higher education), Clarion State College (library science), and Illinois State University (sociology).

RUSH G. MILLER has served as university librarian and director of the university library system, University of Pittsburgh (271 Hillman Library, Pittsburgh, PA 15260, rgmiller@pitt.edu) since 1994. He also holds a joint appointment as professor in the Department of Library and Information Science. In addition, he holds the Hillman Endowed Chair. He holds M.A. and Ph.D. degrees in medieval English history and the MLS in library science. Before coming to the University of Pittsburgh, he was dean of libraries at Bowling Green State in Ohio. Since joining the University of Pittsburgh, Dr. Miller has led the development of innovative uses of information technology including providing access to a comprehensive array of electronic publications for faculty and students at the university. These new resources have been provided without lessening the commitment of the ULS to comprehensive research collections. In fact, the university achieved its 4 millionth volume during the fiscal year 2000. A major expansion and renovation of library facilities is underway. His programs in opening Chinese resources to world scholars through a collaborative with the key universities in China have had a profound effect on scholarly access to remote resources and have become a model for international global resource sharing. Dr. Miller has been active as a speaker and writer on issues as diverse as digital libraries, global library resources, collection development of digital libraries, organizational development, diversity, and management.

SARAH M. PRITCHARD was appointed the university librarian at Northwestern University (University Library, 1970 Campus Drive, Evanston, IL 60208–2300, spritchard@northwestern.edu) in September, 2006. From 1999 to 2006, she was the university librarian at the University of California, Santa Barbara, and a key leader in the development of systemwide library services for the University of California. Her earlier positions include director of libraries at Smith College; associate executive director at the Association of Research Libraries in Washington D.C., and several public service positions at the Library of Congress. She has a B.A. from the University of Maryland, and master's degrees in French and in library science from the University of Wisconsin-Madison.

Ms. Pritchard has been actively involved in professional associations and projects, notably in the Association of Research Libraries and the American Library Association. She has been a leader in state library networks in Massachusetts and California, and was appointed by the governor to the board of the Library of California. She is currently a member of the national steering committee for the Scholarly Publishing and Academic Resources Coalition (SPARC). She is the author of more than 60 articles and other publications; has lectured and consulted on various library topics in North America, Europe, and Asia; and has won many professional and academic awards.

DONALD E. RIGGS has served as vice president for information services and university librarian (Nova Southeastern University, Alvin Sherman Library, Research, and Information Technology Center, 3100 Ray Ferrero, Jr. Blvd., Fort Lauderdale, Florida 33314–7796, driggs@nova.edu) since 1997. Before this appointment, he served six years as dean of university libraries and senior professor of information at the University of Michigan. Before going to the University of Michigan, he was dean of libraries at Arizona State University for about 12 years.

Dr. Riggs has served in several leadership capacities in the library profession (e.g., president of three different state library associations, president of the Library Administration and Management Association-LAMA, and two terms on the ALA Council representing LITA and as a member-at-large). He is the author/editor of eight books, 46 book chapters, and about 100 journal articles. He has served as editor of *Library Administration and Management, Library Hi Tech,* and *College & Research Libraries.* He was invited to write the "library leadership section" for the four-volume *Encyclopedia of*

Leadership (Sage Publications). In 1991, he received the prestigious Hugh
C. Atkinson Memorial Award for his innovation in library technology and
risk-taking leadership.

NANCY ROSSITER is an assistant professor at Simmons College, Graduate School of Library and Information Science (300 The Fenway, Boston,
MA 02115–5898, nancy.rossiter@simmons.edu), where she teaches management classes, including principles of management, contemporary management theory, marketing the library, and information entrepreneurship. Before
joining the Simmons faculty, she taught for eight years at Bay Path College,
Bryant University, Providence College, and Roger Williams University. She
was instrumental in developing an entrepreneurship program for women at
Bay Path College. Before teaching on the college level, Dr. Rossiter owned
a publishing company in East Greenwich, Rhode Island. She has also been a
consultant, with clients including GTECH, Bryant's Small Business Development Center and Center for Management Development.

CANDY SCHWARTZ is a professor at Simmons College, Graduate School
of Library and Information Science (300 The Fenway, Boston, MA 02115–
5898, candy.schwartz@simmons.edu), where she teaches courses in the
organization of information resources, including subject analysis, classification, Web development, information architecture, and digital libraries.
Dr. Schwartz received her Ph.D. from Syracuse University in 1986. She is the
co-editor of *Library & Information Science Research,* has published articles in
journals such as *The Journal of Academic Librarianship* and the *Journal of the
American Society for Information Science and Technology,* and is the author,
co-editor, or co-author of several monographs, including *Sorting out the Web*
(2002) and *Revisiting Outcomes Assessment in Higher Education* (2006).
Dr. Schwartz has held numerous offices in the American Society for Information Science & Technology (ASIST), including director and president, and
has received local and national ASIST awards for teaching and service.

ARTHUR P. YOUNG is dean emeritus of university libraries, Northern
Illinois University. He is the author of more than 200 publications, including 8 books and 40 refereed articles. He serves on the editorial boards of the
Journal of Academic Librarianship, Library & Information Science Research,
and *Library Quarterly.*